Karen Jeppe

MISAK

AN ARMENIAN LIFE

(Karen Jeppe's story of an orphan who became a son)

translated, edited and introduced by

Jonas Kauffeldt

Gomidas Institute
London

ISBN 978-1-909382-18-3

Gomidas Institute
42 Blythe Rd.
London W14 0HA
United Kingdom
www.gomidas.org
info@gomidas.org

For Dr. Peter P. Garretson,

Department of History, Florida State University

Acknowledgements

The origins of this short book date back to 2001, the year when I spent numerous months in the halls of the Danish Royal Library and the Danish State Archives. First encountering Jeppe's writings while perusing the pages of the journal *Armeniervennen*, I came to realize that this story about Misak needed a new and wider audience. However, as the date of publication indicates, it took me many years to complete this project, hampered as it was by other research interests, changes of employment, and so on.

Firstly, I would like to thank Dr. Betsy L. Nies of the Department of English at the University of North Florida in Jacksonville and Dr. Kristin G. Kelly, also a professor of English, and a colleague of mine at the University of North Georgia near Atlanta. They both provided invaluable comments, corrections, and recommendations that helped to improve the final version of this edited translation. In addition, a number of my former students, namely Max, Jefferson, Ashley, Jessica, and Christian, all contributed insightful suggestions and advice. Thanks very much to all.

Secondly, my closest family members, namely my parents and brother, were very supportive and helpful during the lengthy process of getting this project prepared and finalized for submission to prospective publishers. In particular, my father, Jørgen Kauffeldt, provided invaluable commentary and advice over the final months of the editing process.

Finally, I wish to thank Ara Sarafian and everyone at the Gomidas Institute for agreeing to publish this English-language version of Jeppe's story. They recognized the significance of her work and perspective, an acknowledgement for which I will always be grateful.

TABLE OF CONTENTS

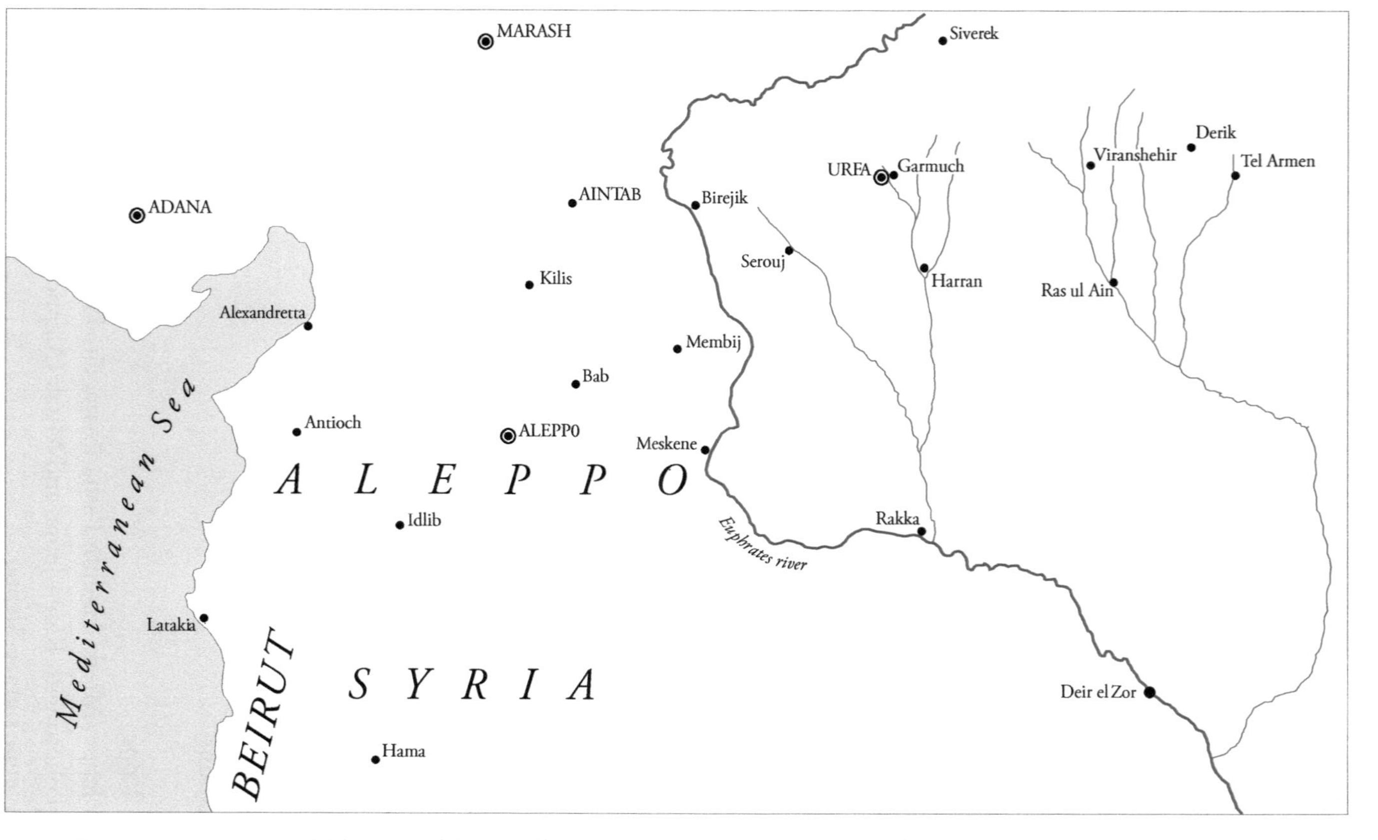

Ottoman provinces of Aleppo and Syria. Most of these territories were absorbed into modern Syria after WWI.

Preface

The purpose of this translation is to make Karen Jeppe's words and sentiments known to a much wider audience, both academic and popular. Danish is after all a language only accessible to a limited population, so making her work available in English will serve to greatly expand the number of people who can appreciate and learn from it. Moreover, the story Jeppe tells is a very personal and unique account not only of her own experiences in Urfa, a city in upper Mesopotamia, and surrounding areas during the closing years of the Ottoman Empire, but also those of her adoptive son, Misak (given name Misael Melkonian). Jointly, their stories told as one, provide a rare perspective on lives improbably intertwined and on experiences at once horrifying but also captivating and inspirational.

In my effort to translate Jeppe's account, I have sought to render as unchanged as possible her words, phrases, and sentiments. At times, however, as is common in translation, minor modifications were needed to assure for clarity and greater readability. For example, at times Danish turns of phrase needed to be altered because a direct translation into English would have made very little sense.

Changes were also made in terms of place-names and words used to describe items and titles specific to the region of the Middle East. Spellings were updated to reflect customary modern usage and italics were routinely employed when terms were used that do not commonly appear in English (i.e. *mutassarif* in italics, but mullah not).

The footnotes included in the translated text are mine unless otherwise indicated. Jeppe provided only very few notes of her own, so I have resolved to expand her manuscript where it seemed beneficial to provide further explanation and clarification. Specifically, notes providing biographical details, historical context, and general information and commentary are provided throughout.

Jonas Kauffeldt
Flowery Branch, Georgia
July 2013

Karen Jeppe

Introduction[*]

The Author: Karen Jeppe

It is rare for common people to stand out in history. Most often such individuals and their stories get lost in the grand sweep and intensity of major events, leaving unclear the full ramifications of those same events on regular people and obscuring the sacrifices and challenges they made and experienced. Scholars have in recent decades done much to address this shortfall in historical knowledge and significantly furthered our collective insight, but much research remains to be done in uncovering the full spectrum of experiences and struggles of the great multitudes of humanity. However, it is equally true that in times of crisis and unprecedented hardship, remarkable, yet still common individuals, can and do rise to the challenge and assert themselves, forcing history to include them in the narrative of momentous events.

One such crisis, with both domestic and international repercussions, unfolded in the Ottoman Empire over the final decades of its existence, from the latter half of the nineteenth century through to the conclusion of the First World War. Beset by fundamental and debilitating conditions, such as wars and internal instability, economic weakness and a limited commitment to fundamental systemic reforms, questions were increasingly raised about the viability and survivability of the empire. Many voices within its diverse population, seemingly no longer willing or able to coexist within the prevailing, though antiquated, multicultural and multi-confessional framework, were clamoring for real and tangible reforms that would be more reflective of the needs of a modernizing society. However, a government commitment to such change did not manifest itself, and instead censorship, repression and retribution met

* This introductory essay is an expanded and revised version of the fourth chapter in the author's dissertation, *Danes, Orientalism and the Modern Middle East: Perspectives from the Nordic Periphery*, unpublished Ph.D. dissertation, Florida State University, 2006.

those and their organizations that called for positive change. In particular, the Armenian population, increasingly branded a fifth column threat to Ottoman imperial survival, was punished severely in successive campaigns over the course of the final decades of the empire's existence.* It was in the wake of the first of these onslaughts, during which many tens of thousands of Armenians lost their lives or were left destitute, that there emerged an international call for some measure of Western intervention to address the evolving humanitarian crisis.

But the obligation to respond in a concerted and effective manner to the human tragedy was assumed most effectively by private organizations and individuals rather than state institutions or government officials. Regular civilians, moved by the gruesome events and by propaganda, joined relief efforts that sought to provide housing,

* Fridtjof Nansen, *Armenia and the Near East* (New York: Duffield, 1928), 285-89; Richard G. Hovannisian, ed., *The Armenian Genocide in Perspective* (New Brunswick: Transaction Books, 1986), 25; M. C. Gabrielian, *Armenia: A Martyr Nation* (New York: Fleming H. Revell, 1918), 231. One of the most contentious debates of the past many decades concerns the fate of the Armenians of the Ottoman Empire. In the turmoil that tore at the realm over the last years of its existence, ranging from revolts to invasions, a steady breakdown of imperial loyalties was replaced by new ideologies of identity that increasingly split the diverse Ottoman population. Fear, suspicion and incitement fueled tensions and left the empire ripe for collapse during the First World War. The Armenians were particularly hard hit by the conflict as their numbers in Anatolia were reduced from 1.5 million in 1914 to only 70,000 a decade later. Many fled to escape the instability and the fighting, but far more were expelled or even murdered by Ottoman gendarmerie units and Kurdish paramilitaries. The exact number of fatalities is fiercely contested by historians who either favor the Turkish claim of 400,000 or the Armenian estimate of over a million. William L. Cleveland, *A History of the Modern Middle East*, 2d ed. (Boulder: Westview, 2000), 148; Justin McCarthy, *Muslims and Minorities* (New York; London: New York University Press, 1983), 121; Stanford J. Shaw and Ezel Kural Shaw, *Reform, Revolution, and Republic*, vol. 2, *History of the Ottoman Empire and Modern Turkey* (Cambridge: Cambridge University Press, 1977), 316. Also see Donald Bloxham, *The Great Game of Genocide: Imperialism, Nationalism, and the Destruction of the Ottoman Armenians* (Oxford: Oxford University Press, 2005).

education, and employment opportunities for the Armenians who remained within the Ottoman Empire. Mostly directed and staffed by Christian missionaries, the motivation to offer assistance was primarily religious, but individuals also chose to act based on distinctly personal grounds. Women, especially those who were single and educated, would make their mark in this international relief work, finding in the foreign postings a certain liberty and independence from the constraints and limits placed on them domestically.[*] From North America to Scandinavia, they journeyed to Ottoman Armenia to not only rescue and inspire but also to perform selfless acts that would eventually make many of them larger than life. The Dane Karen Jeppe (1876-1935) was one such person, who, despite being a devout Christian, never sought to convert Armenians to her faith, Lutheran Protestantism, and instead felt drawn to the crisis-ravaged region to fulfill a religiously-inspired duty to help others and realize her own obligation to God.[†] This acceptance of the Eastern Christian as an equal exhibited a progressive, perhaps even unique, worldview and an appreciation of cultural diversity defiant of conventional Orientalism.[‡] However, Jeppe too endorsed the popular Western demonization of the Turk as bestial and blood-thirsty, reflecting the entrenched view of the Other. Over the years she would be slow to purge herself of that latter assessment, even as she settled into a decades-long residency in the region, first in Anatolia and later in Syria, and also adopted Armenian children as her own, including a son, Misak (Misael) Melkonian. But during the more than thirty years that Jeppe served as an aid worker focused on Armenian affairs, including six as a League of Nations commissioner for refugees, she did embrace new, perhaps even groundbreaking, thinking and contributed to the development of the modern system of humanitarian assistance. Her

* Inger Marie Okkenhaug, "Scandinavian Missionaries, Gender and Armenian Refugees during World War I. Crisis and Reshaping of Vocation," *Social Sciences and Missions* 23 (2010): 64-65.

† Svend Cedergreen Bech, ed. *Dansk Biografisk Leksikon* 7 (Copenhagen: Gyldendal, 1981), 340-41.

‡ Okkenhaug, "Scandinavian Missionaries, Gender and Armenian Refugees...," *Social Sciences and Missions*, 67-68. For a full discussion and definition of Orientalism, see Edward Said. *Orientalism*. New York: Vintage Books, 1978.

emphasis on preserving the ethno-cultural identity of refugees, combined and balanced with efforts at resettlement and integration on foreign soil, were elements of policy that today are standard. The fate of the Armenians in the Ottoman Empire served, even if belatedly, to instruct the international community in how it should manage and aid a displaced and victimized population.

The Urfa Years

On a cold and dreary winter's day in late February 1902, Aage Meyer Benedictsen (1866-1927), an ethnographer and historian, addressed a gathering of fellow Danes, including teachers and students, at a hall in Copenhagen.[*] The subject of his presentation was the plight of the Armenian community inside the Ottoman Empire, whose conditions he had witnessed just the year before and could therefore describe in compelling detail. Thousands were suffering from the repercussions of a violent campaign that descended on the Armenians during the mid-1890s, when forces loyal to Sultan Abdülhamid II cracked down on the minority population. Armenian revolutionaries and a regional uprising in 1894 had certainly provoked the government response, but the authorities also overreacted and were tacitly responsible for numerous massacres.[†] At the forefront of this violence were the irregular cavalry forces known as the Hamidiye, units of which were organized several years before the repression ensued and largely in its anticipation. These selfsame contingents became synonymous with the horrific events, and across Europe and in North America the "Hamidian massacres" served

* De Danske Armeniervenner, *Bestyrelses Protokol,* December 1923 – May 1935, 48-49, De Danske Armeniervenner Collection (hereafter DDA), Danish State Archives; Karen Jeppe, "Urfa," *Armeniervennen* 1, no. 3-4 (1921): 10; Ingeborg M. Sick. *Pigen fra Danmark* (Copenhagen: Nordisk Forlag, 1928), 57; Svend Cedergreen Bech, *Hos et folk uden land: Karen Jeppe – armeniernes ven* (Copenhagen: G. E. C. Gads Forlag, 1982), 12; Manuel Vigilius, "Pigen fra Danmark," *Kristeligt Dagblad,* 12 July 1996.

† M. Sükrü Hanioglu, *A Brief History of the Late Ottoman Empire* (Princeton: Princeton University Press, 2008), 131; Taner Akcam, *A Shameful Act* (New York: Henry Holt, 2006), 40-41; Lord Kindross, *The Ottoman Centuries* (New York: Morrow Quill, 1977), 556-558.

for many as a call to action.[*] Benedictsen's voice became just one more in that chorus, articulating how trauma, despair and insecurity now haunted many in the Armenian community.

Karen Jeppe was one of the people in the audience that February day and, feeling deeply moved by Benedictsen's speech, she began to seriously contemplate joining the nascent Danish aid effort in the region. Though burdened with frail health, she felt duty-bound to help relieve the suffering of the distant Armenians, leading her in 1903 to join the recently established *De Danske Armeniervenner* (DDA – The Danish Friends of Armenia).[†] Only a year old, the DDA was a fledging organization, but its leadership, including Benedictsen, was determined to carve out a role for Danes in the international campaign to aid the Ottoman Armenians. However, prevented by limited funding from establishing themselves independently in the region, the DDA forged a partnership with the *Deutsche Orientmission* (DOM), founded by Johannes Lepsius, whose activities centered around the town of Urfa in upper Mesopotamia. There the Germans operated an orphanage and a carpet factory, providing both education and employment for the local Armenians. The Danes resolved to contribute to the effort by sponsoring ten children under DOM care and to dispatch Jeppe, a teacher by training, to work for the Germans and be the DDA's representative in Urfa.[‡] Alongside the DOM, U.S. missionaries were also active in the town, having established a mission station as early as 1892 under the direction of Corinna Shattuck (d. 1910).[**] During the 1895 massacres in Urfa, Shattuck had valiantly sheltered Armenians from harm and,

* Merrill D. Peterson, *"Starving Armenians"* (Charlottesville: University of Virginia Press, 2004), 25-26; Peter Balakian, *The Burning Tigris* (New York: HarperCollins, 2003), 114-115; Armen Garo, *Bank Ottoman* (Detroit: Armen Topouzian, 1990), 96-99; Kindross, *The Ottoman Centuries*, 562-563.

† Jeppe, untitled account, 1929, DDA, bundle 10, folder D, Danish State Archives.

‡ H. F. Ulrichsen, "De første 25 År," *Armeniervennen* 8, no. 5-6 (1928): 17-19.

** Karen Jeppe, "Under Aaget," *Armeniervennen* 1, no. 9-10 (1921): 38; Ephraim K. Jernazian, *Judgment Unto Truth* (New Brunswick: Transaction Books, 1990), 37-38.

after the killings, she worked tirelessly to reestablish their community by supporting the revival of local industries and providing sound education and training for orphans.* The legacy of Shattuck's courage and commitment would serve as an inspiration for Jeppe, who, years after their first meeting, wrote that "[Shattuck] was one of the strong, one who had stood firm in a time of need without fear or concern for her own safety...."† The Dane would strive to emulate that determination and sacrifice, and from the day she arrived in Urfa in November 1903, and incidentally was greeted by Shattuck, she took the first steps toward mirroring, perhaps even eclipsing, the American's reputation.

The drive to educate and strengthen the Armenian community was central to the purposes of the foreign missions, and Jeppe embraced that cause with vigor. She immediately set about learning the local languages (Armenian, Arabic, and Turkish) and, in addition to assuming responsibility for directing the operations at the German orphanage, Jeppe committed her expertise as a teacher to the innovation of the methods of instruction and the types of curricula traditionally used in Armenian schools.‡ Focused particularly on improving the rate at which children learned to read and write, she introduced such effective reforms that they were soon adopted by Armenian teachers at other institutions and gradually became part of an established system used across the region.** The attention devoted to education was also extended to developing vocational training programs that emphasized high skill levels to better guarantee that the Armenian boys who completed their

---

* Dana L. Robert, "The Influence of American Missionary Women on the World Back Home," *Religion and American Culture: A Journal of Interpretation* 12, no. 1 (2002): 78; Jeppe, "Under Aaget," *Armeniervennen* 1, no. 9-10 (1921): 38; Sick, *Pigen fra Danmark*, 40-41; Balakian, *The Burning Tigris*, 83-84. Urfa was the scene of violent clashes in both October and December 1895. It was during the second incident that several thousands of Armenians were killed.

† Jeppe, "Misak: Et livsbillede fra Armenien," *Armeniervennen* 2, no. 7-8 (1922): 32.

‡ Matthias Bjørnlund, "Karen Jeppe – den glemte heltinde," Danes 93, no. 6 (December 2013): 34.

** Christian Winther, *Armenien og Karen Jeppe* (Copenhagen:), 21; Sick, *Pigen fra Danmark*, 46; Cedergreen Bech, *Hos et folk uden land*, 23.

apprenticeship in the mission workshops could earn enough money to support themselves. A commitment to providing the Armenians with the abilities necessary to assert their independence financially was considered by Jeppe a key function of the Western aid initiatives in the region. She even argued that elements of a positive, social revolution had resulted from the tragic massacres as widows and single women had become heads of households:

> As difficult as it is, the situation is probably in the long run positive for Urfa's women as they thereby [as heads of households] become aware of their own worth, learn to work and generally attain a different role than that which Oriental women usually as a rule occupy.*

Traditional, cultural restraints on the empowerment of women as well as the simple opportunity for individuals to realize their potential had consequently been reduced, and Jeppe was determined to contribute further to that trend by petitioning the DDA to provide funds for a loans program that would help free people from debt and predatory usury rates. Such a program, she argued, would offer a type of assistance that neither the German nor U.S. missions were providing, and therefore promote a Danish role in spurring self-help.† The notion of an expanded, more independent DDA presence in Urfa seemed even more warranted later in the year when financial difficulties plagued the German mission and the number of children at its orphanage plummeted from a peak of three to four hundred to less than one hundred. Both Jeppe and Benedictsen came to see the DOM as mismanaging its resources, and he further expressed a profound disagreement with nascent German plans to shift their focus away from aid work and instead concentrate on the conversion of Muslims, especially Kurds.‡ Benedictsen considered such an approach dangerous, and he increasingly favored that the DDA should withdraw from its

* Jeppe to the DDA Committee, Urfa, 18 February 1905, DDA, bundle 10, folder B, Danish State Archives.

† Ibid.

‡ Aage M. Benedictsen to the DDA Committee, Urfa, 2 January 1906, DDA, bundle 10, folder B, Danish State Archives; Jeppe to the DDA Committee, Urfa, 18 February 1906, DDA, bundle 10, folder B, Danish State Archives.

partnership with the Germans in Urfa and seek out a different community to support. He had in mind a move to the north into traditional Armenian lands where he had visited a town, Ahkavank, located on Lake Van, in which work was afoot to develop a teachers college.* Through his conversations with the local leaders, Benedictsen found they were eager to receive foreign assistance and technical advice as long as they retained sovereign control over the religious content of the education. The Dane, reflecting DDA policies, fully endorsed such a restriction and saw the opportunities for independent work in the town as too promising to forego. With this in mind, he recommended that Jeppe should immediately transfer to Ahkavank where her expertise in education would make her ideal to lead the Danish efforts at the college.† However, she resisted any speculation of her abandoning the work at Urfa, declaring that she could not leave until called to do so. "My place is in Urfa," she wrote to the committee, "and here I feel suited to be in every way and I wish nothing else."‡ In fact, by 1906 Jeppe was developing ambitious plans to improve and expand the existing workshops and even procure a piece of land for the purposes of raising cattle.** She was determined to help create a diverse range of economic opportunities for the Armenians and to stress that the quality of work and products should be second to none in the town. Yet skills alone, she warned, were not enough to ensure survival, because the conditions prevailing in Urfa and the dangers of illness preyed on the population. The funds made available to Jeppe from the DDA were therefore essential in allowing her to dispense to people, who were otherwise independent, needed aid for medical treatment, food, and clothes.

But through initiative and hard work the economic foundations for the relief effort in Urfa steadily improved as an ever widening array of

---

* Benedictsen to the DDA Committee, Ahkavank, 17 September 1905, DDA, bundle 10, folder B, Danish State Archives; Benedictsen to the DDA Committee, Urfa, 2 January 1906, DDA, bundle 10, folder B, Danish State Archives.

† Benedictsen to the DDA Committee, Urfa, 2 January 1906, DDA, bundle 10, folder B, Danish State Archives.

‡ Jeppe to the DDA Committee, Urfa, 18 February 1906, bundle 10, folder B, DDA, Danish State Archives.

** Ibid.

workshops and ventures flourished. The establishment of a tannery, a weaving mill, and a dye works all served to provide not only needed employment but also generated income to support the mission's institutions. Efforts to manufacture clothing were also initiated, and Jeppe secured patterns and designs from Denmark to bring new ideas and innovation to the production of garments locally.[*] Yet an emphasis on traditional Armenian crafts and techniques was hardly neglected, because the Dane recognized the cultural importance of people maintaining the skills to do such work, and she was sure an export market could be created in her native country. Jointly with another Danish woman, Ingeborg M. Sick, yet independent of the DDA which initially deemed the venture risky, Jeppe started an immediately successful program of procuring Armenian handicrafts and selling them at bazaars organized in Denmark.[†] Her sense of initiative in finding and developing local means to raise money for the aid work allowed Armenians to participate in the recovery of their own community and to contribute to its improvement.

The dual benefit of providing employment and generating income was similarly achieved through Jeppe's 1909 purchase of a farm outside Urfa. Located a few kilometers northeast of the town, in the hill country of Medjeidé near the Armenian village of Garmuch, the farm would serve both as an annual summer retreat for Jeppe and a select group of orphans, and as a place where Armenians could receive training and gain experience in cultivating the soil.[‡] With the help of her young adopted son, Misak Melkonian (1893-1978), the property was developed into a vineyard, and, through hard work, the farm became a stabilizing

---

* Jeppe to Lars Boisen Rützou, Urfa, 30 June 1906, DDA, bundle 10, folder B, Danish State Archives; Jeppe to Lars Boisen Rützou, Urfa, 19 December 1906, DDA, bundle 10, folder B, Danish State Archives.

† Ingeborg M. Sick, "Karen Jeppe of Denmark and Armenia," *American-Scandinavian Review* 25, no. 1 (March 1937): 20-21.

‡ Jeppe, "Armenierne i Euphrat-Egnen," *Armeniervennen* 11, no. 3-4 (1931): 10; Jernazian, *Judgment Unto Truth*, 39.

influence in the area.* Jeppe, ever conscious of the need to reestablish dialogue and trust between the Armenians and their Muslim neighbors, strove to reach out to the Kurds and Arabs who lived in the surrounding countryside or simply traveled past the farm. The Dane helped to develop the rural setting as a point of friendly contact and hospitality between the disparate communities in an effort to ensure the safety of the Armenian presence.† Such dedication to cultivating local relations was needed, because despite the promises of the 1908 Constitutional Revolution in which Armenian opposition movements had joined forces with other progressive Ottoman groups to restore constitutional government, events just the following year had badly shaken hopes of ethnic harmony within the empire. The killing of thousands of Armenians in Cilicia, southeastern Asia Minor, revived the fears of widespread persecution, and Jeppe, who traveled to the region in the aftermath to collect orphans and bring them to Urfa, was ever sensitive to the dangers lurking within Ottoman society in spite of the new regime.‡ Writing years later that she believed the Young Turk government was initially sincere in its commitment to reforms, she too sensed that it lacked the needed experience to foster profound change within the empire.** In fact, insiders, such as Armen Garo, a leading Armenian activist and a delegate to the post-1908 Ottoman Parliament, held that any hopes of substantive reform were lost already during 1910, leaving the prospects for a progressive and united Ottoman Empire fleeting.†† And even as Jeppe acknowledged that some political freedoms and economic opportunities served to improve the lives of the Ottoman Armenians, she had little confidence that attitudes about them were altered for the better in the minds of the wider population. Similarly, she

---

* Misak Melkonian, "Meine Mutter," March 1946, copy in DDA, bundle 10, folder D, Danish State Archives; Sick, *Pigen fra Danmark*, 82-83; Cedergreen Bech, *Hos et folk uden land*, 33, 61.

† Hebe Spaull, *Women Peace-Makers* (London: George G. Harrap, 1924), 53; Sick, *Pigen fra Danmark*, 82-83.

‡ "Miss Karen Jeppe," *Times* (London), 2 October 1935; Nansen, *Armenia and the Near East*, 296.

** Jeppe, "Solglimt mellem Bygerne," *Armeniervennen* 1, no. 3-4 (1921): 14-15.

†† Garo, *Bank Ottoman*, 182-183.

found that even the changes that were seemingly beneficial to the Armenian community included dangers as the secularization and Westernization of society threatened to separate its members from their traditions.[*] In an attempt to mitigate the most harmful aspects of that process, Jeppe committed herself to help regulate the levels of foreign influence on the Armenians under her care and responsibility, and she worked to incorporate the people as partners in the recovery of their community. By late 1911, she could take comfort in the contributions and assistance that Armenians were providing the relief effort and in the fact that the quality of craftsmanship in the workshops was improving.[†] Yet Jeppe also lamented that the ongoing financial constraints on the mission made it difficult to address significantly the poverty in Urfa, and she noted that "all the suffering one must witness has a depressing effect on the mind…."[‡] Little did she know that events of a horrific nature were on the horizon, events that would do far more than merely weigh heavily on her mind but also stretch the very limits of her sanity.

Witnessing the Unimaginable

The advent of the First World War and the Ottoman decision to join the conflict on the side of the Central Powers intensified existing suspicions, justified or not, about the possible disloyalty of non-Turkish and non-Muslim people within the empire. Fears that minority groups might collaborate with the Allies and encourage desertions from the Ottoman armed forces prompted the leadership of the Committee of Union and Progress (CUP), the empire's ruling party, to develop plans to address the perceived threat.[**] However, by the summer of 1915, even after very real setbacks both in the Sinai and the Caucasus, Ottoman military fortunes had stabilized and the serious, internal dangers imagined had largely dissipated. In fact, at Gallipoli, in the face of determined Allied efforts to advance up the peninsula and capture the

---

* Jeppe, "Solglimt mellem Bygerne," 14-15.

† Jeppe to Henrik Scharling, Urfa, 30 November 1911, A.I.3, bundle 2, Danish State Archives.

‡ Ibid.

** Raymond Kévorkian. *The Armenian Genocide: A Complete History* (London: I.B. Tauris, 2011), 241.

Ottoman capital, some of the most dedicated defenders were Arabs, making it clear that even as other Arabs would later join a revolt against the Ottoman authorities in 1916, non-Turks were prepared to fight for the empire.* Many Armenians felt similarly disposed to emulate such efforts, perhaps still hopeful that the promises of the 1908 Constitutional Revolution could yet be achieved, but events would not afford them that opportunity.† Circumstances would instead see the regime order the arrest and disarmament of Armenian soldiers, the seizure and imprisonment of Armenian civic leaders, and the forcible removal of Armenian civilians from their homes, even from areas that could not possibly be characterized as strategically sensitive or threatened by wartime conditions. These collective steps constituted part of a concerted CUP effort to implement ideological goals, namely the Pan-Turanist dream, and stipulated security policies, "necessitating" the decision to expel and ultimately eliminate the Armenian population from all of Asia Minor, including even the eastern provinces and upper Mesopotamia.‡ Beginning in the late spring of 1915 the first deportations were organized, sending thousands eastwards with only the personal items they could carry and forced to leave everything else behind.** One observer, the U.S. Ambassador Henry Morgenthau,

---

* A. L. Macfie. *The End of the Ottoman Empire, 1908-1923* (New York: Addison Wesley Longman, 1998), 130. 142-143. Armenian soldiers also fought in the so-called Battle of the Dardanelles, and there would still be Armenians fighting in the Ottoman army as late as 1918 on the Palestinian front. See Kévorkian, *The Armenian Genocide*, 241.

† Vahakn N. Dadrian, "The Documentation of the World War I Armenian Massacres in the Proceedings of the Turkish Military Tribunal," *International Journal of Middle East Studies* 23, no. 4 (1991): 562. The proceedings of the postwar tribunal established that the Ottoman assertions of widespread Armenian disloyalty and rebellion were generally exaggerated and most often false.

‡ Kévorkian, *The Armenian Genocide*, 241, 251-254; Akcam, *A Shameful Act*, 202-204; Donald Bloxham, The Armenian Genocide of 1915-1916: Cumulative Radicalization and the Development of a Destruction Policy," *Past & Present* 181 (2003): 142-143.

** Akcam, *A Shameful Act*, 130.

related that the entire landscape practically became alive with the masses of humanity on the march:

> For the better part of six months, from April to October 1915, practically all the highways in Asia Minor were crowded with these unearthly bands of exiles. They could be seen winding in and out of every valley and climbing up the sides of nearly every mountain – moving on and on, they scarcely knew whither, except that every road led to death.*

A temporary destination for some of these columns of unfortunates was the town of Urfa, where the crackdown on the Armenian community had yet to begin in earnest. However, the flood of refugees, the first of whom arrived in June 1915, was an ominous sign, and the Ottomans had already moved to arrest leading Armenian citizens and had confiscated the DOM orphanage for use as a temporary barracks.† Forced to relocate to a villa near the mission hospital, Jeppe refused to be dissuaded from continuing her work despite the mounting obstacles imposed by the Ottoman authorities. Determined to use her relatively protected status as a neutral European affiliated with the German presence in the town, Jeppe demanded access to the refugees whenever a new column arrived, and she distributed food and water to the people, administered rudimentary medical care and arranged to have cobblers available to repair or provide shoes. In a desperate effort to alleviate their suffering and show them a little kindness, even if just for a day or two before they again were marched off, Jeppe repeatedly braved crowds of

---

* Henry Morgenthau, *Ambassador Morgenthau's Story* (New York: Doubleday and Page, 1918), 314. The neutrality of United States during the initial years of the war provided American diplomatic personnel with a unique opportunity to witness the unfolding events. In addition to Ambassador Morgenthau, men like Consul Leslie A. Davis in Kharput and Consul Jesse B. Jackson in Aleppo wrote powerful and detailed reports about the deteriorating situation impacting the Armenians. See Balakian, *The Burning Tigris* and Leslie A. Davis, *The Slaughterhouse Province: An American Diplomat's Report on the Armenian Genocide, 1915-1917*, ed. Susan Blair (New Rochelle: Aristide D. Caratazas, 1989).

† Sick, *Pigen fra Danmark*, 92; Jakob Künzler, "Dit Folk er mit Folk: Stormen bryder løs over Asien," *Armeniervennen* 19, no. 5-6 (1939): 18; Kévorkian, *The Armenian Genocide*, 614.

the weakened, the emaciated, and the dying, enduring scenes that devastated her emotionally.* Ephraim K. Jernazian, an Armenian Protestant pastor in Urfa who visited Jeppe at her home, was greatly moved by her dedication to his people, deeming her services as "invaluable" and attributing to her "inexhaustible wisdom and indomitable courage."† Such an assessment was apt, because not only did Jeppe strive to help the wretched refugees, she also actively worked to hide and spirit away to safety a handful of Armenians.

In the face of considerable personal risk, Jeppe made the decision to defy Ottoman policies and construct underground shelters beneath her Urfa residence in order to provide a temporary refuge for Armenian adults. Having already bribed local officials to exempt her adopted son, Misak, from the draft and having hidden him in the house, she expanded her resistance efforts to offer sanctuary to dozens of others, including a wanted Gregorian priest, over the course of the next few years.‡ This proactive embrace of subversive and illegal activities was perhaps uniquely facilitated by the breakdown of the traditional hierarchy within the foreign missions during the war years, as independent-minded women like Jeppe and others took personal initiative to address the calamity unfolding before their eyes.** However, the dangers of concentrating too many people under one roof, such as health risks and the greater likelihood of detection, meant that arranging to smuggle people out and away from the town was imperative. With the help of area Kurds and Bedouins a network of escape routes was developed and, in the countryside around Jeppe's vineyard, an element of protection was extended to her and the Armenians courtesy of a local outlaw, a reputed shaykh from the village of Garmuch, who provided the Dane with provisions and helped shield her farm from harassment by the Ottoman

* Misak Melkonian, "Karen Jeppes sværeste Tid: Misak Melkonians Erindringer," *Armeniervennen* 16, no. 9-10 (1936): 35-36.

† Jernazian, *Judgment Unto Truth*, 65-66.

‡ Melkonian, "Karen Jeppes sværeste Tid," *Armeniervennen* 16, no. 11-12 (1936): 47; Sick, *Pigen fra Danmark*, 89-90.

** Okkenhaug, "Scandinavian Missionaries, Gender and Armenian Refugees…," *Social Sciences and Missions*, 87-88.

gendarmerie.[*] Such a sense of security was lacking in Urfa where the authorities, despite having eased their presence in the town following the brutal clearing of the Armenian Quarter in October 1915, continued to suspect Jeppe of engaging in illegal activities and conducted repeated, yet unsuccessful, searches of her villa.[†] The constant fear that the Ottomans might discover the secret rooms and unravel the efforts to help Armenians flee, exerted on her considerable physical and emotional strain. Struggling to maintain her health under the difficult conditions, Jeppe ultimately lost that battle as she succumbed to the pressures and suffered a nervous breakdown.[‡] One Armenian youth living in the house even alleged that she became so distraught and overwhelmed by the many months of grueling work that she attempted suicide on several occasions.[**] In symbolic action, as he described it, she had sought to emulate Jesus by sacrificing her life for that of the Armenian people. But each time Jeppe recovered to continue her work and, even after she fell seriously ill in early 1917 and the DDA committed funds to bring her back to Denmark, she refused to depart from Urfa as long as there still remained Armenians in need of rescue.[††] Instead she moved from the town to the better climate and safer conditions at the vineyard and endured for another year the burdens of failing health and limited access to proper medical care. That decision would affect the rest of Jeppe's life

---

* Melkonian, "Karen Jeppes sværeste Tid," *Armeniervennen* 19, no. 3-4 (1939): 11-12.

† Jakob Künzler, *In the Land of Blood and Tears*, trans. Geoffrey Steinherz (Arlington: Armenian Cultural Foundation, 2007): 58-59.

‡ Kevork Garabedian, "Miss Koren Yeppe: The Mother," December 1946, DDA, bundle 10, folder D, Danish State Archives; L. F. Gaszczyk, "Miss Karen Jeppe," *Times* (London), 2 October 1935.

** Garabedian, "Miss Koren Yeppe: The Mother," December 1946, DDA, bundle 10, folder D, Danish State Archives. The evidence of such mental and physical strain was not unique to Jeppe alone. A fellow Urfa resident, the Reverend F. H. Leslie of the United States, eventually committed suicide in 1915 as a consequence of the horrors he had witnessed and after having been brutalized in Ottoman detention. See Künzler, *In the Land of Blood and Tears*, 47-48; Kévorkian, *The Armenian Genocide*, 619; Balakian, *The Burning Tigris*, 255.

†† Cedergreen Bech, *Hos et folk uden land*, 45; Sick, "Karen Jeppe of Denmark and Armenia," *American-Scandinavian Review*, 21-22.

as her body was so severely strained during her extended stay that it took fully two years for her to recuperate after the return to Denmark in 1918. Yet Jeppe never regretted the choice she made, because even though the experience damaged her health permanently, the ordeal also strengthened her emotionally and spiritually. She came to identify herself with the Armenian people and saw their ability to overcome repeated persecutions as a model for her own efforts to endure through sheer will and determination.*

A Working Recovery

The passion Jeppe felt for the Armenian cause was hardly dampened by her obligation to temporarily depart from the region. Within a year of her return to Denmark, she was deeply involved in committee work with the DDA and their efforts to help Armenians assert their national rights and territorial claims. Encouraged by Johannes Lepsius of the DMO, who called for the Scandinavian supporters of Armenia to take a leading role in organizing European-wide backing of Armenian interests, Jeppe eagerly dedicated her energies to that end.† Armenian leaders responded to such prospective Nordic involvement by approaching the DDA with proposals to assert a greater regional role, one suggesting the settlement of Scandinavian farmers in the eastern provinces to serve as a buffer against Turkish aggression, and another calling for the possible establishment of a Nordic mandate over Armenia.‡ Jeppe, characterized by one scholar as "a fervent [postwar] Armenian nationalist," would have endorsed such plans, because, as she wrote years later, even before the outbreak of the First World War, she recognized that the real tragedy faced by the Armenian people was not just the massacres and the multitude of orphans in need of aid, but rather their lack of an independent country.** "[C]learly all oppression is evil," she declared, "but nothing can compare

* Jeppe, untitled account, 1929, DDA, bundle 10, folder D, Danish State Archives.

† De Danske Armeniervenner, *Bestyrelses Protokol*, 1919-1923, 15, DDA, Danish State Archives.

‡ Ibid., 24-25.

** Okkenhaug, "Scandinavian Missionaries, Gender and Armenian Refugees…," *Social Sciences and Missions*, 89.

with what a more advanced race suffers when it is brutalized by one that is inferior."[*] In her mind, the Turks were unsuited to govern the Armenians, and she was adamant that violent resistance to their rule was legitimate. Jeppe even asserted, on the occasion of the Armenian decision in Urfa to defy the Ottoman deportation order of 1915, that if only the entire Armenian population in the empire had risen as one, they could have prevented much of the suffering that followed.[†] And though the fight in Urfa was to be a desperate and futile act, what Jeppe termed their "last battle of despair," she still reportedly danced and was overjoyed upon hearing the church bells that summoned the people to resist, and was quoted as declaring that "now the Armenians have found the right way of dying like heroes."[‡]

Jeppe's celebration of the defiant Armenians contrasted sharply with her condemnation of the Turks for orchestrating the massacres and of Islam for inciting people to participate. Religion rather than nationalism, she argued, was the fundamental factor in the killings, and she saw the persecution of Armenians during the First World War as merely a continuation of the policies of the former regime. In fact, even in 1922, in the dramatized biographical account of her adopted son's life, *Misak: An Armenian Life*, Jeppe asserted that upon her arrival in the Ottoman Empire in 1903, she sensed that a dark shadow covered the realm.[**] She identified that ominous presence as the spirit of Islam and related how her visit to a mosque had been a horrifying experience as she felt enveloped by that spirit. Just months later, Jeppe further argued that Islam and Christianity were "diametrically opposed" and were separated by a gaping chasm.[††] Unlike Christians, she argued, Muslims were prone to fatalism, were largely indolent, discriminated against women, and were scarred by a reliance on selective morality. "There could be an

---

* Jeppe, untitled account, 1929, DDA, bundle 10, folder D, Danish State Archives.

† Garabedian, "Miss Koren Yeppe: The Mother," December 1946, DDA, bundle 10, folder D, Danish State Archives.

‡ Ibid; Kévorkian, *The Armenian Genocide*, 618.

** Jeppe, "Misak: Et livsbillede fra Armenien," *Armeniervennen* 2, no. 7-8 (1922): 28.

†† Jeppe, "Armenien," *Tidens Kvinder* 1, no. 12 (31 May 1923): 6-7.

unending amount more to point out," Jeppe wrote, "but I have yet to penetrate the Mohammedan (sic) mentality sufficiently to do the issue justice." However, "these are but the obvious differences," she continued, "those that shape their society and their actions so clearly that one cannot help but notice them."* In no uncertain terms, Jeppe was delivering to Danish readers a powerful message, one reinforced by her many years in the region, that Islam was an overtly flawed religion. The barbarism and suffering she had witnessed in Urfa was weighing heavily on her mind, and her assessment of the faith and the people reflected that sense of intense outrage and pain. Over time, Jeppe would ease her general condemnation of Islam and Muslims as she forged strong bonds with Arab Bedouins in the French Mandate of Syria, but the Turks she never forgave as their persecution of the Armenian community continued throughout her lifetime.

A Home for a People

The month of April, 1921 saw Jeppe return to the Middle East and settle in Aleppo, Syria, a town with a large concentration of recent Armenian refugees from across Asia Minor. Estimated at no less than 8,000, the displaced peoples included many former residents of Urfa, among them Jeppe's adopted daughter and son and countless of her acquaintances.† Feeling invigorated by the reunification with family and friends, she immediately set about organizing employment opportunities for the refugees, but the influx of humanity was complicating the economic situation in the city and surrounding area. Though long the center of an established Armenian community, Aleppo was in the aftermath of the First World War hard-pressed to accommodate an increase in population as new borders cut the urban area off from its traditional markets in Asia Minor and Persia, and commercial activities were further

* Ibid., 7.

† Jeppe, "Account of the situation of the Armenians in Syria," Baalbek, 24 August 1922, DDA, bundle 10, folder A, Danish State Archives; Jeppe, untitled account, 1929, DDA, bundle 10, folder D, Danish State Archives; Jeppe, "Atter i Orienten," *Armeniervennen* 1, no. 5-6 (1921): 18; Jeppe, "Frk. Jeppe i Syrien," *Armeniervennen* 2, no. 9-10 (1922): 33.

hampered by ongoing tensions across the region.[*] Rival French and Turkish territorial claims led to fierce clashes around Urfa in 1920, and by the time of Jeppe's arrival in Syria, the political situation had eased only slightly and she reported that the countryside around Aleppo was unsafe and rather short of the necessary stability to absorb and employ thousands of foreigners.[†] The ever-growing pool of available labor, coupled with a dwindling supply of jobs, prompted the local population to actively shun the Armenian refugees as workers. Jeppe immediately recognized that overseas funds and initiative were needed to help mitigate the emergent crisis and, within just weeks of her arrival in the city, she opened a sewing hall to provide employment for Armenian women. Putting them to work, she asserted, was important since they far outnumbered the men within the refugee community. In fact, Armenian males of working age constituted less than ten percent of the displaced population and, with many having more than a dozen dependents, they were in desperate need of support from their female relatives to help shoulder the burden of providing for the entire family.[‡]

The urgency to funnel refugee women into the workforce intersected with Jeppe's determination to revive traditional Armenian arts and crafts. Having worked for years in Urfa to support local industries that produced high-quality embroideries and dyed silks, she saw the restoration of such enterprises following the war as not only vital to the creation of jobs but also as a means to celebrate and sustain Armenian culture and identity.[**] "Indeed, it is the handicraft, the skill," she

---

* Philip S. Khoury, *Syria and the French Mandate* (Princeton: Princeton University Press, 1987), 17; Peter A. Shambrook, *French Imperialism in Syria 1927-1936* (Reading: Ithaca Press, 1998), 295; Jeppe, "Hjemløse," *Armeniervennen* 2, no. 3-4 (1922): 10.

† Jeppe, "Account of the situation of the Armenians in Syria," Baalbek, 24 August 1922, DDA, bundle 10, folder A, Danish State Archives; Jernazian, *Judgment Unto Truth*, 118-19; "French Losses at Urfa," *Times*, 28 April 1920.

‡ Jeppe, "Account of the situation of the Armenians in Syria," Baalbek, 24 August 1922, DDA, bundle 10, folder A,
Danish State Archives.

** Jeppe, "Et par billeder fra arbejdsmarken," *Armeniervennen* 2, no. 11-12 (1922): 44.

stressed, "which always assist the Armenian to recover every time he is knocked down."* Jeppe's colleagues on the DDA committee shared those concerns and in May 1921, with funds provided from various chapters across Denmark, she was able to found the sewing hall.† Soon the effort also secured financial support from a Swedish charity and began attracting investment interests from Armenians in Syria.‡ The Dane was particularly happy about the latter development as she anticipated such local involvement could help to ensure success. However, access to sources of capital could not mask that a concerted effort was still needed to recover and cultivate the creative skills and artistry that were in danger of being lost following years of destruction and population displacements. To spearhead that drive, Jeppe recruited an initial core group of ten experienced women whose talents were used to develop designs and patterns that would form the basis for future production.** That work was further bolstered by the fortuitous discovery in an Aleppo warehouse of a large crate of Armenian fabrics and embroideries that Jeppe had shipped to the city during the early years of the war.†† Originally intended for export to Europe, the recovered items became a treasured source of ideas and inspiration for the women at the sewing hall. Within only four months, they had developed eighteen separate designs and seen their collective workforce expand to forty seamstresses. Such progress was matched by Jeppe's commitment to authenticity and high quality. Intent on securing export markets based on a reputation for delivering the finest products, she worked tirelessly, often visiting the sewing hall twice daily, to verify that

* Jeppe, "Account of the situation of the Armenians in Syria," Baalbek, 24 August 1922, DDA, bundle 10, folder A, Danish State Archives.

† Jeppe, "Oversigt over Aarets Arbejde," *Armeniervennen* 7, no. 7-8 (1927): 33.

‡ Ibid; De Danske Armeniervenner, *Bestyrelses Protokol*, 1919-1923, October 1921, DDA, bundle 1, Danish State Archives.

** Horome Gaszczyk, "Eine Liebe Erinderung," Aleppo, 3 February 1946, DDA, bundle 10, folder D, Danish State Archives; Spaull, *Women Peace-Makers*, 58.

†† Jeppe, "Account of the situation of the Armenians in Syria," Baalbek, 24 August 1922, DDA, bundle 10, folder A, Danish State Archives; Jeppe, "Frk. Jeppe i Syrien," *Armeniervennen* 2, no. 9-10 (1922): 35.

standards were maintained and that the workers used only the best materials and those made to closely match the colors and texture of Armenian originals.*

Jeppe's contribution to the revival of Armenian handicrafts joined idealism and preservation of culture with an emphasis on shrewd business practices and an understanding of economic realities. Credited by Henriette "Henni" Forchhammer (1863-1955), a fellow feminist and an influential figure in her own right, with having "saved from annihilation" the art form of Armenian embroidery, Jeppe too assumed a role as a hard-nosed business manager guiding a nascent venture through the treacherous shoals of local and international trade.† Ever conscious of the need to build a business that was sound economically, rather than merely serving as a charitable employer sustained mostly by subsidies, she knew that revenues generated from sales overseas were imperative. And through persistence and negotiation such commercial links with importers emerged from Europe to as far afield as Australia and the Americas. However, markets in Scandinavia would from the outset be seen as having a pioneering responsibility. Thus, in December 1921, Jeppe advocated the formation of chapters across Denmark and Sweden that would commit to purchase for resale set quantities of product on an annual or biannual basis.‡ Such a network of supporters, it was argued, could serve to provide a stable and reliable market and in turn draw needed attention to the goods Armenians had to offer. Within a year this speculation and effort bore fruit as the DDA successfully concluded arrangements to supply handicrafts to Daells Varehus, a large department store in Copenhagen, and also staged a successful bazaar in

* H. Gaszczyk, "Eine Liebe Erinderung," Aleppo, 3 February 1946, DDA, bundle 10, folder D, Danish State Archives.

† Henni Forchhammer, *Et besøg hos Karen Jeppe* (Copenhagen: De Danske Armeniervenner, 1926), 13; Cedergreen Bech, ed., *Dansk Biografisk Leksikon* 7, 223.

‡ Jeppe to the DDA, Aleppo, 9 December 1921, reprinted in "Breve fra Karen Jeppe," *Armeniervennen* 21, no. 1-2 (1941): 2. Following Jeppe's death in 1935, the editors of the DDA's journal moved to publish a great many of her letters. This effort was not only a tribute to Jeppe's many years of work but also a recognition that her words and spirit remained central to the organization even after her passing.

the capital.[*] In time, Jeppe would cite developments like these as evidence of the strong support her work enjoyed among Danes, a fact which she reinforced by asserting that the sewing hall was essentially "an entirely *Danish* venture."[†] Notice of her and the DDA's efforts, what could be termed their national signature in the region, was also made by other aid organizations, among them Near East Relief which already in April 1923 approached Jeppe with an interest to adopt her approach in the development of embroidery workshops.[‡] One aspect of her success in that venture was the discipline she exhibited in not expanding local production beyond the export capacity despite the pressing need to employ more Armenian refugees. Though troubled by the need to show restraint, Jeppe accepted it as unavoidable as earlier efforts to establish a weaving business alongside the sewing hall had ended in failure, forcing its closure in 1922 after less than a year in operation.[**]

The challenges of creating sufficient economic development in northern Syria were aggravated in late 1921 when the French agreed to cede Cilicia back to Turkish control. Thousands of Armenians resident in the region, fearful of their fate in the absence of French protection, streamed into Syria as refugees.[††] Many made their way to Aleppo, only a short distance from the new border, and settled in the town already straining to accommodate its existing population. Jeppe would later estimate that as many 150,000 Armenians had entered Syria by 1925, and she observed that within months of the renewed influx, conditions in the northern city deteriorated as wages declined, prices for food

---

* De Danske Armeniervenner, *Bestyrelses Protokol*, 1919-1923, November 1922, 42-43, DDA, bundle 1, Danish State Archives; *Armeniervennen* 3, no. 11-12 (1923): 45-46.

† Jeppe, "Oversigt over Aarets Arbejde," *Armeniervennen* 7, no. 7-8 (1927): 33. Italics in the original.

‡ Jeppe to the DDA, Aleppo, 21 April 1923, reprinted in "Breve fra Karen Jeppe," *Armeniervennen* 26, no. 2 (1946): 8.

** Jeppe, "Account of the situation of the Armenians in Syria," Baalbek, 24 August 1922, DDA, bundle 10, folder A, Danish State Archives.

†† Stephen H. Longrigg, *Syria and Lebanon under French Mandate* (London: Oxford University Press, 1958), 138; Ellen Marie Lust-Okar, "Failure of Collaboration: Armenian Refugees in Syria," *Middle Eastern Studies* 32, no. 1 (1996): 56; Nansen, *Armenia and the Near East*, 317.

increased, and employment opportunities evaporated.* The refugees in particular were forced to cope with hardships, and she found that "they are suffering from every distress that can be endured by man, when he is homeless and destitute."† A concerted campaign of relief, financed both by the French Mandate authorities and international aid organizations, would be needed to alleviate the growing burdens on Syrian society. European activists sympathetic to the Armenian cause also lobbied the League of Nations to become involved in the recovery of refugees who were cut off from their families and ethnic roots. In fact, the League's hopes of "bringing peace and security to the region through a moral and political reordering along modern liberal nationalist, Wilsonian lines" were seen by many as inherently connected with a mission to assist the displaced Armenians and an effort warranting the recruitment of capable and dedicated activists.‡ Attention therefore soon fell on Jeppe as a person whose experience and ongoing work could well serve the wider relief efforts, and an active campaign of lobbying by Scandinavian delegates at the League ensued.** However, already approached early in 1921 by leading Armenians in Paris, who wanted her to assume a high-profile role in the League's activities, Jeppe expressed initial misgivings about taking on the responsibilities that such work demanded.†† She also voiced concerns that adequate funds would be lacking to properly resettle and rehabilitate the people rescued from across the region. And if that was the case, she noted, then it would be better to leave them in

---

* Jeppe, "Landbrugs-kolonien ved Eufrat," *Armeniervennen* 4, no. 11-12 (1924): 49.

† Jeppe, "Account of the situation of the Armenians in Syria," Baalbek, 24 August 1922, DDA, bundle 10, folder A, Danish State Archives.

‡ Keith David Watenpaugh, "The League of Nations' Rescue of Armenian Genocide Survivors and the Making of Modern Humanitarianism, 1920-1927," *American Historical Review* 115, no. 5 (2010): 1318.

** Ibid, 1326-1327.

†† Jeppe to the DDA, Paris, 30 February 1921, reprinted in "Breve fra Karen Jeppe," *Armeniervennen* 20, no. 11-12 (1940): 29-30; Henni Forchhammer, "Karen Jeppe og Folkenes Forbund," *Armeniervennen* 23, no. 7 (1943): 18.

captivity rather than give them false hope and insufficient support.[*] Yet by the late spring, after seriously considering the matter and feeling increasingly obligated to accede to the Armenian calls, she agreed to be a candidate for the new body, the Commission for the Protection of Women and Children in the Near East. Having come to realize that her fate, even her very essence, was really joined with that of the Armenian people, and having summoned from their indomitable nature the strength and courage needed to face the immense challenges that lay ahead, Jeppe gradually embraced her prospective role within the League.[†]

In September 1921 Jeppe accepted the post of commissioner, becoming part of a three-member team tasked with overseeing the recovery and welfare of Armenian refugees within the territories of the fledgling Ottoman state.[‡] Immediately upon assuming the new appointment she began work even though the projected service as yet lacked an approved budget and adequate infrastructure. Determined to seize the moment and forge ahead now that she had committed herself fully to the task, Jeppe acted to implement plans already under development months earlier. In her mind, Aleppo should become a center for the recovery work, serving as a beacon for the entire region south of the Taurus Mountains.[**] Feeding its flame should be the bright

* Jeppe, "Account of the situation of the Armenians in Syria," Baalbek, 24 August 1922, DDA, bundle 10, folder A, Danish State Archives; Henni Forchhammer, *Minder om Karen Jeppe* (Copenhagen: J. Frimodts Forlag, 1945), 14;

† Jeppe to the DDA, Aleppo, 15 May 1921, reprinted in "Karen Jeppe og Folkenes Forbund," *Armeniervennen* 23, no. 7 (1943): 19; Jeppe, "Mine Oplevelser blandt Armenierne," 1, no. 2 (1921): 6; *Armeniervennen* 1, no. 11-12 (1921): 41.

‡ The other two relief workers and League commissioners were Emma Cushman, an American nurse, and Dr. W.A. Kennedy, an Anglo-Irish physician, who were both based in Istanbul. See Watenpaugh, "The League of Nations' Rescue of Armenian Genocide Survivors…," *American Historical Review*, 1323, 1329.

** Jeppe to Inga Nalbandian, Aleppo, 13 July 1921, reprinted in "Karen Jeppe og Folkenes Forbund," *Armeniervennen* 23, no. 8 (1921): 21; Forchhammer, *Minder om Karen Jeppe*, 18.

lights of safety and promising opportunities offered by temporary housing and job creation in the city and surrounding countryside. And channeling escapees to the Syrian safe haven should be a network of recovery stations, each staffed with agents dedicated to assist Armenians in flight to freedom. However, Jeppe's idealism about the League's work was significantly tempered by her views on the manner in which such captives should be released and the quality of person her agents should entice to escape. Rather than endorse a wholesale and forcible liberation of all such Armenians held across the region, estimated by Jeppe at no less than 30,000 women and children in her zone of operation from Syria to Mesopotamia, she advocated a much more calculated and selective approach.[*] In fact, she believed that many Armenian captives had been debilitated and corrupted by their years in Muslim households and would therefore fail to be assets in the effort to reconstitute the Armenian community. Such people, Jeppe argued, were often heavily "Turkified" and should consequently be avoided, and children who grew up in urban areas ought to be particularly so as they had "been the victims of an unlimited licentiousness, and have mentally and physically been infected and spoiled."[†] A lesser stigma was attached to those Armenians who endured their captivity in the rural areas with either Arab or Kurdish tribes, because that latter setting was seen as harboring at least aspects of moral and pure living. However, in either context, she argued, the Armenians were subjected to a process of dehumanization and "de-civilization" as they found themselves immersed in Islam and removed from Christianity. Under such pressures, Jeppe believed, "weak and degenerate individuals yield more easily and become Mahometans (sic)," but as a people, she continued, "the Armenian nation could never stoop to embrace Islam and instead held true to Christianity even through to the most incredible sufferings."[‡] It was therefore imperative to discriminate between the individuals in Muslim hands and only seek

* Jeppe, "Account of the situation of the Armenians in Syria," Baalbek, 24 August 1922, DDA, bundle 10, folder A, Danish State Archives; Jeppe, "Armenien," *Tidens Kvinder* 1, no. 12 (1923): 6.

† Jeppe, "Account of the situation of the Armenians in Syria," Baalbek, 24 August 1922, DDA, bundle 10, folder A, Danish State Archives; Jeppe, "Frk. Jeppe i Syrien," *Armeniervennen* 2, no. 11-12 (1922): 45.

‡ Ibid.

to liberate those who retained a devotion to their identity and harbored the sense of initiative and commitment needed to free themselves.

Jeppe's cautionary and selective approach to her work suggests both contradiction and the influence of ideology, but it also underscores the very real limits imposed by funding constraints and uncertain prospects for success. Seeking to do more than just rescue and assist, she was further driven by a passionate commitment to see the Armenian nation revived, a mission which could best be achieved and sustained by Armenians of strong character and ethnic devotion.[*] Limited resources only reinforced the need to focus selectively and, though able to immediately solicit additional financial support from both Swedish sympathizers and the Armenian Red Cross in Britain upon her accession to the prestigious League of Nations appointment, Jeppe lacked the necessary resources to be widely effective.[†] Conscious that a mass flight of Armenian captives could not be accommodated, and ever fearful that such a flood of escapees might further inundate the Syrian economy and aggravate local animosities, she emphasized patience as a policy.[‡] The League's legislated authority to actively enforce the recovery of the unfortunates ought therefore to be avoided, and efforts should instead be made to negotiate, where possible, for their release.[**] Such an approach would promote understanding over deception and dialogue over force, and help to cultivate in the local population an acceptance of the Armenians as people with rights. However, it is clear that such harmony was not always forthcoming as many local Muslim Arab elites and

* Okkenhaug, "Scandinavian Missionaries, Gender and Armenian Refugees...," 89; Watenpaugh, "The League of Nations' Rescue of Armenian Genocide Survivors...," 1327.

† League of Nations, "Work of the Commission for the Protection of Women and Children in the Near East," Geneva, 11 September 1923, A. 69. 1923. IV. *League of Nations Documents, 1919-1946*. New Haven: Research Publications, 1973. Jeppe's included report was dated 16 August 1923.

‡ Jeppe to the DDA, Aleppo, 19 December 1922, reprinted in "Breve fra Karen Jeppe, *Armeniervennen* 26, no. 1 (1946): 3; Jeppe to the DDA, Aleppo, 21 April 1923, reprinted in "Breve fra Karen Jeppe," *Armeniervennen* 26, no. 2 (1946): 7.

** Sick, *Pigen fra Danmark*, 187.

intellectuals saw the rescue efforts as invasive, sometimes misguided, and generally as an unwanted extension of the French administrative regime in Syria.[*] But complications and challenges aside, Jeppe believed that there existed "a very strong will for flight among the Armenians in Muslim homes," and she did not foresee that its intensity was likely to fade.[†] Hence, the need for urgency was absent as it was estimated that over the subsequent four to five years, as the young captives matured, most would retain their passion for their Armenian roots and still seek to be reunited with family members. In fact, Jeppe held that there was a ten-year window, a period when the youths were aged between their teens and early twenties, during which time it was entirely possible to reintegrate them into their culture and society.[‡] However, within that group it was further asserted that boys aged fourteen to eighteen years old were particularly motivated for escape as were unmarried girls and young women who had yet to be tied down with a husband and the duties of motherhood. The League's mission, as Jeppe saw it, was consequently to facilitate rather than enforce the repatriation of Armenians, and to help gather the scattered but hearty seedlings of a Christian nation in revival.

But as the Dane assumed her official position as a League commissioner in March 1922, she was increasingly uneasy about the future prospects of the Armenian community in the region. The challenges of establishing an out of place people in a new land weighed heavily on Jeppe as she lamented their loss of a national home. "I am not at all satisfied," she declared, "with the Armenians settling in Syria. It is not their country," she continued, "and living among entirely foreign peoples, one cannot know if they might not be at risk of their lives and property here."[**] Her recognition of their vulnerabilities as refugees

---

* Watenpaugh, "The League of Nations' Rescue of Armenian Genocide Survivors…," 1328-1329, 1336.

† Jeppe to the DDA, Aleppo, 30 May 1922, reprinted in "Endnu nogle Breve fra Karen Jeppe," *Armeniervennen* 25, no. 5 (1945): 23.

‡ Jeppe to the DDA, Aleppo, 26 June 1922, reprinted in "Breve fra Karen Jeppe," *Armeniervennen* 22, no. 7-8 (1942): 16.

** Jeppe, "Account of the situation of the Armenians in Syria," Baalbek, 24 August 1922, DDA, bundle 10, folder A, Danish State Archives; Jeppe, "Frk. Jeppe i Syrien," *Armeniervennen* 2, no. 11-12 (1922): 46.

made it clear that League efforts needed to be focused on far more than the release of captives, including a commitment to equip the displaced population with needed training and skills and furthering integration. The founding in Aleppo of the League's recovery home in September 1922 was a minor if significant step to address that pressing need. In fact, Jeppe had managed to convince her fellow commission members that she should remain in Syria rather than head to Istanbul as first intended, because reputed multitudes were concentrated across the region within reach of the city. Further aggravating the state of affairs between 1922 and1923 was the arrival of as many as 25,000 Armenian refugees to Aleppo even as the international effort to alleviate their suffering seemingly wavered.[*] The large aid organization Near East Relief decided in 1923 to abandon its efforts in Syria proper and consolidate its resources in Lebanon, leaving Jeppe and her fledgling League operation to cope with the mounting crisis.[†] Such developments made it imperative that additional financial support be forthcoming to supplement the insufficient funds made available by the League, and the Dane estimated in late 1922 that in the upcoming year she would need £4,000 in private contributions to bolster the meager £1,500 budgeted from Geneva.[‡] Much of that money she hoped to raise in Scandinavia, calling on her Nordic compatriots to assume the responsibility of funding the daunting task at hand. And though those resources were woefully inadequate to address the entirety of needs, Jeppe described the assistance coming from overseas as fuel sustaining the faint Danish flame of her work, a proverbial light in the darkness that was helping to call and draw determined Armenians to seek their salvation.[**]

The passion and dedication she felt for the rescue and rehabilitation effort led her to defend it vigorously against those, even including delegates within the League itself, who advocated that the limited

---

* Longrigg, *Syria and Lebanon under French Mandate*, 138; Lust-Okar, "Failure of Collaboration…," *Middle Eastern Studies*, 56.

† Jeppe, "Hjemløse," *Armeniervennen* 2, no. 3-4 (1922): 10.

‡ Jeppe to the DDA, Aleppo, 7 December 1922, reprinted in "Karen Jeppe og Folkenes Forbund," *Armeniervennen* 24, no. 1 (1944): 1.

** Jeppe, "Et par billeder fra arbejdsmarken," *Armeniervennen* 2, no. 11-12 (1922): 44.

assistance provided should be suspended as it fell outside the purview of the international organization.* In the face of such criticism, Jeppe was adamant that the aid, however scarce, was symbolically significant, and in a famed thirteen-word phrase uttered at a League session in September 1923, she declared that "Yes, it is only a little light, but the night is so dark."† To her the League's involvement and presence, that flickering flame, needed to be sustained until it burned brightly, because it represented hope and "more than anything else, it is this feeling of security, of having gotten a good and big home, sheltered by the greatest moral authority of the world, that gives them [the Armenians] force and courage."‡ Those powerful yet simple words captured Jeppe's deep and intense conviction about the virtue of the humanitarian work being conducted, and her proclamations served to shore up and strengthen the support for ongoing League funding of the Aleppo-based operation. Over the subsequent years, from the 1923 re-approval of the initial budget until the last allocation of payments in 1926, monies flowed from Geneva as a stable, dependable, yet ever dwindling share of the overall resources available to Jeppe. And even after the suspension of direct assistance from the organization, she retained her title as League commissioner for another year and all the property purchased using League funds passed to her ownership. The resources provided by the organization were therefore vital assets in Jeppe's strides to build the infrastructure of an effective humanitarian aid agency.

With the advent of 1923, the foundations of the next decade's Danish-led relief efforts in Aleppo were quickly taking shape. Having merged the modest commercial ventures that she began upon her arrival in early 1921 with the League plans for a large-scale rescue and recovery

* Forchhammer, "Karen Jeppe og Folkenes Forbund," *Armeniervennen* 24, no. 1 (1944): 2.

† Jeppe to Johannes Ravn, Aleppo, 10 April 1931, Johannes Ravn Collection, Danish State Archive; Christian Winther, *Armenien og Karen Jeppe*, 27.

‡ League of Nations, "Work of the Commission for the Protection of Women and Children in the Near East," Geneva, 11 September 1923, A. 69. 1923. IV. *League of Nations Documents, 1919-1946*; Jeppe, "Et par billeder fra arbejdsmarken," *Armeniervennen* 2, no. 11-12 (1922): 44.

program, Jeppe soon became an indispensable figure in the rehabilitation of Armenian refugees. Even before the doors of the League's relief institutions in the city were opened, more than a hundred people, the vast majority of them children, had already streamed into Aleppo to seek the prospective shelter that it offered.* About half of these were soon reunited with family, thereby removing them as a drain on the venture's limited resources, but the rest were either too young to fend for themselves or in desperate need of skills to function independently in an urban environment. The immediate response was to provide temporary lodgings in the form of tents until additional funds could be gathered to pay the high rents prevailing in the city, and night classes and training was begun to provide the boys over fourteen with a rapid, six months of education. Financial constraints simply prevented Jeppe from housing the older refugees for longer periods of time, because as 1923 progressed the number of people having used her services had climbed to over three hundred.† However, a measure of much needed assistance was soon forthcoming from the Armenian Red Cross in London which generously allocated £800 towards the construction of numerous buildings, including a large barracks that could house as many as 200 people.‡ Jeppe praised such efforts by the Armenians to participate in the restoration of their nation and marveled at the level of communal organization that saw aid dispersed through local and regional networks and coordinated the reunification of refugees in Syria with relatives as far away as the United States. In her mind, this served to underscore yet again the indefatigable nature of the Armenian people and their ability to persevere and flourish against all odds, to literally "create bread from

---

* Jeppe, "Account of the situation of the Armenians in Syria," Baalbek, 24 August 1922, DDA, bundle 10, folder A, Danish State Archives; Jeppe, "Frk. Jeppe i Syrien," *Armeniervennen* 2, no. 11-12 (1922): 45.

† League of Nations, "Work of the Commission for the Protection of Women and Children in the Near East," Geneva, 11 September 1923, A. 69. 1923. IV. *League of Nations Documents, 1919-1946.*

‡ Ibid; League of Nations, "Protection of Women and Children in the Near East," Geneva, 1 September 1924, A. 46. 1924. IV. *League of Nations Documents, 1919-1946*; Jeppe, "Paa vej til Syrien – Hjemme igen," *Armeniervennen* 4, no. 3-4 (1924): 11.

stones."[*] Strengthened by those core qualities of pride and courage, the Armenians seemingly constituted the ideal population to embrace Jeppe's humanitarian principle of providing help for self-help, of enabling a people to restore their own dignity and identity.

Central to realizing that policy was the expansion of the vocational programs that she organized immediately upon her return to the region in 1921. Determined to provide the Armenians with the skills to become self-supporting, Jeppe not only strove to increase the workforce at the sewing hall, which rose to 150 women and girls in the mid-1920s and twice that number in later years, but she also founded additional businesses.[†] A tannery and carpentry workshop were both in operation by 1923, and an emphasis on top quality production served to give those enterprises a solid reputation in Aleppo.[‡] Such efforts helped to partially meet the rising need for jobs as Armenians continued to arrive in the city, but additional resources were also required to relieve the ever-worsening conditions in the surrounding and expanding refugee camps. Léopold Gaszczyk, a Pole hired in 1923 by Jeppe to serve as an assistant, would two decades later describe the impromptu settlements as sites where the unfortunate residents, if abandoned to rely only on their own limited means, were in serious danger of compromising their health and losing their identity:

> In the years 1923-1924 immense camps of barracks and all kinds of huts were erected of empty petrol and gasoline tins held together by bandelets (sic) or old boards and in some cases made with sun dried bricks....
>
> [T]hese settlements grew overnight out of the earth just like mushrooms covering larger and larger spaces on the outskirts of

* Jeppe, "Account of the situation of the Armenians in Syria," Baalbek, 24 August 1922, DDA, bundle 10, folder A, Danish State Archives.

† H. Gaszczyk, "Eine Liebe Erinderung," Aleppo, 3 February 1946, DDA, bundle 10, folder D, Danish State Archives; Jenny Jensen, "Brev fra Aleppo," *Armeniervennen* 5, no. 5-6 (1925): 17.

‡ De Danske Armeniervenner, *Bestyrelses Protokol*, 1919-1923, DDA, bundle 1, Danish State Archives; Jeppe, "Oversigt over Aarets Arbejde," *Armeniervennen* 7, no. 7-8 (1927): 33.

> Aleppo....[E]xtremely unhealthy [and] lacking of every privacy, they were harmful morally just as well as physically.*

Pressing needs for direct assistance in the form of medical care, hot meals, and money for refugee families therefore prompted Jeppe to solicit additional Danish aid. The DDA soon responded to this call and resources were raised in 1925 to open a soup kitchen as part of a feeding program to provide for the poorest children in the shantytowns during the winter months. Within the year, Jeppe was calling on the organization to double its commitment of funds in order to extend the program from three to six months annually, thereby further ensuring the well being of the 500 children under their care.† An increasing level of support for the aid work also allowed Jeppe in 1926 to disperse over £150 directly to Armenian refugee organizations in Aleppo.‡ And with funds initially raised exclusively from Danish-Americans, she opened the following year a medical clinic with the express aim of keeping refugee families intact by guaranteeing the health of the parents.** Through such preventive measures, including the distribution of used clothes collected overseas, the hope was to improve the lives of the refugees sufficiently to prevent a descent into worsened conditions that in turn would demand greater resources to remedy. The effort to sustain tolerable living standards and maintain the health of the displaced population was also imperative if attempts to educate the refugee children were to be successful. Without access to proper diet, housing, and clothes, the Armenian children would constitute a very poor student body incapable of absorbing the education provided by the local schools. The Jeppe-led approach to helping the people beyond her immediate care was therefore rather multifaceted, involving a broad range of measures meant to limit the problems facing the refugees and intended to create an environment where unfettered access to education was a symbolic prize for the population. In very idealistic terms, she envisioned the pursuit of

---

* L. Gaszczyk, untitled circular, Aleppo, 1 February 1946, DDA, bundle 10, folder D, Danish State Archives.

† Jeppe, "Nu maa der hjælpes," *Armeniervennen* 6, no. 9-10 (1926): 34.

‡ Jeppe, "Vor Virksomhed i Syrien," *Armeniervennen* 6, no. 3-4 (1926): 13.

** Jeppe, "Blandt de Syge og Fattige i Barak-Lejren, *Armeniervennen* 9, no. 3-4 (1929): 14.

learning as a testament to the nobility and commitment of the people, conveying to her readers and supporters images of young children defying the everyday struggles to pursue their studies, of underpaid but dedicated teachers guiding their learning, and of devoted parents who sacrificed to keep their offspring in school.[*] The ability to provide the Armenian people with a future rather than merely keeping them alive was consequently a matter of key importance, and Jeppe was throughout her career in Aleppo adamant that the efforts to rescue and recover individuals were largely wasted if aid was not forthcoming in the aftermath to assure them of access to opportunities and intellectual and spiritual development.

Agents of Hope

The League of Nations decision to make Jeppe a commissioner and fund her work in Syria committed the organization to an ambitious program of restoring Armenian refugees to their families and nation. Convinced that thousands of women and children were forcibly confined to Muslim households across the region, trapped, as Jeppe put in, behind "the prison doors" of the harems, the international body moved to empower the Dane to spearhead a network of agents and recovery stations.[†] Jeppe immediately channeled this promised authority into action as within only months of her appointment, yet long before she officially assumed the position, she was hard at work organizing and coordinating the efforts of a number of men who had previously acted independently to bring Armenians out of captivity.[‡] Paralleling this initiative was the establishment during the summer of 1922 of a rescue post at Jarablus, located right on the Turco-Syrian border.[**] Intended to serve as a magnate for Armenians across the divide, the station attracted fifty children and young women over only a brief period of four to five weeks in July and August, constituting a significant portion of the two hundred

* Jeppe, "Sennepskornet," *Armeniervennen* 10, no. 9-10 (1930): 34.

† Jeppe, "Armenien," *Tidens Kvinder* 1, no. 12 (31 May 1923): 6.

‡ Jeppe to the DDA, Aleppo, 16 December 1921, reprinted in "Breve fra Karen Jeppe," *Armeniervennen* 22, no. 3-4 (1942): 7.

** Jeppe, "Et Aar i Folkenes Forbunds Tjeneste," *Armeniervennen* 3, no. 3-4 (1923): 11.

and twenty-five people recovered across the region during the entire first year.[*] Such success made it clear that the placement of recovery posts close to the estimated concentration of Armenians increased significantly the number of people who chose to flee. By September 1924, a string of three posts along the Mardin-Hasakah-Dayr az Zawr line in eastern Syria had helped to elevate the recovery numbers to over six hundred, including one hundred eighty-seven in just the first six months of the year.[†] That level of progress was in part attributable to the assistance offered by the French Mandate authorities and local Arab officials who helped to provide identity papers and general protection for the escaped refugees. Jeppe's adopted son, Misak Melkonian, and the Pole Gaszczyk too were praised by her as playing important roles in the initial successes, routinely touring the network of countryside stations and overseeing the vital links with their network of agents and informants whom they relied on to establish contact with the captive Armenians.[‡] Melkonian would eventually even lead "a team of armed Armenian and Arab horsemen that embarked on search and rescue expeditions in the contiguous areas, sometimes penetrating Turkish territory."[**] And jointly, the two men's efforts helped to maintain and coordinate a system that strived to inform the unfortunates across the region that hope and promise was within their reach if they had the will, opportunity, and courage to grasp it.

During the course of 1925 more than three hundred people seized that chance, ballooning the League's tally of recovered Armenians to well over one thousand since the rescue efforts first began four years earlier.[††]

---

* Ibid.

† League of Nations, "Protection of Women and Children in the Near East," Geneva, 1 September 1924, A. 46. 1924. IV. *League of Nations Documents, 1919-1946*.

‡ Jeppe to the DDA, Aleppo, 14 February 1923, reprinted in "Karen Jeppe og Folkenes Forbund," *Armeniervennen* 24, no. 1 (1944): 2; Jeppe to the DDA, Aleppo, 29 March 1924, reprinted in "Breve fra Karen Jeppe," *Armeniervennen* 26, no. 5 (1946): 19; Forchhammer, *Minder om Karen Jeppe*, 28.

** Vahram L. Shemmassian, "The League of Nations and the Reclamation of Armenian Genocide Survivors," in *Looking Backward, Moving Forward*, ed. Richard Hovannisian (2003), 101.

†† Jeppe, "Frk. Jeppes Rapport: Arbejdet i Folkeforbunds-Kommissionen," *Armeniervennen* 6, no. 3-4 (1926): 11.

Constituting the largest group collected as yet during a twelve-month period, the numbers reflected the accelerating success of the League's activities but also the growing financial burdens weighing on the relief efforts. At a cost of about £9 per recovered refugee, the cumulative expense of £2,700 far outstripped the £1,800 allocated from Geneva for the year, and, while private funds easily covered the budget shortfall, the trend suggested that a scarcity of resources might soon undermine both the pace and scope of the work yet needing to be performed.* Jeppe feared such developments in what she described as the eleventh hour of the recovery effort and a time when commitments needed to be doubled rather than restrained. The mistakes of the past, the Dane argued, when too few resources were made available and thousands of Armenians were effectively abandoned to their fates, should not be repeated, and she was adamant that the League's agents under her leadership should be sent ever further afield to rescue more people. Even as she conceded that the station at Dayr az Zawr ought soon to be closed as the surrounding area had largely been "cleaned," her passion for the cause pushed her to call for a replacement station at Ras al Ayn located just on the border with Turkey.† There she predicted that as many as two thousand Armenians were poised to seek their escape, needing only the proximate presence of the League's representatives to seal their decision. From Ras al Ayn her agents could also conduct with greater ease covert forays into Turkish territory, traveling the countryside disguised as Arab Bedouin or Kurdish tribesmen and spreading the news that a better life awaited them across the border in Syria. A favored destination of such secretive trips was the region around Mardin, a heavily Kurdish area centered about 20 km inside Turkey. One agent in particular, Vasil Sabagh, a Catholic Armenian and former merchant from Urfa, who managed the station at Hasakah, used his prior commercial connections and familiarity with the regional countryside to establish a range of contacts that facilitated the

* Ibid.

† League of Nations, "Commission for the Protection of Women and Children in the Near East," Geneva, 5 September 1925, A. 32. 1925. IV/ C. 451. 1925. IV. *Official Journal. Special Supplement 38. Records of the 6th Assembly. Meetings of the Committees. Minutes of the Fifth Committee*, 157, 159.

release of Armenians from the local Kurdish communities.[*] Among that latter population, Jeppe envisioned yet another frontier of rescue work since those lands had until then remained neglected due to the League's reluctance to directly and officially challenge conditions within the Turkish Republic. Prospects for the liberation of Armenians were further worsened by the outbreak of a Kurdish revolt in 1925, cutting the League's agents off from the area. Yet as the fighting raged, thousands of Kurds sought refuge in Syria, bringing with them the very people that Jeppe and her network were empowered to rescue. Out of conflict, in turn, sprang forth opportunity and the recovery service quickly sought to exploit the emergent conditions even as dangers persisted in the countryside.

In the hinterlands of northeastern Syria and the areas along the disputed border with Turkey, Jeppe's agents encountered an environment that was both harsh and immensely challenging. Tasked with being the face of the League of Nations on the margins of settled society, the men enlisted by her and her closest assistants, Misak Melkonian and Gaszczyk, were a valiant group of individuals whose courage and dedication allowed them to defy the calamities that lurked in the unfamiliar wilderness. By 1928, as the network of stations and agents was in its final months of operation, Jeppe could report that several of the men had died over the years from either overwork or the ill-effects of the tough conditions under which they lived. Local opposition to the rescue work too posed a danger as people saw their families and interests threatened by the League's interventions. In a 1926 interview, Jeppe even alleged that she was a target of Turkish assassination plots, preventing her, out of fear for her life, from venturing into certain districts along the border.[†] Whatever the veracity of such claims, the safety of League personnel was an ever-pressing concern that was only heightened with the murder of the famed agent Vasil Sabagh. Having committed himself to save at least forty children from captivity, he was bringing his thirty-seventh ward to safety in Aleppo when he was cut down in the Syrian Desert by disgruntled

* Ibid,159; Jernazian, *Judgment Unto Truth*, 130, 156-57; Shemmassian, "The League of Nations…," 100.

† "10,000 mennesker, som maa dø af sult," *København*, 3 October 1926.

Arabs.* The Dane greatly lamented this loss to her network because men of such experience and valor were scarce. His passing also underscored the need to proceed with caution and to always be mindful of not inciting the local population. In fact, Jeppe's final report to the League in July 1927 stressed that the modest number of people recovered was attributable to a deliberate and calculated policy of restraint:

> This accounts for the comparatively small numbers rescued. If we had been unscrupulous, we could have had very different figures to show. As it is, we know that, *although the scope of our work has been limited, within those limits it has done nothing but good.*†

Rather than provoke and inflame, the aim was to negotiate and persuade, working to humanize the captive Armenians in the eyes of those holding them and thereby secure their release. Jeppe too acknowledged that not everyone ought to be removed from their life among the Muslims, noting that many were indeed part of loving families and had dependent children.‡ The genuine bonds forged, however artificial and unnatural their origins, should not be arbitrarily cut as this could disrupt lives unnecessarily and also undermine the League's moral authority. Even when such ties were severed voluntarily by women who desired to rejoin Armenian society, Jeppe felt sorry about the resultant tragedies left in its wake as Arab and Kurdish men and children lost wives and mothers.** She, in fact, described the experience of Armenians in Muslim households as a spectrum in which both mercy and simple self-interest motivated those among whom they lived. Tales of rape, abuse, and mental anguish might abound, but there were also accounts reflecting compassion and affection, such as the one in which an Armenian boy was adopted by a wealthy Arab and eventually inherited his fortune, or the one about a young woman whose Arab husband taught her to read and helped her recover a lost child. These

---

* Jernazian, *Judgment Unto Truth*, 130, 156-57.

† League of Nations, "Report of the Commission for the Protection of Women and Children in the Near East," Geneva, 28 July 1927, A. 29. 1927. IV. *League of Nations Documents, 1919-1946*. Italics in the original.

‡ Ibid.

** Jeppe, "Fra vort Optagelseshjem," *Armeniervennen* 3, no. 5-6 (1923): 19.

alternative narratives served to broaden Danish understandings of the conditions prevailing in the Syrian Desert and the Turkish hinterland, adding complexity and nuance to an issue often imbued with moral indignation. Even the Arab Bedouin practice of tattooing their Armenian women, a tradition denounced by Danish commentators as burdening them with enduring shame and marking them permanently as property, was actually explained years later to the readers of *Armeniervennen*, as evidence of integration and inclusion.*

But whatever positives could be salvaged from the experiences of Armenians across the countryside, nothing diminished the calamity that had befallen the population as a whole. The events of the First World War devastated the community within the Ottoman Empire, and Jeppe was astounded by the ability of the people to persevere:

> That catastrophe that befell them was in relation to population size and available relief efforts so overwhelming and frightful that one wonders why they did not perish entirely. When a people loses 80% of its men and all its physical property, and further is driven from the lands it has occupied for centuries, one should think they were surely doomed.†

Convinced that one million Armenians died during the regional conflict, a sentiment she shared with Fridtjof Nansen, her famed Scandinavian colleague, Jeppe found that the people were straining under the tremendous and lasting burdens of having experienced such debilitating losses.‡ Displaced, impoverished, and psychologically wounded, the Armenians were, in her view, sustained only by their

---

* Inger Christensen, "Fra mit besøg i Aleppo," *Armeniervennen* 4, no. 5-6 (1924): 22; Sick, *Pigen fra Danmark*, 165-66; Jenny Jensen, *Armeniervennen* 5, no. 5-6 (1925): 18; Künzler, "Dit Folk er mit Folk: Stormen bryder løs over Asien," *Armeniervennen* 19, no. 7-8 (1939): 30.

† Jeppe, "Hvor længe endnu," Lyngby, 31 August 1929, DDA, bundle 9, Danish State Archives.

‡ Jeppe, "Armenierne i Euphrat-Egnen I," *Armeniervennen* 10, no. 9-10 (1930); Nansen, *Armenia and the Near East*, 318.

"never failing will to live."[*] That innate spirit made them a uniquely noble people and a tremendously important asset to the West, constituting a virtual bulwark against the Orient. "The Armenians," asserted Jeppe, "are for our race the furthest most outpost in the struggle against Asia."[†] The quintessential "Eastern people," whose very roots were so firmly embedded in the region, had, in her mind, since evolved into the first and critical line of defense for Western civilization. Their struggle should hence be supported without restraint and Jeppe resisted vehemently those who argued otherwise. When articles critical of the Armenians appeared in the Danish press, as happened in 1930, many of which were written by Danish railway engineers who had spent years in Turkey, she staunchly defended the community against such attacks and was simply incredulous that the villainous Turk could be favored over the noble Armenian victim. Determined to dismiss and discredit those responsible, she used her decades-long residence in the region as an instrument to diminish the validity of commentary and assertions made by those with far fewer years of experience:

> [T]here are many who come to the Orient *with a preconceived understanding*, and who also believe that they have it confirmed. The shorter the time they remain here, and the less insight they have in the actual conditions, the more convinced they are in their judgment.[‡]

In terms that preempted by decades the anti-Orientalist discourse, Jeppe was striking at the heart of Western misconceptions of the East by condemning those who generalized widely based on their own narrow experiences and asserted as fact that which was solely attributable to perception. However, in almost the same breath, she too placed herself squarely within the sphere of Orientalism by emphasizing that the East was almost insurmountably foreign and alien:

---

* Jeppe, "Hvor længe endnu?," Lyngby, 31 August 1929, DDA, bundle 9, Danish State Archives.

† Jeppe to the DDA, Aleppo, 9 February 1925, reprinted in "Breve fra Karen Jeppe," *Armeniervennen* 27, no. 1 (1947): 8.

‡ Jeppe, "De bagtalte Armeniere: Europas onde Samvittighed," *Armeniervennen* 10, no. 11-12 (1930): 41. Italics in the original.

> The Orient is so impenetrable for outsiders that they cannot tell the different races apart, and they do not comprehend the particular way that Orientals act.*

Jeppe, in her fervor to assert herself as an unassailable authority in contrast to other commentators, was effectively solidifying the popular perception that the East was a realm of the mysterious Other and fraught with dizzying complexity. Danes were consequently encouraged, if not obligated, to turn to her for guidance in order to explore and understand the murky, distant world of the Middle East. That perceived role as gatekeeper to genuine knowledge was further emphasized, even to the point of the ridiculous, by one of Jeppe's many supporters who witnessed her work in Syria:

> She [Jeppe] had acquired that rare skill among Westerners to be able to penetrate the soul of the Oriental, this almost debilitating sensitivity that is necessary to win his trust, and a talent which has made her into [one of] our century's most remarkable Western female figures in the Orient....†

Again the region was described as otherworldly, as inhabited by people who were at their core profoundly different from Westerners. Only a small number of people, such as the famed Dane, could supposedly bridge that chasm and reveal what was otherwise obscured, and explore the private lives and spectrum of personalities within the alien populations. But for Jeppe, the proclaimed arbiter between truth and fiction about the East, the Armenians constituted a people apart from the rest, a people possessing qualities, such as honesty and sense of duty, which tied them more to the West than to their native soil.‡ A broad acceptance of such links, it was argued, should generate more support for the relief efforts and foster greater involvement by France, the power administering the Syrian Mandate.

The French relationship with Jeppe and the League's mission to recover Armenian refugees revealed the complexities of European rule in the region. Having swiftly crushed the emergent forces seeking Syrian

---

* Ibid.

† Elizabeth Meyer, "Armeniens ukronede droning," *Politiken*, 17 June 1934.

‡ Forchhammer, *Minder om Karen Jeppe*, 9.

independence in 1920, France worked to legitimize its occupation of the area through a manipulation of the many regional and ethnic centers of power within the Mandate, even separating Lebanon from Syria and creating a split that would endure. Geopolitical interests similarly motivated the French decision in 1921 to cede traditionally Syrian territory to the Turkish Republic, serving to further dismember the former Ottoman province.[*] In fact, by war's end, France was a weakened country entirely unsuited to oversee a mandate as it lacked the necessary resources to foster regional economic development.[†] French policy was instead focused on generating revenues from the territory and securing internal security. A vital agency in achieving that latter goal was the intelligence service, the *Service des Reseignements*, whose small corps of officers worked tirelessly and skillfully to promote factional and sectarian identities rather than a unified, national ethos.[‡] The Armenians constituted one such community within the Mandate, and the French sought for a time during the 1920s to establish it as an allied population upon whom they could rely for support. Through aid and favored access to government employment it was hoped to link the fortunes of the Armenians, both native and refugee, to the ongoing French presence in the region, and they soon emerged, both out of need and in pursuit of opportunity, as an unequivocal "client community of the state," by 1925 even receiving full political rights within the Mandate.[**] This relationship between an ethno-religious minority, including significant numbers of foreigners, and the occupation forces of a European power served to alienate the Armenians from the broader Syrian population, a development that in many ways worked at cross-purposes with the objectives of Jeppe and the League of Nations. After all, while she would ultimately praise the role of the French intelligence officers in having facilitated and actively protected the recovery work, the close Armenian ties, even outright collaboration, with the occupiers served to poison the prospects of integrating permanently that community into Syrian

* Tabitha Petran, *Syria* (New York: Praeger, 1972), 61.

† Khoury, *Syria and the French Mandate*, 46-47.

‡ Ibid, 55-56, 77-78.

** Ibid, 206-07, 364; Lust-Okan, "Failure of Collaboration…," 58, 60.

society.[*] Those concerns were further aggravated by the role of Armenian armed forces in the suppression of the Great Arab Revolt (1925-1927), the conduct of irregular units in the Maydan district of Damascus generating particular notoriety.[†] Concerted efforts were therefore needed to reverse the debilitating process of alienation and instead institute measures that could ensure the minority and refugee population permanence within the Mandate.

New Lands for an Ancient People

In the wake of the failed Arab uprising against French rule, the authorities moved to reform and hone their approach to governing Syria. The policy of supporting non-Arab minorities was rapidly disbanded in favor of a more astute system that sought to co-opt elements within the Arab community rather than maintain an adversarial relationship reinforced by alliances with minorities.[‡] As regarded the Armenians, French administrators worked, in response to the shifting policy, to gradually reduce their concentration within the cities and to disperse them across the sparsely populated countryside. Jeppe favored such changes, having as early as May 1921 argued that the Armenians held captive throughout the rural areas, and the target of future recovery efforts, were largely agrarian people in need of resettlement in farming communities.[**] And while she also expressed misgivings, as late as October 1926, about the promise of a future for Armenians in Syria, hoping instead for the successful revival of an independent Armenia, she felt that in the interim, before the dream was realized, resources should

---

* League of Nations, "Protection of Women and Children in the Near East," Geneva, 24 September 1926, A 106. 1926. IV. *League of Nations Documents, 1919-1946*; Jeppe, "Fra Rednings-arbejdet," *Armeniervennen* 8, no. 1-2 (1928): 4.

† Khoury, *Syria and the French Mandate,* 191; Lust-Okan, "Failure of Collaboration...," 61.

‡ Lust-Okan, "Failure of Collaboration...," 61-64.

** Jeppe to the DDA, Aleppe, 15 May 1921, reprinted in "Breve fra Karen Jeppe," *Armeniervennen* 20, no. 11-12 (1940): 30-31; Forchhammer, *Minder om Karen Jeppe*, 15.

be committed to fund settlements.* However, such ambitious plans would require financial support from sources other than the League of Nations, and in 1923 Jeppe opened negotiations with the Swedish chapter of the International Fellowship for Peace and Reconciliation, an organization intent on fostering positive relations between refugees and their neighbors.† During those talks, the Swedes became convinced that Jeppe was the right person to direct the spending of their contributions. Impressed by both her experience and regional reputation, the organization's directors were also soon persuaded by the Dane's ability to deliver Armenian settlers who were tied to her personally and willing to assume the risks of venturing into the countryside as pioneers.

Over the winter months of 1923-24 there arrived in Aleppo a community of Armenians who were well suited to form the vanguard of the Danish-directed effort to found farming villages in the Syrian hinterland. Hailing from the village of Garmuch near Urfa, they were native to the region of Medjeidé, where Jeppe had once owned a farm and she and her son had helped foster an almost idyllic relationship between the Armenians and local Muslim inhabitants.‡ That positive environment was later crushed by the events of the First World War and the conflict's aftermath, leading to the eventual expulsion of the last elements of Armenian settlement in the Turkish-controlled region. But vestiges of cross-cultural cooperation remained, the remnants of which Jeppe would cultivate and later transplant to the rural areas of Syria where the prewar contacts between Arab Bedouin and the Garmuch Armenians served as a reservoir for the reestablishment of stable farming communities. Intent on recapturing the idealism developed in Medjeidé, Jeppe seized the opportunity to rapidly channel the expelled Armenians into the countryside once she was approached with settlement proposals

* Jeppe to the DDA, Aleppo, 9 December 1921, reprinted in "Breve fra Karen Jeppe," *Armeniervennen* 21, 11-12 (1941): 23; "10,000 mennesker, som maa dø af sult," *København*, 3 October 1926.

† Jeppe, "Landsbrugs-Kolonien ved Eufrat," *Armeniervennen* 4, no. 11-12 (1924): 50-51; Jeppe, "Armenierne i Euphrat-egnen, II," *Armeniervennen* 11, no. 1-2 (1931): 3.

‡ Jeppe, untitled account, 1929, DDA, bundle 10, folder D, Danish State Archives; Jeppe, "Garmudsch-Bønderne og deres Skæbne," *Armeniervennen* 7, no. 3-4 (1927): 15.

by Bedouin shaykhs of the Aneze tribe. They coveted Armenian colonization in their tribal lands as a way to better protect their holdings from possible French expropriation or even encroachments by rival tribes.* And having learned that the experienced Garmuch Armenians were in Aleppo, one of the shaykhs, Hadjim Pasha, entered negotiations with Jeppe in early 1924, seeking their assistance in helping his people transition from nomadism to sedentary agriculture.† Jeppe embraced this initiative and praised the Arab chief as a visionary who recognized the benefit the Bedouin could derive from association with Armenian farmers. In fact, she was convinced that the Armenians were poised to revolutionize agriculture in Syria and would through their presence in the Mandate help to bolster the rural economy by improving efficiency and increasing yields.‡ This sense of promise led Jeppe to describe the emergent partnership with the Syrian Bedouin as a surreal moment, and as she traveled in April 1924 to Tel Samen, the future site of the first Armenian settlement, to finalize the negotiations, her thoughts were dominated by the symbolism of the event. "[H]ow curious it was," mused Jeppe, "this connection between the League of Nations, the very newest institution of these modern times, and the Bedouin Pasha, the representative of one of our most ancient levels of cultural development."** The cutting-edge and the traditional were in essence coming together to forge something new at a place far removed from Jeppe's base in Aleppo. Located beyond the Euphrates River in the western desert, Tel Samen was to constitute the center of a League and DDA presence in the remote countryside, capable of serving as a link in the chain of rescue stations established across the region. It would also be a model for the settlements to follow as the agreement called for shared investment and the establishment of the Armenians as tenant farmers under the protection of the local Arabs. In exchange for £250 to cover half the expense of constructing a dam needed to expand irrigation

* Shemmassian, "The League of Nations…," 101.

† Jeppe, "Armenierne i Euphrat-Egnen, III," *Armeniervennen* 11, no. 3-4 (1931): 10.

‡ Jeppe, "Landbrugs-Kolonien ved Eufrat," *Armeniervennen* 4, no. 11-12 (1924): 49.

** Jeppe, "Armenierne i Euphrat-Egnen, III," 11.

and increase the amount of arable land, Hadjim Pasha committed himself and his tribe to cover the costs of relocating and housing an initial group of thirty Armenians.* Within months these pioneers were joined by their dependents and, as the summer drew to a close, the community came to number fully sixty families. This rapid success was touted by Jeppe as compelling evidence that settlement was a solution to the growing refugee problem and a natural extension of the League's funding of rescue work:

> No element could ever be more suited to colonization in this country than these young Armenians with all the energy of their race tingling in their veins, acclimatized and accustomed to the village life among the Arabs. The colony would attract them in thousands and enable them to become Armenians again under the most favorable conditions, with a prospect of future prosperity before them, utilizing that which seemed the greatest obstacle, their 'arabisation,' (sic) to build up a strong and thriving peasantry fit to understand and to be understood by the native population. Then we would have erected in this remote place a monument to give evidence of the salutary activity of the League of Nations in the world.†

Through a commitment to fund and support colonization, Jeppe argued that the League could truly realize its calling and channel resources into a project by which Armenians would genuinely be integrated and absorbed into Syrian society. Their transition from impoverished refugees competing for limited employment in the cities to productive farmers helping to develop a vibrant agricultural economy in the Mandate, would help to remove them as a burden on the wider community. Access to land would also bestow on the Armenians a tangible stake in the country and enhance their abilities to help themselves. Jeppe believed passionately that such benefits were self-evident and, together with Henni Forchhammer, her tireless ally and compatriot at the League, she advocated an immediate allocation of

* Ibid.

† League of Nations, "Protection of Women and Children in the Near East," Geneva, 1 September 1924, A. 46. 1924. IV. *League of Nations Documents, 1919-1946.*

£2,000 to found an additional colony in late 1924, money that she believed would be returned in multiples based on the economic activity generated and the relief provided to refugees otherwise confined to the shanty-towns.[*] Those calls continued and were widened during 1925 as Jeppe asserted the League could best achieve its role by "inaugurating a conspicuous colonization scheme" and foster, through its full-fledged support, an increased flow of the funds needed to make the ambitious program succeed.[†] Donors across Europe and other Western countries would more readily contribute to the effort if it was wholly endorsed by the League, and the physical manifestations of Armenian settlement would similarly induce investment from their own communities in the cities. An ever greater internationalization of the project would also reassure the prospective settlers of guarantees and tangible protections in the countryside. "Our example and the moral support of the League of Nations," she stressed, "were sufficient to encourage them to leave the frightful refugee camp in Aleppo."[‡] The fears of danger and victimization in the countryside had gradually been replaced by an evolving confidence in Jeppe's leadership and reputation coupled with a growing belief in the reliability of stable, League-supported assistance and the provision of adequate security supplied by the armed forces of France.[**]

---

* League of Nations, "Protection of Women and Children in the Near East," Geneva, 25 September 1924, A. 85. 1924. IV. *Official Journal. Special Supplement 23. Records of the 5th Assembly. 20th Plenary meeting. Text of the debates*, 446-447; League of Nations, "Protection of Women and Children in the Near East," Geneva, 18 September 1924. *Official Journal. Special Supplement 28. Records of the 5th Assembly. Meetings of the Committees. Minutes of the Fifth Committee*, 46-47; Jeppe, "Frk. Jeppe og koloni-tanken," *Armeniervennen* 5, no. (1925): 20.

† League of Nations, "Commission for the Protection of Women and Children in the Near East," Geneva, 5 September 1925, A. 32. 1925. IV/ C. 451. 1925. IV. *Official Journal. Special Supplement 38. Records of the 6th Assembly. Meetings of the Committees. Minutes of the Fifth Committee*, 160.

‡ Ibid.

** Jeppe, "Landbrugs-Kolonien ved Eufrat," *Armeniervennen* 4, no. 11-12 (1924): 50.

But just as Jeppe was mobilizing to seize the colonization initiative, the French were becoming increasingly wary of ceding power to the League of Nations. Adamant that the pace and scope of Jeppe's settlement program fell under the exclusive authority of the Mandate government, France worked to limit her freedom of action across the Syrian countryside.* Such restrictions were largely prompted by French concerns that the new settlements imposed additional administrative and economic responsibilities on the Mandate's institutions and personnel. In their mind, a policy of restraint and caution, slowing the spread of Armenian settlements, was needed, and by 1925 such imposed limits were instrumental in fostering a minor diplomatic crisis between Jeppe, the League of Nations commissioner, and General Maurice Sarrail, the High Commissioner of Syria. The Dane was in fact so frustrated by French obstructions that she characterized the Mandate government as "unusually difficult" and pledged to Benedictsen, the man who first inspired her two decades earlier to aid the Armenians, that she would work to unseat the General.† And within months, though seemingly unaffected by her efforts, fortune smiled on Jeppe as the army officer was ousted, in large measure blamed for the outbreak of the Arab Revolt, and replaced by a civilian, Henri de Jouvenel.‡ The new high commissioner was a far more approachable figure and one with experience as a former delegate to the League, so immediately Danes both within the organization and in the diplomatic corps moved to repair Jeppe's relations with the Mandate authorities, an action which

---

* League of Nations, "Commission for the Protection of Women and Children in the Near East," Geneva, 5 September 1925, A. 32. 1925. IV/ C. 451. 1925. IV. *Official Journal. Special Supplement 38. Records of the 6th Assembly. Meetings of the Committees. Minutes of the Fifth Committee*, 158; League of Nations, "Protection of Women and Children in the Near East," Geneva, 23 September 1925, A. 111. 1925. IV. *Official Journal. Special Supplement 38. Record of the 6th Assembly. Meetings of the Committees. Minutes of the Fifth Committee*, 163; Forchhammer, "Karen Jeppe of Folkenes Forbund," *Armeniervennen* 24, no. 4 (1944): 14.

† Jeppe to Aa. M. Benedictsen, Breslenberg, 12 August 1925, DDA, bundle 9, Danish State Archives.

‡ Khoury, *Syria and the French Mandate*, 182-83.

very quickly succeeded in patching the rift that had developed.* Yet problems remained regardless of those efforts since the French still harbored fears about allowing thousands of Christian foreigners to occupy lands in traditionally Muslim Arab areas.† Developments to the south in the British Mandate of Palestine represented to them a poignant warning about the tensions that might emerge if the government sanctioned unregulated settlement and seemingly disregarded concerns by the native population.

Jeppe and her colleagues, however, viewed the Zionist venture in a far more favorable light and even considered the movement a source of inspiration. The spirit of initiative and optimism that pervaded the ranks of European settlers streaming into the Mandate captivated Jeppe from the very moment she first observed Jews, mainly young Poles, disembarking at Jaffa and being ferried to shore.‡ Expressing a deep sympathy for their efforts to recover a homeland lost long ago, she wondered if the Armenians could emulate that drive and similarly restore their nation. But regardless of their ultimate fate, she took great comfort in observing that the very boatmen transporting the Jews that last bit of distance to their coveted destination were in fact Armenian. Their participation in the endeavor, mused Jeppe, underscored the enduring Armenian sense of enterprise and revealed a relationship rich in symbolism as one displaced peoples was extending a helping hand to another.** Jointly, the Armenians and European Jews, were perceived as a population endowed with the skills and initiative needed to transform the region along the lines deemed necessary in the West. For Jeppe that emerging transformation was abundantly clear when she traveled through Palestine in 1924, confirming in her mind the benefits of Mandate policy:

---

* Danish ambassador, Berlin to Count Moltke, Danish Foreign Minister, 14 December 1925, L. #6079, "Dansk Missionsvirksomhed i Syrien," bundle 2, 43. F. 5. Udenrigsministeriet; Forchhammer, *Minder om Karen Jeppe*, 37.

† Shemmassian, "The League of Nations…," 102.

‡ Jeppe, "Atter i Orienten," *Armeniervennen* 1, no. 5-6 (1921): 18.

** Ibid.

> All the while it is exceedingly interesting to see the two worlds meet. At times one passes through orange groves, interspersed with vineyards, olive gardens, and swaying palm trees, and within the gardens one can see well-built houses; everything is enveloped in prosperity. Those are the Jewish colonies. Right next to them lies clusters of filthy, clay huts without a tree, reflecting the familiar image of the Oriental landscape.
>
> Those are the Arab villages. The English surely know what they are doing by "bringing in" Jews to Palestine. Now I truly understand the issue at its core.[*]

In unambiguous terms, Jeppe was embracing the civilizing logic of Zionist immigration even as she distanced herself from the myth of Palestine being a depopulated land. Her focus was instead on the role of European influence as a counterbalance to the stagnant and ossified society that existed in the Mandate. "Shall the Orient ever again blossom," she wondered, "it does not seem to be lacking the natural preconditions, but rather it is Islam that has laid its dead hand over everything."[†] The region's people were, in other words, being held back by their adherence to a debilitating religion that kept them from asserting their potential. And the influx of vibrant foreigners, it was suggested, would therefore help to release them from that grip and remove the shackles of tradition. Armenians were projected to have much the same effect in Syria as the Zionists in Palestine, with Jeppe suggesting that the effort would be as much about cultural influence as settlements.[‡] Their mere presence and freedom to flourish was anticipated to have a transformative impact even if the resources available to invest in the enterprise were significantly less than those committed by Jewish immigrants. Forchhammer, in fact, calculated that as little as £10 was spent to settle an entire family of Armenians and concluded that "when one compares with the enormous sums expended on the Zionist colonies in Palestine, [our costs] are quite remarkably

* Jeppe, "Paa vej til Syrien – Hjemme igen," *Armeniervennen* 4, no. 3-4 (1924): 10.

† Ibid.

‡ Jeppe to the DDA, Aleppo, 22 May 1925, reprinted in "Karen Jeppe og Folkenes Forbund," *Armeniervennen* 24, no. 3 (1944): 10.

affordable."[*] But the scarcity of resources did not dampen the optimism about the impact that Armenian settlement could have on societal reform. However, Jeppe's strong reservations toward Islam, a remnant of the devastating memories she retained of the persecution of Armenians inside the former Ottoman Empire, would gradually dissipate as she spearheaded the colonization drive in Syria. Intent on making the settlement of her wards a success, she needed to forge stable relationships with local Muslims and cultivate in them a vested interest in the wider project. In the years following the failed Arab Revolt those efforts were aided by the growing cosmopolitan makeup of the population in Jazira, the triangular area of Syria lying east of the Euphrates River and enclosed by the borders with Turkey and Iraq. Displaced Kurds and Armenians found the underdeveloped region offered them refuge and opportunities, and the French worked to improve the economic conditions by building a rail link between Aleppo and the key, emerging commercial center of Qamishli.[†] A coalescing of interests during the late 1920s therefore helped to promote the colonization effort that in many ways was regarded as Jeppe's most memorable accomplishment in her work to assist the Armenian community.

The drive to develop farming communities and settlements in the countryside resonated with donors and supporters because it constituted a romantic yet tangible achievement. With the settling of refugees at Tel Samen in 1924 and the establishment of a neighboring community at Tel Armen (Armenian Hill) later in the year, Jeppe made clear her ability to marshal the necessary resources and support to realize the stated goals of improving Armenian lives. Those skills similarly sustained the effort as French doubts about the enterprise briefly surfaced during 1925 and the emphasis momentarily shifted to consolidation rather than expansion. But once the crisis was over, the program resumed with renewed vigor as Jeppe's son, Misak, took up near-permanent residence in the countryside to oversee the ongoing project, and she proclaimed with confidence that great prospects for expansion beckoned. Trumpeting in early March 1926 that one hundred families were already

* Forchhammer, *Minder om Karen Jeppe*, 30; Forchhammer, "Kolonierne i Syrien," *Armeniervennen* 6, no. 7-8 (1926): 31.

† Khoury, *Syria and the French Mandate*, 525-27.

settled and that another one hundred were poised to join them, the Dane too noted that the existing farms were largely self-supporting and therefore not in need of subsidies that would drain away the funds required to found new villages.* The colonization scheme was consequently evolving successfully from a purely financial and investment perspective, providing partial vindication for the calculated risks assumed just two years earlier. More importantly, the evidence of sound development and local stability suggested that the conditions were ripe for growth, and Jeppe projected that the area could absorb another 200-300 families, the bulk of whom would be the last of the displaced people from the Urfa and Garmuch areas. By 1926 Jeppe therefore intended to more than double the Armenian presence in the countryside and, early that year, in pursuit of that goal, she and Misak jointly secured a three-year lease of land near the Turkish border where they helped found the colony of Charb Bedros.† Within only months, and buoyed not only by French support but also donated funds to procure both seeds and some cattle, the new settlement had blossomed, having attracted forty families from Garmuch and thirty youths from the recovery home in Aleppo.‡ Such numbers revealed that the colonies were serving as far more than merely alternative homes for displaced farmers from Turkey, but were also emerging as important outlets for the thousands of refugees wallowing in camps encircling Syrian cities.

Yet a need for restraint in channeling Armenians to the countryside was equally recognized by Jeppe and her colleagues. Enthusiasm for the colonization drive had to be balanced with the critical objective of also accommodating the Arab Bedouin population in the area. Enough farm land and sufficient water resources needed to be reserved for non-

---

* Jeppe, "Vor Virksomhed i Syrien," *Armeniervennen* 6, no. 3-4 (1926): 13.

† Jeppe, "Armenierne i Euphrat-Egnen, III," *Armeniervennen* 11, no. 3-4 (1931): 12.

‡ Ibid.; League of Nations, "Work of the Commission for the Protection of Women and Children in the Near East," Geneva, 1926, A. 25. 1926. IV. *Official Journal. Special Supplement 49. Records of the 7th Ordinary Session of Assembly. Meetings of the Committees. Minutes of the Fifth Committee*, 97; Forchhammer, "Karen Jeppe og Folkenes Forbund," *Armeniervennen* 24, no. 5 (1944): 18.

Armenian settlers with whom a strong and lasting partnership was being sought. At Charb Bedros that aim was emphasized from the outset as Arabs were among the pioneers working to create a successful agricultural community.* Efforts to deepen the relationship further focused on making sure that Armenian access to medical care and education in the villages was also extended to the local Arabs.† Through the availability of such services, along with the technical assistance offered by Armenian farmers, elements that collectively underscored their "civilizing" effect, it was anticipated that the Armenians would be seen as indispensable. The DDA even made funds available to aid Arab farmers directly, providing Misak, who was the resident representative of the Armenians in the rural areas, with the necessary resources to alleviate poverty and cultivate good will.‡ Such innovations built on the initial sound foundations forged in 1924 by Jeppe and Hadjim Pasha, two unlikely allies in a partnership that sought to realize goals of practical cooperation but tapped into Western ideals of building Christian-Muslim fellowship. Serving to unlock the purse strings of captivated donors, the promise of Arab-Armenian bliss in the Syrian countryside became a critical aspect of Jeppe's aid work, the coveted pursuit of which celebrated her regional role like no other aspect of the relief efforts. And while she commended the Bedouin chiefs as critical figures in the initiative, her supporters touted her as the linchpin in making the settlement dream a reality:

> No one but she can at this moment in time assume responsibility for such a task [colonization]. Beloved by the Armenians, treated with courteous trust by the Bedouin, with kind respect by the French and supported by her position as a

* Jeppe, "Garmudsch-bønderne og deres skæbne," *Armeniervennen* 7, no. 3-4 (1927): 16.

† Jeppe, untitled report, 1929, DDA, bundle 10, folder D, Danish State Archives; Jeppe to the DDA, Aleppo, 21 January 1925, reprinted in "Breve fra Karen Jeppe," *Armeniervennen* 27, no. 1 (1947): 6; Forchhammer, *Minder om Karen Jeppe*, 43.

‡ Jeppe, "Urfa-bøndernes kolonisation i Syrien, *Armeniervennen* 9, no. 5-6 (1929): 21; Jeppe, "Armenierne i Euphrat-egnen," *Armeniervennen* 11, no. 5-6 (1931): 18.

League of Nations commissioner this woman possesses a level of influence which few could have imagined.*

Deemed a critical figure in balancing all the interests and concerns of the myriad of parties affected, Jeppe seemingly vindicated that praise and confidence through her tireless commitment to have the Armenian communities entrenched beyond challenge. By 1929, after nearly five years of physical and material investment, and a time during which drought, locusts, and other challenges had been overcome, she could proudly proclaim that the Armenians had become an integral part of rural society in one region of Syria.† Jeppe even related that the Bedouin adopted the Armenians as tribal members, reflecting that they were no longer perceived as a foreign element in the countryside. In fact, not only were their settlements spreading across the Jazira, but the population was increasingly engaged in everything from farming to commercial and professional activities, helping to create the beginnings of a vibrant economy. And Armenians were also selected by the French to take a leading role in helping to develop an expanded cotton production in the Amq plain, south of Aleppo.‡ Such developments reflected the shifting perception of the Armenians from mere refugees to important and contributing members of society.

The League and DDA-directed settlement project was consequently a spectacular success as the anticipated role of the Armenians was seemingly realized. Their joint efforts were helping to revitalize the rural economy, and Jeppe could proudly report in 1931 that the region around Tel Samen, the inaugural farming community, had flourished since the initial commitment of investment.** The amount of land under cultivation was by then twice the size of the original area developed, transforming the countryside into one dominated by lush gardens and groves. Just a year earlier, in 1930, the growing ambition and

* Forchhammer, "Kolonierne i Syrien," *Armeniervennen* 6, no. 7-8 (1926): 31.

† Jeppe, "Urfa-bøndernes kolonisation i Syrien," *Armeniervennen* 9, no. 5-6 (1929): 21.

‡ Ibid., 22; Khoury, *Syria and the French Mandate*, 50-51.

** Jeppe, "Armenierne i Euphrat-egnen," *Armeniervennen* 11, no. 5-6 (1931): 18.

sophistication of the colonization effort was also reflected in the moves to develop a model-farm and village at Tineh.[*] Planned as largely a commercial venture involving the hiring of an agricultural expert to oversee the planting and cultivation of vineyards, the project marked a transition by Jeppe's network from a primary focus on supporting subsistence and small-scale farming to an emphasis on plantation-style agriculture. Tineh was also poised to assume a government-sanctioned, vanguard role in the region as plans were afoot to build and operate in the town a state-funded Arab school, the first of its kind in the area.[†] Such a decision suggested an official and growing endorsement of Armenian influence and local leadership, as well as constituting a formal recognition of their achievements as a community. One Dane who in 1931 visited the one-year old settlement even remarked that in conversations with the neighboring Bedouin he found that they expressed an admiration for Western customs and laws and coveted becoming as industrious as the Armenians.[‡] Jeppe echoed that assessment and asserted that such attitudes reflected the rewards of a concerted campaign to forge positive ties. "We put so much emphasis," she declared, "on ever deepening and expanding our friendly relations with the Arabs."[**] In her mind, that effort was vindicated by evidence of a profound rapprochement across ethnic lines. Over time, Jeppe claimed, the Muslim Arabs had come to recognize their error in viewing the Christians as unbelievers and untrustworthy, blaming such misdeeds on deception and poor influence from the Turks.[††] Now purged of the xenophobia that fueled the Ottoman-incited persecutions of Armenians, the local Arabs were open to reassess their views and become more accepting of others. A dynamic of integration and tolerance, requiring duties of both the arriving and existing populations, developed around the settlements. The once poisonous environment had been replaced by

---

* Jeppe to the DDA, Aleppo, 14 October 1930, reprinted in "Breve fra Karen Jeppe," *Armeniervennen* 22, no. 11-12 (1942): 23.

† Ibid.

‡ R. Munksgaard, "Landet hinsides Euphrat," *Armeniervennen* 11, no. 5-6 (1931): 21-22.

** Jeppe, "Armenierne i Euphrat-egnen," *Armeniervennen* 11, no. 5-6 (1931): 19.

†† Ibid.

one in which Misak and the Armenians were the Arab farmer's best friends and his most reliable source of assistance, a gesture that was reciprocated through genuine friendship and loyalty.* In fact, as a serious drought plagued the Jazira in 1932, Jeppe reported that the crisis spurred greater cooperation rather than leading to conflict.† The carefully crafted bond withstood the strains imposed by nature and prior tradition, proving beyond doubt that the relationship was based on far more than narrow self-interests.

The transformative idealism attached to the Armenian colonization of the remote reaches of rural Syria colored Jeppe's passion for the enterprise and the legacy others constructed for her. As late as 1934, less than a year before her death, Jeppe contrasted the rural setting of the settlements with life in Aleppo, highlighting the health benefits of the countryside and the hearty attributes of working in a farming community.‡ Even in the face of environmental challenges and other setbacks that forced the DDA to commit considerable funds to restore communities devastated by poor harvests and the death of livestock, Jeppe never wavered from her conviction that the frontier areas were the future for the Armenians.** That determination was rewarded as "Karen Jeppe's villages became of great value culturally for the plains. Even many years after her death," the commentator continued, "people will consider her achievement and speak of her exploits, even among the Bedouin."†† A similar sense of profound legacy was expressed almost a decade earlier by another admirer of Jeppe's tireless work in the countryside:

> Thus, one day, when the account of Mesopotamia's small-holder's movement is to be written, the story will include 'the Girl from Denmark,' she who traveled a great distance to

* Jeppe, "Et Uaar," *Armeniervennen* 12, no. 7-8 (1932): 31.

† Jeppe, "Et Uaar," *Armeniervennen* 12, no. 5-6 (1932): 19.

‡ Jeppe to Major General L. Ernst, Aleppo, 13 October 1934, DDA, bundle 9, Danish State Archives.

** Jeppe, "Tørke," *Armeniervennen* 13, no. 7-8 (1933): 28-29; Jeppe, "Fra landsbyen Tine," *Armeniervennen* 13, no. 7-8 (1933): 29-31.

†† Künzler, "Dit Folk er mit Folk," *Armeniervennen* 19, no. 7-8 (1939): 30.

> foreign lands in order to found perhaps the largest small-holder's movement the world will ever witness.*

It was, in other words, far from the great Syrian cities that the Danish woman and her supporters saw the fulfillment of their role. In contrast to the open spaces and sense of opportunity beckoning in the rural areas, the urban environment was one where the struggle against poverty, disease, and squalid conditions seemed constant and ever needed to preserve the Armenian community.

The Work in Aleppo

Humanitarian concerns for the lives of refugees residing in Syria demanded that relief efforts in the urban centers be focused on medical services, food aid, and proper housing. Committed to avert a greater crisis than that entailed by the simple displacement of thousands, aid organizations strove to preserve the health and morale of the people, thereby preventing a further deterioration of conditions. Jeppe and the DDA were heavily engaged in such activities that were largely reactive or defensive in nature, ever responding to the challenges emerging among the Armenian population in the refugee camps. Programs delivering preventive medical care and basic nutritional needs were instituted by the Danes to stave off calamities that would put even heavier strains on the refugees as well as the aid workers themselves and the donor community. Over the initial period of Danish-funded medical services, spanning twenty-one months from April 1927 to the close of 1928, about one thousand people received care, an accomplishment cited by Jeppe as evidence of the strides being made to reassure the most vulnerable members of society that a safety net existed for their benefit.† Funds were also dispensed to feed the dependents of patients and pay for improvements to their homes, measures deemed necessary to speed and better assure their recovery. A concerted initiative to institute permanent food aid for the poorest Armenians was similarly begun and repeatedly

* R. Munksgaard, "Landet hinsides Euphrat," *Armeniervennen* 11, no. 5-6 (1931): 22.

† Jeppe, "Blandt de syge og fattige i barak-lejren," *Armeniervennen* 9, no. 3-4 (1929): 14.

expanded to cover as many as 1,400 individuals, mostly children, by the spring of 1927.* Jeppe believed that such a service, if sustained for a few years, could be an important factor in saving many of the next generation, and by the summer of 1928, she was proud to report that the entirely Danish-run and funded kitchen was feeding an average of 190 people daily.† The DDA came to see their responsibility for this service and its dependable delivery of warm meals as so important that, even as other funding wavered in the early 1930s, the committee approved additional monies to keep the kitchen open.‡ Denmark was also the source of other supplemental funding that in 1927 allowed Jeppe to purchase a large parcel of land outside Aleppo. Intended not only as the DDA's new location locally, the property too became the site of forty specially built houses for widows and their children.** She felt passionately about the need to help such women and allow them to retain their families, providing temporary lodgings for the most at risk widows and allocating funds to aid those who were only marginally better able fend for themselves.†† Such aid served to give the women the ability to assert their independence and gain the confidence to be successful heads of households.

An emphasis on improved housing and expanded opportunities similarly influenced the campaign to grant Armenian refugees access to the resources and materials needed to construct their own homes. Determined to mitigate and even end the poor conditions of the refugee camps, Jeppe worked tirelessly to raise the issue with donors. In 1929 the need for action was heightened by a new French Mandate policy to raze shacks in the shantytowns in order to thin the population in the camps

---

* Jeppe, "Oversigt over årets arbejde," *Armeniervennen* 7, no. 7-8 (1927): 33.

† Ibid., 34; Jeppe, "Af årets arbejde," *Armeniervennen* 8, no. 5-6 (1928): 19.

‡ De Danske Armeniervenner, *Bestyrelses Protokol*, 1923-1935, DDA, entry for 1 September 1932, bundle 1, Danish State Archives.

** Jeppe, "Husvilde i fremmed land: Karen Jeppes opråb til Armenierdagen," *Armeniervennen* 7, no. 9-10 (1927): 38-39.

†† Jeppe, "Børneforsogen i Aleppo," *Armeniervennen* 8, no. 11-12 (1928): 42.

and create space for limited urban renewal.* Jeppe both favored and disapproved of this action as she recognized the deplorable health conditions prevalent in the poorest neighborhoods, but also feared the people might be left homeless. To help avert such an eventuality, money was desperately needed to procure land for replacement housing, and a body administered by the League of Nations, the Nansen Fund, emerged as an important source of aid and loans for Armenian refugees. However, the money available was often insufficient to meet demand, leaving many people with only the shell of a home that consisted of little more than the bare walls. The DDA moved to fill that gap by raising funds to secure building materials, such as lumber and windows, which would allow the Armenians to complete work on sturdy, permanent houses.† Such assistance was increasingly needed during the early 1930s as economic conditions worsened and Armenians became unable to repay loans provided by the Nansen Fund. Declining wages, growing unemployment, and ongoing shack demolitions stunted efforts at communal recovery, and by 1934 currency devaluations led Jeppe to conclude that the resources she and the refugees had available were a mere one-third of 1929 levels.‡ The challenges facing her and the DDA therefore lingered as the years progressed, leaving her supporters and associates ill-prepared to sustain the intensity of commitment and resolve needed to continue the aid work once she had passed from the scene.

An Organization Fades

On 7 July 1935 Karen Jeppe died in Aleppo, fostering a seemingly irreversible void in the Danish humanitarian presence in Syria. Having struggled for years with the difficulties of failing health and the burdens

* Jeppe, "En tak og en bøn," *Armeniervennen* 9, no. 11-12 (1929): 45; Jeppe, "Hedelodden fra Varde i Aleppo," *Armeniervennen* 10, no. 7-8 (1930): 26; Lust-Okar, "Failure of Collaboration," *Middle Eastern Studies*, 62-63.

† Jeppe to H. F. Ulrichsen, Hjørring, 28 September 1929, DDA, bundle 9, Danish State Archives; Jeppe, "En tak og en bøn," *Armeniervennen* 9, no. 11-12 (1929): 45.

‡ Jeppe, "I skyggedalen," *Armeniervennen* 14, no. 9-10 (1934): 34-35.

of demanding relief work, she finally succumbed to a combination of exhaustion and illness during the summer of her fifteenth year in the Mandate. Evacuated from Tineh, one of the Armenian villages she help found, to Aleppo in late June and admitted to the French hospital of St. Louis, Jeppe was diagnosed with severe fever attributed to an attack of malaria, as well as problems with her liver and lungs.[*] Tests at the hospital also confirmed aggravating circumstances as they revealed the presence in her system of coli bacteria, related to typhus.[†] And despite valiant efforts by the medical staff, Jeppe lacked the constitution to overcome her ailments, passing away within about a week of her hospitalization. What followed was an outpouring of grief among the Armenians over the loss of a tireless advocate for the most vulnerable in their community and a great supporter of their cause. In a public and well-attended funeral at the Armenian church of Gregory the Illuminator, located near the DDA compound, people came to pay their respects and file past the coffin draped with *Dannebrog*, the Danish national flag.[‡] Jeppe's remains were next interred in a humble grave, but, as one commentator noted, the hearts of the Armenians became her true mausoleum.[**] Cherished for her unwavering spirit and love in defense of the people, she achieved a reputation, still evident today among Armenians in Syria, as someone who committed herself to the cause without regard for the consequences, like a mother to her children.[††] Misak Melkonian suggested that sense of attachment was genuine and intense, asserting that she was in essence consumed by the affairs of the Armenians, becoming as much his parent as the parent of all

---

* Gaszczyk to J. Malmstrøm, Aleppo, 27 June 1935, DDA, bundle 10, folder D, Danish State Archives; Gaszczyk to J. Malmstrøm, Aleppo, 29 June 1935, DDA, bundle 10, folder D, Danish State Archives.

† Gaszczyk, "Beretningen derudefra: Karen Jeppes sidste dage," *Armeniervennen* 15, no. 7-8 (1935): 28.

‡ Ibid.

** Winther, *Armenien og Karen Jeppe*, 40; Forchhammer, *Minder om Karen Jeppe*, 63. This recognition of Jeppe's standing in Armenian hearts is also reflected by the inclusion of her name on the Wall of Remembrance at the Armenian Genocide Museum in Yerevan, Armenia.

†† Bjørnlund, "Karen Jeppe – den glemte heltinde," *Danes*, 37.

Armenians.* Another young man to benefit from Jeppe's tenderness was Dr. Kevork Garabedian, a dentist settled in Iraq and a former refugee, who praised her in much the same terms: "Sweet is the word mother, much sweeter when applied to an unmarried lady by hundreds and thousands in love and reverence." "Miss Koren Yeppe (sic)," he continued, "is one such lady who was called mother by a whole community."† Armenians who knew Jeppe therefore came to regard her as exceptional and in possession of most praiseworthy qualities.

The DDA regarded Jeppe's passing as a similarly monumental development, viewing her contributions and leadership as almost irreplaceable. Within just days of her death, the Committee met to discuss the implications for the organization, concluding that:

> ...the loss we have sustained is of such a magnitude that one must immediately begin to consider seriously the impossibility of even continuing, because Karen Jeppe was not only our leader but the very standard, the very banner under which the entire enterprise was conducted.‡

Their sense of misgivings about the sustainability of the work was further reinforced as the year progressed and reports surfaced about mismanagement and unfavorable developments. An audit of the DDA's finances in Syria and an inspection tour of its facilities concluded that Misak had been less than forthright about local activities and could not account for the use of 20,000 crowns received from Denmark.** In August questions also emerged about the ongoing economic viability of the Armenian villages as new assessments suggested they were too distant

---

* M. Melkonian, "Meine Mutter," March 1946, DDA, bundle 10, folder D, Danish State Archives. The use of the title "Mother" in reference to the foreign women who played the role of saviors was quite common throughout the Armenian community. See Okkenhaug, "Scandinavian Missionaries, Gender and Armenian Refugees...," *Social Sciences and Missions*, 89-90.

† K. Garabedian, "Miss Koren Yeppe: The Mother," December 1946, DDA, bundle 10, folder D, Danish State Archives.

‡ De Danske Armeniervenner, *Bestyrelses Protokol*, 1935-1949, DDA, entry for 17 July 1935, bundle 1, Danish State Archives.

** De Danske Armeniervenner, untitled document, 1935, DDA, bundle 9, Danish State Archives.

from Aleppo to export produce to the city, and fears were raised about faltering relations with the local Arabs.[*] However, despite the difficulties, the DDA continued its work even as it failed to find another personality to generate the popular support Jeppe could command. By 1940, the Committee surrendered to that reality and initiated a campaign to raise funds by republishing Jeppe's correspondence in *Armeniervennen*, emphasizing how essential she had been to the organization.[†] That effort continued over the subsequent years, in part to sustain the Danish connection to the aid work, yet the ever dwindling financial support prevented the DDA from dispatching another Dane to Aleppo. Finally, in the wake of the Second World War, the organization recognized the impossibility of continuing its activities, voting in December 1946 to end operations by the close of the following year.[‡]

A Woman and Her People

The accomplishments of Karen Jeppe during her decades of work with the Armenians ranged from the mundane to the spectacular. Focused not only on the traditional relief sectors of food aid, medical care, housing and education, she also was empowered both by the League of Nations and the DDA to actively seek the recovery of Armenians from captivity and found farming settlements in the Syrian countryside. Those latter endeavors, that saw Jeppe's agents rescue almost 1,900 people and establish half a dozen villages, were elements in a new humanitarian drive to resolve refugee crises through a concerted international effort.[**] With the League providing moderate funding and

* J. Malmstrøm to H. F. Ulrichsen, Aleppo, 28 August 1935, DDA, bundle 9, Danish State Archives.

† "Breve fra Karen Jeppe," *Armeniervennen* 20, no. 11-12 (1940): 29. Ironically, one of the letters chosen for republication revealed her distinct discomfort with being regarded as indispensable and vital to the relief effort.

‡ Malmstrøm, "Nu slutter vi: meddelelse fra styrelsen," *Armeniervennen* 27, no. 1 (1947): 5.

** Jeppe to Johannes Ravn, Aleppo, 10 April 1931, Private Archive, Danish State Archives; Jeppe, untitled report, 1929, DDA, bundle 10, folder D, Danish State Archives.

the all-important forum to debate strategy and bestow legitimacy, the relief work was bolstered by a network of privately-organized aid groups that supplied the dedicated personnel and balance of resources needed to be successful.* Part of a transition away from smaller, mission-based programs that were focused jointly on assistance and conversion, striving to change the people being helped, the new generation of internationally-coordinated, large-scale efforts intended to dispense aid as an end in itself. The Orientalist vision of the West needing to tame and alter the East was deemphasized in favor of policies to promote welfare and development. In the Syrian context, Jeppe combined the authority of her League office with the available funds to create the necessary conditions to foster integration of the refugees into the existing society. But ever-conscious of the need for the Armenians to retain their identity, she was adamant that the people should neither be converted nor assimilated to the point of losing the uniqueness inherent in their distinct culture.† That level and intensity of commitment to the Armenians as Armenians came to resonate with the refugees.

In Jeppe and the Danish organization she spearheaded, the people came to recognize the bond that could be forged between small nations, each equally vulnerable to the whims of their powerful neighbors or sovereigns. And even as those ties seemingly weakened with her death and the DDA's gradual withdrawal from regional involvement, a new basis for cooperation and understanding was evolving in the form of an institution of higher learning. The Karen Jeppe College of Aleppo, founded in 1947 and constituting a clear tribute to the late Dane's memory, also came to symbolize the effort to cultivate and develop the existing links between Denmark and the Armenians.‡ In the words of Bishop Zareh, head of the Armenian Apostolic Church in Aleppo, the Danish woman represented the special relationship tying the two peoples together, and the decision to name the school after her was as

---

* League of Nations, Secretariat, *The Refugees* (Geneva: Information Section, 1938), 22-23, 35.

† Winther, *Armenien og Karen Jeppe*, 39; "Karen Jeppe i Danmark," *Armeniervennen* 13, no. 7-8 (1933): 25.

‡ Forchhammer to Dame Rachel Crowdy, Copenhagen, 20 October 1948, Box 1, FF12, Crowdy Papers, Wichita State University Archives.

much a tribute based on the past as a statement about the future. "The spiritual bonds," he declared, "that bind us to our Danish friends have not been severed, they have simply altered character and been reshaped into cultural bonds, [so] that with these new ties our college does not constitute an end but rather a new beginning."* That which was once founded on pity, sympathy, and charity had matured into a relationship of equals, sustained both by the emotional attachment of common memories but also by the promise of tomorrow's intellectual and educational developments.

The Story - *Misak: An Armenian Life*

In the 1920s Jeppe authored an account about her adopted son, Misak Melkonian. The dramatized but biographical story was published in *Armeniervennen* (The Friend of Armenia), the main journal of the Danish Friends of Armenia, and served as both a tribute to her son and a celebration of Armenian resilience and nobility. The story was serialized in the bi-monthly journal in well over two dozen segments across several years, beginning in mid-1922 and concluding with the final installment in 1928. It has not appeared in print elsewhere or been translated in the years since.

Jeppe began and introduced her account in 1903 with her journey to the Ottoman city of Urfa in eastern Asia Minor or upper Mesopotamia. Feeling compelled to venture far from Denmark to help alleviate the plight of the Armenian community, she would find in the people and in the young boy Misak her true purpose and sense of fulfillment. In fact, between Jeppe and Misak an unlikely relationship would be forged between individuals born seemingly worlds apart and shaped by the events of an Ottoman Empire passing through its final tumultuous decades of existence. It is precisely that instability, violence, and uncertainty, as well as how it devastatingly impacted the young Misak's life, which constitutes the basis for the story.

The opening chapter, "A Friend in Need", introduces the reader to Misak (given name Misael). Jeppe has shifted the setting a decade into

---

* "Fra indvielsen af Karen Jeppe College," *Armeniervennen* 28, no. 1 (1948): 5.

the past, to mid-1890s, where we find Misak living as a wretched beggar on the streets of Urfa and under the "care" of his aunt and uncle. They exploit his predicament of having lost his parents and consider him as nothing more than a means to an end. He is the friend in need, and it is Hovagim Biredjiklian, an unmarried head of household, who comes to his aid and becomes his adoptive caretaker. The rest of the chapter introduces the reader to all the members of the Biredjiklian family and describes how Misak begins to live again, leaving his troubles behind.

But over Jeppe's subsequent chapters, covering the latter half of 1895, it is made plain that grave challenges are emerging. Hovagim and his sister-in-law's brother, Krikor, attend a summer time community meeting where they are informed about violence and incitement against Armenians that is spreading in Urfa's direction. Quietly but determinedly the Armenians prepare themselves for what seems inevitable, and when the anticipated attack comes in October, they are able to jointly deflect it from their section of town. However, in the wake of the violence the community is convinced to disarm in a bid to show their loyalty to the authorities, hoping this gesture will sustain them. Krikor, on the other hand, is unconvinced and prepares an underground hiding place beneath his home.

The scene next shifts to late December 1895, when the disarmed and defenseless Armenian community was massacred. The onslaught culminated with the burning of the city's Gregorian Cathedral, where hundreds had sought refuge in a futile attempt to escape the violence. Misak and his new family remained at home, almost resigned to their fate, and when the mob burst into the Biredjiklian house tragedy ensued. Hovagim and his brothers are killed and only the women and children are spared. But Hovagim is described as dying with honor and facing his killers fearlessly and unarmed, serving to represent the righteousness and dignity of the Armenian people. It is also revealed that Krikor's ruse has worked, saving he and his brothers from death.

In the aftermath of the massacre a measure of normalcy is restored. Ottoman government troops oversee the reestablishment of order and the provisioning of rudimentary relief supplies to the survivors. But the true savior of the community is Corinna Shattuck, the legendary American missionary of Urfa, who not only sheltered hundreds at her compound during the violence, but now provides leadership, morale boosting encouragement, and organizational discipline. Partly through her efforts foreign relief aid is distributed effectively and new economic initiatives are established, such as an export trade in handicrafts produced by the local Armenian women. Jeppe also points out, significantly, that numerous Armenian men were saved from sure death by random Muslim residents who hid them in their homes.

Misak begins a new life after the massacres, as he is first turned over to Corinna Shattuck's care and then eventually placed with the newly established German orphanage in Urfa. This latter relief effort is spearheaded by the German Orient Mission, the organization led by the famed Dr. Johannes Lepsius (1858-1926). It is this turn of events that will bring Misak and Jeppe together, as she will arrive in the coming years to partner with the Germans in Urfa. His new life will also bring him a new identity, as the name "Misak" is bestowed upon him when he is registered with the orphanage. In time, as events progress, he will officially become Misael again, but "Misak" will remain the name under which Jeppe knows and refers to him.

Jeppe next focuses on the efforts of the Armenian community members in Urfa to rebuild their lives. Not only do they restore the cathedral, but educational reforms are also being pushed through, led in part by the activism of the foreign missions and those Armenians who favor Western-style education. Jeppe also describes how Misak adapts happily to life at the orphanage and that he finds both warmth and comfort there, as well as a renewed pride and confidence in being Armenian.

In late 1903 Jeppe reintroduces herself to the story with her arrival in Urfa. All the orphans greatly anticipate her joining the staff, but Misak especially yearns for her to become his mother. This does not happen straight away and instead, in the spring of 1905, Misak leaves the orphanage and rejoins the household of the Biredjiklians, his adoptive family. Now barely into his teens, Misak must seek full-time employment as the family does not have the funds to care for him. But Jeppe soon comes to his aid, finds him an apprentice position with an Armenian merchant, and covers the costs for his new training.

Jeppe and Misak's relationship only grows stronger as time passes, culminating in her decision in 1906 to adopt him as her son. She also brings him along on a summer journey to the Taurus Mountains in the same year, and en route they travel through the southeastern city of Diyarbakir, where Misak takes in the bustling commercial life and dreams to one day bringing such prosperity to Urfa. The journey also serves as a framework for explaining events in the region and their overall meaning, as Misak and Jeppe discuss the rivalries between local Kurdish tribes, the reputed hidden hand of Sultan Abdülhamid II in the local troubles, and the uncertainties about the future.

Positive change, or at least the prospects for it, is the main subject of this chapter. It considers the repercussions of the Constitutional Revolution of 1908, when a coalition of reformers forced an end to autocracy and restored constitutional government in the Ottoman Empire. These changes promised a better future for all Ottoman subjects, the Armenian minority included, and fostered an anticipated expansion of their civil rights. Included in those changes were both civic benefits but also obligations, such as mandatory military service for all young men. However, many wanted to escape this burden and, in Misak's case, that entailed purchasing forged identity papers. With Jeppe's help, he obtained papers that resurrected his true name, Misael Melkonian, but also advanced his age to twenty-nine and hence beyond the group generally eligible and selected for military service.

The closing chapter, entitled "The Final Feast", spans from about 1910 until 1913. It emphasizes Misak's evolution into an increasingly important partner in Jeppe's work and how she came to depend on him. This trend would, of course, only grow and intensify over the following two decades as they truly became mother and son, sharing both a mutual affection but also a dedication to a common cause. However, despite that ongoing relationship and bond, Jeppe's specific story about Misak, *Misak: An Armenian Life*, ended symbolically in 1913, a decade after it began with Jeppe's arrival to the region in 1903. In the looming shadow of the Ottoman Empire's ultimate defeat and disintegration, she described the joyous celebration of Misak's wedding to Lucia, an Armenian assistant to Jeppe and also an adopted former orphan. Jeppe thereby concluded the account by contrasting the promise and possibilities of youth and marital union with the ominous clouds of calamity and destruction that awaited the Armenian community during World War One. In a sense, she seemingly argued, Misak's life was representative of the wider Armenian experience, lodged between tragedy and the drive to survive and endure.

Karen Jeppe, Misak, Hadjim Pasha (Syria, cir. 1925).

Karen Jeppe (sitting, middle), then clockwise, Jenny Jensen, Horome Gaszczyk, Leopold Gaszcyk (Horome's husband), Misak Melkonian, Lucia Melkonian, Karen Bjerre. (Aleppo, cir. 1926).

Karen Jeppe's grave (Aleppo).

SELECTED BIBLIOGRAPHY

Unpublished Archival Sources

Rigsarkivet (The Danish State Archives)

Karl Christian Ludvig Povlsen (KCLP): Correspondence from Karen Jeppe.

Henrik Scharling (HS): Correspondence from Karen Jeppe.

De Danske Armeniervenner (DDA): Protocols, correspondence, and documents related to the Danish aid mission for Armenian refugees in Syria. Includes a great volume of papers pertaining to Karen Jeppe, the woman directing the organization's Aleppo-based efforts.

Udenrigsministeriet (UM): Official correspondence, reports, and documents from the Danish Foreign Ministry. Includes papers from consulates and embassies, files on Danish citizens in the Middle East, and affairs dealing with Danish missionary activity in the region.

Det Kongelige Bibliotek (The Danish Royal Library)

Armeniervennen, 1921-1948: Bi-monthly journal of the DDA, The Danish Friends of Armenia.

Wichita State University

Dame Rachel Crowdy Papers (RC): Correspondence from and concerning Karen Jeppe.

Published Sources

Akham, Taner. *A Shameful Act*. New York: Henry Holt, 2006.

Badeau, John S., and Georgiana G. Stevens. *Bread from Stones: Fifty Years of Technical Assistance*. Englewood Cliffs, N.J.: Prentice Hall, 1966.

Balakian, Peter. *The Burning Tigris: The Armenian Genocide and America's Response*. New York: Harper Collins, 2003.

Barton, James L. *Story of Near East Relief 1915-1930: An Interpretation*. New York: Macmillan, 1930.

Bedoukian, Kerop. *Some of Us Survived: The Story of an Armenian*. New York: Farrar Straus Giroux, 1978.

Benedictsen, Aage Meyer. *Armenien: Et Folks Liv og Kamp gennem to Aartusinder*. Copenhagen: De Danske Armeniervenner, 1925.

Berg, F. Fris. "The Share of Scandinavia in Christian Missions to Moslems." *Moslem World* 14, no. 1 (January 1924): 30-36.

Berkes, Niyazi, ed. *Turkish Nationalism and Western Civilization*. New York: Columbia University Press, 1959.

Bjørnlund, Matthias. "Karen Jeppe – den glemte heltinde." Danes 93, no. 6 (December 2013): 34-37.

____. "Karen Jeppe, Aage Meyer Benedictsen, and the Ottoman Armenians: National Survival in Imperial and Colonial Settings." *Haigazian Armenological Review* 28 (2008): 9-43.

Bloxham, Donald. *The Great Game of Genocide: Imperialism, Nationalism, and the Destruction of the Ottoman Armenians*. Oxford: Oxford University Press, 2005.

____. "The Armenian Genocide of 1915-1916: Cumulative Radicalization and the Development of a Destruction Policy." *Past & Present* 180 (2003): 141-191.

Boisen, Ingolf. *Tyrkiet og Danmark gennem Tiderne*. Copenhagen: Kampsax, 1962.

Bruun, P. Daniel. *Paa de Tyrkiske Fronter 1914-1915: Dardanellerne – Gallipoli*. Copenhagen: Vilhelm Tryde, 1922.

Cedergreen Bech, Svend. *Hos et folk uden land: Karen Jeppe – armeniernes ven*. Copenhagen: G.E.C. Gads Forlag, 1982.

____, ed. *Dansk Biografisk Leksikon*. 3rd ed.16 vols. Copenhagen: Gyldendal, 1979- 1984.

Christensen, Arthur. "Det nye Tyrki." *Gads Danske Magasin* 25 (1931): 193-201.

Cleveland, William L. *A History of the Modern Middle East*. 2d ed. Boulder: Westview Press, 2000.

Dadrian, Vahakn N. "The Documentation of the World War I Armenian Massacres in the Proceedings of the Turkish Military Tribunal." *International Journal of Middle East Studies*. 23, no. 4 (1991): 549-76.

____. "The Secret Young-Turk Ittihadist Conference and the Decision for the World War I Genocide of the Armenians." *Holocaust and Genocide Studies* 7, no. 2 (1993): 173-201.

Davis, Leslie A. *The Slaughterhouse Province: An American Diplomat's Report on the Armenian Genocide, 1915-1917*. Edited by Susan Blair. New Rochelle: Aristide D. Caratazas, 1989.

Davison, Roderic H. "The Armenian Crisis, 1912-1914." *American Historical Review* 53, no. 3 (April 1948): 481-505.

Forchhammer, Henriette. *Et Besøg hos Karen Jeppe: Skildring fra en Rejse til Syrien.* Copenhagen: De Danske Armeniervenner, 1926.

____. *Minder om Karen Jeppe.* Copenhagen: J. Frimodts Forlag, 1945.

Gabrielian, M. C. *Armenia: A Martyr Nation.* New York: Fleming H. Revell, 1918.

Garo, Armen. *Bank Ottoman: Memoir of Armen Garo – The Armenian Ambassador to America from the Independent Republic of Armenia.* Translated by Haig T. Partizian. Detroit: Armen Topouzian, 1990.

El-Ghusein, Fa'iz. *Martyred Armenia.* London: C. Arthur Pearson, 1917.

Hacobian, A. P. *Armenia and the War.* London: Hodder and Stoughton, 1917.

Hanioglu, M. Sükrü. *A Brief History of the Late Ottoman Empire.* Princeton: Princeton University Press, 2008.

Hovannisian, Richard G., ed. *The Armenian Genocide in Perspective.* New Brunswick: Transaction Books, 1986.

Jensen, Jensine. *Billeder fra Østerland.* Copenhagen: O. Lohses Forlag, 1939.

Jeppe, Karen. "Armenien." *Tidens Kvinder* 1, no. 12 (31 May 1923): 6-7.

Jernazian, Ephraim K. *Judgment Unto Truth: Witnessing the Armenian Genocide.* Translated by Alice Haig. New Brunswick: Transaction Books, 1990.

Kévorkian, Raymond. *The Armenian Genocide: A Complete History.* London: I. B. Tauris, 2011.

Khoury, Philip S. *Syria and the French Mandate: The Politics of Arab Nationalism 1920-1945.* Princeton: Princeton University Press, 1987.

Künzler, Jakob. *In the Land of Blood and Tears.* Translated by Geoffrey Steinherz. Arlington: Armenian Cultural Foundation, 2007.

League of Nations. *League of Nations Documents, 1919-1946.* New Haven: Research Publications, 1973.

League of Nations, Assembly. *Official Journal. Records of the 1st-21st Assembly. Plenary meetings. Text of the debates.* 21 vols. Geneva, 1920-1946.

____. *Official Journal. Records of the 1st-21st Assembly. Meetings of the Committees. Minutes.* 21 vols. Geneva, 1920-1946.

League of Nations, Secretariat. *The Refugees.* Geneva: Information Section, 1938.

Lepsius, Johannes. "The Armenian Question." *Moslem World* 10, no. 4 (October 1920): 341-55.

Lewy, Guenter. *The Armenian Massacres in Ottoman Turkey.* Salt Lake City: University of Utah Press, 2005.

Lockman, Zachary. *Contending Visions of the Middle East: The History and Politics of Orientalism.* Cambridge: Cambridge University Press, 2004.

Longrigg, Stephen H. *Syria and Lebanon under French Mandate.* London: Oxford University Press, 1958.

Lust-Okar, Ellen Marie. "Failure of Collaboration: Armenian Refugees in Syria." *Middle Eastern Studies* 32, no. 1 (January 1996): 53-68.

Macfie, A. L. *The End of the Ottoman Empire, 1908-1923.* New York: Longman, 1998.

McCarthy, Justin. *Muslims and Minorities: The Population of Ottoman Anatolia and the End of the Empire.* New York; London: New York University Press, 1983.

Okkenhaug, Inger Marie. "Scandinavian Missionaries, Gender and Armenian Refugees during World War I, Crisis and Reshaping of Vocation." *Social Sciences and Missions* 23 (2010): 63-93.

Pedersen, Gotfried. "Scandinavian Missions to Moslems." *Moslem World* 22, no. 4 (October 1932): 412-14.

Peterson, Merrill D. *"Starving Armenians": America and the Armenian Genocide, 1915-1930 and After.* Charlottesville: University of Virginia Press, 2004.

Robert, Dana L. "The Influence of American Missionary Women on the World Back Home." *Religion and American Culture: A Journal of Interpretation* 12, no. 1 (2002): 59-89.

Rygaard, Olaf A. *Mellem Tyrker og Kurder: En dansk ingeniørs oplevelser i Lilleasien.* Copenhagen: Gyldendalske Boghandel Nordisk Forlag, 1935.

Said, Edward W. *Orientalism.* New York: Vintage Books, 1978.

____. *Culture and Imperialism.* New York: Vintage Books, 1994.

Shambrook, Peter A. *French Imperialism in Syria 1927-1936.* Reading: Ithaca Press, 1998.

Shemmassian, Vahram L. "The League of Nations and the Reclamation of Armenian Genocide Survivors." In *Looking Backward, Moving Forward: Confronting the Armenian Genocide*, edited by Richard G. Hovannisian. New Brunswick: Transaction Publishers, 2003.

Shaw, Stanford J., and Ezel Kural Shaw. *Reform, Revolution, and Republic: The Rise of Modern Turkey 1808-1975.* Vol. 2 of *History of the Ottoman Empire and Modern Turkey.* Cambridge: Cambridge University Press, 1977.

Sick, Ingeborg Maria. *Pigen Fra Danmark: Et Rids af Karen Jeppes Liv og Gerning.* 4th ed. Copenhagen: Gyldendalske Boghandel Nordisk Forlag, 1945.

____. "Karen Jeppe of Denmark and Armenia." *American-Scandinavian Review* 25, no. 1 (March 1937): 18-25.

Smith, Walter George. "The Armenian Tragedy." *Catholic World* 111, no. 664 (July 1920): 485-92.

Spaull, Hebe. *Women Peace-makers.* London; Calcutta; Sydney: George G. Harrap, 1924.

Thompson, Elizabeth. *Colonial Citizens: Republican Rights, Paternal Privilege, and Gender in French Syria and Lebanon.* New York: Columbia University Press, 2000.

Toynbee, Arnold J., ed. *The Treatment of the Armenians in the Ottoman Empire.* London: His Majesty's Stationery Office, 1916.

Watenpaugh, Keith David. "The League of Nations' Rescue of Armenian Genocide Survivors and the Making of Modern Humanitarianism, 1920-1927." *American Historical Review* 115 (2010): 1315-1339.

Winther, Christian. *Armenien og Karen Jeppe.* Copenhagen: Faglig Læsning, 1936.

Newspapers

Berlingske Tidende (Copenhagen)

Kristeligt Dagblad (Copenhagen)

København (Copenhagen)

Manchester Guardian

New York Times

Politiken (Copenhagen)

Times (London)

Karen Jeppe

MISAK

AN ARMENIAN LIFE

(Karen Jeppe's story of an orphan who became a son)

translated, edited, and with an introduction by

Jonas Kauffeldt

Introduction

"Where the Tree of Life Blossomed"

It was the afternoon of 2 November 1903 when I first saw Urfa, the city of King Abgar,* the famed Edessa of the crusaders, and now, most recently, the site of frightful massacres.

With great anticipation I had approached the mountain pass in the belief that I might catch a glimpse of my future home, but even from that location, the city remained hidden from my sight. I could see only the curious lands that lay further beyond the city. It was the Mesopotamian plain which I also was seeing for the first time. It was so unlike the Danish plains with their wild hedges,† small forests, and welcoming villages. Here in Asia it was as if everywhere the earth was barren. One could trace the geological lines and glimpse even older formations as one crossed the region. The Mesopotamian plain reminded me of the sea and the surrounding mountains of the coast; perhaps that is how it once was.

The expanse that lay before us looked like a large bay. Entering the area through the northwesterly corner, we could trace the bordering mountains beginning far to the southwest and running like a great chain round the plain. But to the south there was an absence of mountains where the landscape seemed to become one with the great sea of the plain that continued as far as the eye could see. And beyond where sight could not reach, my imagination continued. I thought I saw the two great rivers

* According to early Christian tradition King Abgar Uchama (Abgar the Black), who reigned between 1 B.C.E. and 37 C.E., exchanged letters with Jesus Christ and became one of the first monarchs to convert to Christianity.

† Such hedges, literally translated as "living hedges," were common in the Danish countryside and served to mark the boundaries between neighboring fields or to shelter crops and homes from the elements.

make their way through the distant countryside, join together as one, and eventually flow into the Indian Ocean.*

But my imagination showed me yet more. It revealed another age, an age when this plain was home to cities and swaying wheat fields, an age when culture flowered here rather than anywhere else. Faint traces of this age were still discernible. The civilization was gone, but its tombs still towered over the plain. They reminded one of our burial mounds, only much larger.† And beneath each of these mounds, which looked like so many mole hills located one next to the other across the plain, one would find not just a chieftain's tomb. It was instead entire cities that rested beneath these mounds, perhaps several cities. How else should they have grown to such heights?

Once in the distant past, cities were located in this plain, where people built homes and lived, married and developed their lives, were born, died and eventually came to rest beneath the turf. Then devastation struck. Hostile hordes moved through the land. The city's men took up arms to resist, but the enemy was too strong. They were killed or enslaved; the city was looted and razed. The place was deserted and left to serve as a testament to its bygone life. Eventually, vegetation came to cover the site until all that remained was just a mound on the plain.

Years later, people again appeared at the site. They uncovered the ancient well, an important discovery, and restored it to working order. Plenty of water made this site a good place to settle down and the people built a few huts on the mound. A city again emerged on the site, built on top of the old. No one contemplated what lay beneath the earth nor did anyone ask who had dug the well. After all, the well now belonged to the new people who were born there.

* The rivers in question are the Tigris and Euphrates which join to form the Shatt al-Arab river delta in southern Iraq. It seems Jeppe confused her geography as the two rivers empty into the Persian Gulf rather than directly into the Indian Ocean.

† Jeppe was here referring to ancient burial mounds that are a common feature of the Scandinavian countryside. Built between the Stone Age and the Bronze Age, these structures were constructed of earth, turf, and stone. *Tel* is the Semitic word commonly used to refer to such city mounds in the Middle East.

In time, that city too lay in ruins and a new city was erected on top of it. The mound grew and grew, but now its summit was covered by only a few wretched mud huts. And the poor Arabs who lived there continued to use the ancient well. It was now their well until someone stronger came and wrested it from them.

Indeed, the plain had a story to tell. It is no wonder that this area caught the eye of many researchers and that they had an intense desire to be permitted to search its soil for traces of the past. I too was attracted to the plain and was eager to be near it.

But as I stood and observed the plain, other images appeared before me. It was Denmark's plains I saw and I asked myself how it was that I had ventured so far from home. What was I seeking in these distant lands? Who had cried out so loudly that I felt compelled to abandon my easy-going life and respond? Ah, now I knew. I heard the summoning voice again, this time much closer. It was the Armenian orphans. Their call affected me so deeply that I severed all other ties in order to be with them.

And so I was off, from *De danske Armeniervenner* (The Danish Friends of Armenia)[*] in Copenhagen to the offices of Dr. Lepsius[†] in Berlin, and then, on a bitterly cold October night, onwards with a Mr. Künzler[‡] into the unknown. Ever southwards we travelled until we reached lands where it was still summer. Far behind us, along with my friends and bright, vivid memories of home, lay the cold and dark north, a place now further

* The organization was established in 1902 as part of the international effort to alleviate the suffering of the Armenians who were victims of persecution in the Ottoman Empire during the 1890s. This Danish aid effort continued until after the Second World War when the organization ceased its activities in 1948.

† Dr. Johannes Lepsius (1858-1926) was a famed German theologian, missionary, politician, and historian who founded the *Deutsche Orientmission* (The German Orient Mission) in 1895. The specific aim of the mission was to aid Armenian children orphaned by political violence in the Ottoman Empire. Jeppe worked with the mission from 1903 to 1918, when poor health and deteriorating wartime conditions forced her to return to Denmark.

‡ Dr. Jakob Künzler (1871-1949) was a Swiss medical missionary who accompanied Jeppe to Urfa. He originally arrived in the city in 1899 and served as an aid worker and later as a medical director of the German mission hospital. In 1934, he also published a biography of Jeppe.

overshadowed by the many strange and extraordinary impressions of the past weeks.

I still felt the chills that [weeks ago] ran through my body as I stood on the deck of the ship on the Black Sea and gazed at the Asian mountains rising out of the horizon. That experience of encountering a new part of the world was for me quite remarkable, and Asia soon won my heart. I was attracted to its wide expanse of territory much as I had always preferred the landscape of Jutland to that of the islands because of its grand scale.* Before such an impressive wilderness, one could feel quite tiny, but that was a feeling I favored, so I came to like Asia.

The arrival in Constantinople too was unforgettable. As the ship moored, a crowd of people rushed onboard and attempted to seize the passengers' luggage. They were dressed in fantastic clothes, were brown, black-haired, and dark-eyed; they all shouted and yelled and smelled of sweat and garlic.† I remained motionless and simply took in the Orient. I was at that moment immersed in the Orient.

Constantinople seemed like a gallery of multi-colored images. Everything I had heard and read about the city was true; but there was yet more, a myriad of things no one had been able to relay. The very life of the city defied description.

But from this brilliant and colorful scene there swelled a dark force. It had so frightened me that it frequently overshadowed all else. It was the spirit of Islam. I had first encountered it when Mr. Künzler took me to visit a mosque. How exactly it transpired I cannot explain, but I felt that force upon me, crowding me from all sides, and at last driving me to flee through the door to the outside. There Mr. Künzler found me, but he could not by any means convince me to again pass through that door. He would have to conduct his future mosque visits without me.

Our departure from Constantinople was probably the most spectacular experience. It was dusk when we weighed anchor and sailed out on the Sea of Marmara. The night descended like a light bluish veil. In the west Stambul's domes and minarets appeared silhouetted against

* Jeppe was contrasting the Jutland Peninsula with the much smaller Danish islands that border the landmass to the east.

† The men described so vividly were porters rushing to compete for the passengers' business.

the night sky, aglow with crimson and gold. But further toward the south the red became yellow and the yellow became green, eventually flowing into the violet in the east.

'A Sunset in the Orient.' Yes, I had heard it mentioned as a global wonder, but as I remained there staring and astounded by the extravagant splendor, I became convinced that the scene was too beautiful to be real; it had to be a dream. My awakening ought to be near; the adorned and colored bubble ought to burst at any moment. But it never did burst. One image simply replaced another.

What a wonder is encompassed in the name Mediterranean Sea. We sailed down along the coast of Asia Minor and passed the Greek Isles. The weather continued to remain clear and beautiful. A light breeze rippled the sea's surface, and the ship glided through ever-darkening blue waters. Dolphins frolicked in it and the flying fish flew across it in long jumps. We remained in sight of land almost continually on either one or the other side of the ship.

Onboard there was a lively companionship. Dr. Kinck was en route to Rhodes together with his young wife. She and I enjoyed each other's company. We did not want for entertainment throughout the day, and in the evenings we gathered on the quarterdeck together with the Greeks and Italians. Certainly we were unable to speak with them, but they played music and sang, and there was much dancing in the southern moonlight.

Following an inimitable sea passage we landed in Asia. We had chosen the city of Mersina, on the Bay of Alexandretta, as the departure point for our travel inland.* Actually we had intended to land at Alexandretta, but it was impossible due to a cholera outbreak in the city. The journey from Mersina was far more difficult, but it was certainly also much more beautiful.

After the short railway ride to Adana,† we travelled by wagon for a couple of days along a quite good road. Then this too ended, and the journey continued on horseback over the Amanus Mountains along often

* Mersina, also spelled Mersin or Mersine, and since renamed Icel, is actually located to the far west of the Bay of Alexandretta (today's Iskenderun).

† Adana is located about fifty miles to the east of Mersina.

indiscernible trails.* Civilization of any kind was now behind us. One could as easily believe it was ancient times or the Middle Ages.

In the evening we arrived at some "khan." That is the term for Turkish hotels. But what a hotel! There are stables for the animals and, if one is lucky, one may get a room for the night and maybe even a light.

Linens and food are one's own responsibility. And the "room" one receives we would consider quite unsuitable even as a stable.

On one occasion, when we stopped at a well, a Kurdish woman approached us.

"Where did you get her?" she asked Mr. Künzler while looking at me.

"I have brought her here from a country far away," he replied.

The woman gazed at me tentatively, much as one woman sizes up another.

"She cannot have been cheap," the woman declared based on her estimation. How could she know that there were women who were neither bought nor sold like chattel?

We made slow progress due to concerns over the cholera outbreak, and we had to repeatedly stop because of quarantine restrictions. Every day we had to switch horses because if the caravan guides moved more than a short distance from their villages, they would be deemed contaminated and prohibited from returning home.† Also, the cavalry soldier who served as our escort caused us numerous delays. But he was considered a necessary evil as there were brigands in the area, something which was true throughout Turkish lands. Cholera and brigands; those are such strangely fantastic concepts. They certainly served to make the journey adventurous and exiting.

Hence we reached the Euphrates. Paradise was supposed to have been located on the other side, but that did not appear to be the case. It looked more like the desert into which Adam and Eve were banished. However, I was still in good spirits. I remained convinced that I would find the gate to Paradise, and as a sign of my confidence, I wrote the following on the

* The Amanus, or Aman Dagh, are a southwestern spur of the Taurus range. The Baylan Pass, also known as the Syrian Gate, which connects Syria and Asia Minor, runs through the Amanus Mountains.

† Jeppe's party, in other words, had to find their own way or somehow arrange to rendezvous en route with caravan guides from their destination villages.

wall of the first khan where we stayed: "Where the tree of life blossomed, it blossoms still." Such was my passage into Mesopotamia, and that was how I had come to stand there and gaze across the great plain.

We began our descent from the heights of the pass down the mountainside via a zigzagging road that ran along a deep ravine. The road was well-built. An enterprising governor (*mutassarif*)* had managed to build it from Urfa† to just the other side of the mountain pass. He was now long gone, and his successors used their time in office to only enrich themselves and otherwise loaf around in the cafés. They did not even maintain the road, and many of the large stone blocks along the edges of the road had since rolled into the ravine. Only a few more years of this neglect would see the people revert to using the old riding trail. By then it would be better than the road.

"When we turn the next corner," said one of my companions, "you will be able to see Urfa." Finally we passed the corner, but I could still not see any city. There was only a cliff to the south with the ruins of an old fortress and two beautiful columns that towered over the mostly collapsed walls. In the corner, just below the fortress, there was a ravine where I could see some trees. Further along stood another steep rock face where there was a windmill. Next came a section of old city wall and, furthest towards the north, an old Turkish graveyard. It looked as if a child had playfully arranged a collection of matchsticks in a sandbox. That was how all the narrow, erect tombstones appeared from the mountaintop. The whole scene was framed by green vineyards and gardens as well as the grey and golden accents of the mountains and the plain that became bluish as evening approached.

No wonder I had to ask disappointingly where the city was. And in response, I was told that the city was located on the eastern face of the mountain with the windmill. I needed to remain patient a little longer, which, of course, I was able to do as now I was busy looking at the multitude of people. It appeared as if half the town had turned out to receive us.

---

* A *mutassarif* administered a *sanjak*, a subdivision of an Ottoman province.

† A city, since renamed Sanliurfa, that lies just to the north of today's Turco-Syrian border.

Mr. Künzler, who was very popular, had already served five years in Urfa. As many of his friends as possible had therefore come out to greet him. I, in contrast, was new to the area, and, as much as I craved seeing Urfa, it seemed the city was no less eager to catch a glimpse of me. It was, in other words, an occasion of mutual entertainment.

Far on the other side of the mountain pass was where the first person, a young Syrian, greeted us. He rode a beautiful horse that was decorated with red, green, and blue cotton tassels and trimmings, a complete caparison. In addition, the horse had a collar of light blue pearls as protection from the "evil eye." The man too was handsome, wearing a black cape embroidered with silver thread and yellow silk that jointly looked like gold. On his head he wore a black silk scarf with silver fringes that was kept in place by a rather heavy ring of black, braided wool.* Mr. Künzler was happy to see him. He had feared that the telegram he sent to announce our arrival had failed to reach Urfa and that no one would have come out to greet us.

The entire hospital staff was present, led by the heavyset pharmacist, and accompanied by the housefathers from the orphanages, people from the American mission, and a large crowd of others from the city.

A din of hooves, neighing, and chatting enveloped the road – as did a cloud of dust.

Hence we sat down to eat as was customary on such occasions.

Scattered around the countryside were small bridges built to cope with the seasonal winter streams. A road was once intended to connect them, but even now the bridges only remained as outposts awaiting that link. Yet at present, during the dry period, the bridges provided suitable hiding places for vagabonds and highwaymen, but peaceful travelers too could, as we did, rest in the shade under the arches.

Blankets were spread out on the ground, and there unfolded before us a feast. Everyone had brought food, and every basket invariably contained a roasted chicken and a watermelon. But, in addition, there was a great variety of meat dishes, cakes and sweets. One simply could not decide where to begin.

---

* Such a ring is known as an *igal* or cord in Arabic.

Meanwhile, Mr. Eckart,* my superior at the orphanage, made his way towards us. When I was told that it was him approaching on the road, I immediately put down the chicken leg I was eating, carefully wiped my fingers, and rose to go and greet my "master." Soon we were both seated and surrounded by lively entertainment and the abundant feast.

But after a while we needed to proceed. Mr. Eckart had brought me a beautiful horse on which I was supposed to make my "entry," but alas, it carried a woman's saddle. I had never ridden before this trip, and on the journey I had become accustomed to the pack saddles. I absolutely refused to ride in that contraption. Besides, I was suspicious of the horses as they seemed so animated by the surrounding festivities. I preferred instead the white donkey I had ridden the previous days. Everyone protested that it was inappropriate to ride a donkey on such an occasion. "Oh," I declared, "better people than I have made their entry into a town in such a fashion." Faced with that compelling argument, the people relented.

The throng of people began to snowball. One small party after the other came riding along the road, greeted us, and joined the entourage. There was no longer time for formal introductions, which for me was just as well as most of the people seemed to look alike. All I could see was the Oriental, hiding all distinctions of race and individuality.

Suddenly the procession halted and everyone dismounted. This time it had to be a person of rank who was approaching.

"Miss Shattuck! Miss Shattuck!"† it sounded through the crowd, and I became quite moved in anticipation.

I knew her name well and knew that she was one of the strong, one who had stood firm in a time of need without fear or any concerns for her own safety, one who had contributed so much that it was hard to fathom.

---

* Franz Eckart (d. 1919) was a German missionary and administrator with the German Orient Mission. His younger brother, Bruno, was also a resident of the city and enjoyed a good reputation within the Armenian community.

† Corinna Shattuck (1848-1910) was a representative of the American Board of Commissioners for Foreign Missions (ABCFM), who had worked in Urfa since 1889. The ABCFM was founded in the early 1800s and became over the subsequent decades very active throughout the Ottoman Empire.

It was a great moment for me to know that I was about to meet and speak to her.

Astride a mule she approached us, a tall, thin, and gray-haired figure. She must have been beautiful in her youth, a beauty still clearly traceable in her fine, intelligent face. She dismounted, and Mr. Eckart escorted me over to meet her. She hugged and kissed me and welcomed me to Urfa. There was something so mothering and loving about her nature and her treatment of me that immediately I felt at home in her company. Soon I was riding contently beside her down the road, and now it was she who was explaining to me all the new things that I encountered.

The closer we got to the city, the more people there were on the road. Miss Shattuck's orphans stood lined up and sang a song for us, the students from the school arrived led by the teachers, and there were also many women. Like large white birds they sat on the slopes on either side of the road, their scarves completely enveloping them.* They had not ventured too far from the city, but they were determined to witness the procession. For them it was like a theatrical production, and they certainly needed to get away from the narrow streets, breathe a little fresh air, and see something new.

In the meantime we had passed through the valley that separates Urfa from the western mountains and had reached the Turkish cemetery. Here there was evidence of a major construction effort as a passage had been dug through the steep hill. We rode between impressive walls that in several places were buttressed with brick. Just before the entrance to this cavernous passage, we again halted, this time before a large crowd of children which had gathered to greet us. It was made up of the children from the German orphanage, those children to whom I was to be a mother. And what a crowd it was. About three hundred children, boys and girls, stood in rows waiting for me. I carefully studied the gathering as thoroughly as time permitted. My first impression was favorable.

But what was one such impression really worth on a day when I was immersed in a new world?

When we exited the tunnel on the other side of the large hill, we found ourselves directly below the walls of Urfa and soon we reached the

* The white worn by the women possibly symbolized their grief over the loss of their relatives.

city's northern entrance, the Samsat[*] Gate. Just outside the gate there was a small mound that appeared man-made and not in keeping with the lay of the land. It chilled me to the core when someone whispered to me that beneath the mound lay buried the victims of the massacres.[†]

We rode on, passing under the arched gate. Gradually the procession thinned; some dispersed already outside the Samsat Gate while others slipped down various side streets. I looked inquisitively down each one. They mostly consisted of a wide, deep gutter where the animals walked. And there was just enough room for one person to pass on the narrow sidewalks between the walls and the gutter. The main street, which was one of the city's most important thoroughfares, was so narrow that just a single heavily laden camel could block it completely. It was a cobblestone road like the side streets of Danish provincial towns, but it was far from clean. Scattered about were piles of garbage, dumped from the houses, and often crowned with a dead cat or chicken that fouled the air.

Down by the Samsat Gate we rode by several open booths, mostly for smiths shoeing horses, but also a café, a bakery, and a Turkish bath. We also passed a large and very dilapidated army barracks where two Turkish soldiers in tattered uniforms sat half-asleep on two stones next to the gate. Next we saw a mosque with a large tree in front of the entrance, and then we entered a strictly residential area. The houses appeared very drab as one could see only the yellowish gray walls and the occasional gateway; not a window, not a bay window, not a balcony were visible. In addition, the houses on the left, meaning the eastern side of the street, were generally much better built than those on the right side. They were, in fact, owned by Turks while on the right lived poor Armenian families. The street, in effect, constituted the border between the two quarters.

* A town located about thirty-five miles to the northwest of Urfa.

† Between 1894 and 1896, the Ottoman Empire conducted an internal campaign against the perceived threat of its Armenian citizens. Known collectively as the Hamidian Massacres, the violence targeted equally those Armenians who simply sought full civil rights within the empire along with the distinct minority of nationalists who were fighting for independence.

We next reached Mastane,* Dr. Lepsius' Oriental carpet factory. Mr. Eckart lived there, and I was to reside with him temporarily. The entrance did not face the main street but instead opened onto the Armenian Quarter, so I got the opportunity to ride along the gutter before we completed our journey.

In the courtyard I was warmly greeted by Mrs. Eckart,† and soon I found myself in a comfortable, European home, partaking of a splendid meal, and, if it had not been for all the foreign noises coming from the street, I would have forgotten that I was in the Orient.

The subsequent days taught me that despite in a sense reaching my goal, there were still obstacles to my getting in contact with these foreign people. There were so many new customs and traditions, so many new ways of thinking that I needed to become familiar with. And then there was the matter of the languages which I needed to learn. That required time and patience. Therefore my initial work was naturally limited to the narrow confines of the mission.

The German Orient Mission, to which I belonged, was only a few years old. It was founded after the massacres, and "mission" was perhaps a deceptive term as the organization was more accurately an aid provider. Dr. Lepsius, who was the organization's founder and leader, was a very open-minded and brilliant man whose activism reflected grand ideas and vision. Therefore, The Danish Friends of Armenia had been drawn to Dr. Lepsius and, since they lacked the resources to establish an independent effort, they had placed the children they sponsored in the German orphanage.

Mr. Eckart was quite young, just twenty-five, when in the spring of 1896 he came to Urfa as Dr. Lepsius' representative to establish an orphanage for the many children who had lost their parents during the massacres. He had been a teacher in the same town where Dr. Lepsius served as a priest and they had become friends. They had also both left their secure positions in government employ in order to dedicate themselves to the aid work.

---

* The factory was also known as Masmana, and F. Eckart, Jeppe's initial host, served as the factory's director.

† Emma Eckart, Franz's wife.

Meanwhile, the scarcity in Urfa was far from relieved with just an orphanage, a fact which Dr. Lepsius fully realized. He sought the counsel of Miss Shattuck, the director of the American mission in Urfa, and moved next to open a medical mission and an Oriental carpet factory.

When I arrived in Urfa, events had left Mr. Eckart the sole administrator of the factory and the orphanage. He was terribly overworked, so there was definitely a need for my services. I would have preferred to immediately move into the orphanage, but Mr. Eckart dissuaded me from doing so. He feared that I might come to feel isolated amongst the foreign peoples and too soon tire of the work. Not before the spring of 1905 did I move out there, and only then did I really come to know the Armenians, first the children and then the adults. And I came to love them.

Out of the multitude at the orphanage I want to emphasize one figure, one of the children there, and through his fate provide an impression of the life and conditions, as I knew them, before the day when the great storm was unleashed and left the land desolate.*

---

* Jeppe is here referring not only to her future adoptive son, Misael "Misak" Melkonian (c. 1891-1978), but also to the great calamity that would descend on the Armenian nation beginning in the spring of 1915.

Chapter One

A Friend in Need

Early in the 1890s, little Misael sat begging in front of the great Gregorian church in Urfa. The church square was the gathering point of the city's Armenians, the center of their public lives. Yet it included much more than just the church. The schools were located there as well, serving at times as facilities where the community could gather for meetings, and there were also a number of rooms for the lodging of Armenian travelers. The whole area was surrounded by a high wall that had only one entrance, a gate about the size of an entire building. It was in this gate complex that Armenians dependent on handouts customarily lived. Only a few of the beggars were from Urfa such as cripples, the elderly, and the blind who really had no other place to go. And their pleas were not ignored as Urfa's citizens were generally affluent and did not passively accept the suffering of the native poor.

The large crowds of beggars from other cities were another matter. There were poor amongst them who, unable to subsist in their own towns, had drifted to Urfa whose citizens were widely known for their prosperity and generosity. Others were unfortunate travelers set upon by highwaymen, who now thanked God that at least their lives had been spared. But most of the beggars were refugees from Ottoman Armenia proper, mostly from the areas around Musch.* Their villages had been attacked by Kurds who had murdered and looted at will and then put everything to the torch. The survivors had since wandered in search of a new place to settle. Many days they had walked on their weary feet, half-starved and clothed in only rags, until they finally reached Urfa and hence now assembled before the church. They hoped to find work, bread, clothes, shelter, and often also medical care for their wounds and relief for the many hardships of refugee life.

---

* It is a district lying about two hundred miles to the northeast of Urfa in the vicinity of Lake Van.

The people of Urfa empathized with their plight and helped them in many ways, but when the refugees spoke at length of their suffering, the city's residents did not believe them. Such calamities had never befallen the citizens of Urfa, and they found it inconceivable that peaceful people would be attacked, robbed, and driven from their houses and homes. They believed the refugees were either exaggerating or had themselves to blame for quarreling with the Kurds.

"Naturally," they told each other, "one must be careful not to provoke the Muslims since we are an oppressed people. There is much we simply must accept and always avoid confrontation."

They too recalled all the instances when they faced unfair and unjust treatment in dealing with their Muslim adversaries. And they thought of how they always had to wear dark-colored, drab clothes in order to avoid provoking any offense.

"So what," they concluded, "we are still living quite well. We enjoy a good income and only rarely are our women harassed or our properties damaged. The refugees must have been careless and allowed Kurdish hostility to emerge. Yet they are still our countrymen and we must help them."

The citizens of Urfa solicited funds while attending church. Those who had a spare room on their farm took in some of the refugees and fed and clothed them. Others helped by providing employment. The refugees settled in and became residents of Urfa. Yet they still yearned for their distant homes, and when they somehow learned that peace was restored, their love for their native regions intensified. They left Urfa and returned to rebuild.

But the steady flow of refugees continued. The residents of Urfa gradually tired of giving, as there seemed no end to the numbers of displaced peoples. In one such subsequent group of refugees, there was a little boy named Misael. He was only about four years old and had neither father nor mother. Instead, he travelled with his uncle and aunt. Why and from where? Those were questions no one was concerned about. En route to Urfa, he rode in a large saddle bag slung over a cow; on the other side were all their remaining possessions. And now, he sat begging under the gate.

In the beginning his life was quite bearable even though he enjoyed no benefit from the money he collected. His aunt took it from him and in exchange gave him only scraps to eat. What he did get in abundance instead were beatings which often left his body black and blue. On the other hand, his aunt was gone most of the day, and frequently he received as charity a little bread rather than money, allowing him to relieve his hunger. In particular one man in his thirties, who attended services at the church every morning and evening, often had something for him. He also always spoke with the boy, giving Misael something to look forward to every day. The man warmed the child's heart, a heart which was otherwise hardened and frightened by a wicked aunt and a lack of contact with caring people.

But at least during the summer, life was bearable even though that season included its share of pests. Misael, who was not kept properly clean, wore a vermin-infested, blue cotton tunic, his only piece of clothing. The dust and the dirt, which whirled around everywhere, lodged in the eyes and at times caused painful infections. And atop the head there was not only vermin in the hair, but also favus* scabs which bled and were very unpleasant. Yet one can become accustomed to enduring many things, and Misael had learned to calmly accept these difficulties and to still laugh and play as a child.

With the arrival of winter it was much too cold to cover oneself with only a thin tunic at night, and Misael froze terribly. During the day he felt so stiff he could hardly stretch out his hand to beg. He also developed stomach problems and steadily lost weight, suggesting the day when he could no longer stand was imminent and that he would soon join the many others who lay beneath the tombstones. Yet he stayed alive, and the man, Hovagim was his name, continued to come by and see him every day. Hovagim recognized that the little food he brought the boy was no longer sufficient. Misael could by now hardly eat anything and simply lay there whimpering.

It had never been pleasant to be close to Misael due to his infestation, but now an added stench worsened conditions. He could no longer go and relieve himself and simply remained lying on the cold ground with

* This is a fungus-borne disease afflicting the human scalp and the skin of mammals and birds.

his thin shirt moist and caked in dirt. Hovagim had seen the boy in that state in the morning, and throughout the day, while he worked, he kept thinking of him.

Hovagim, who was a mason like his brothers, had together with them assumed the work on a building near the church. He was usually a man of few words, but that day his brothers were struck by his utter silence. They thought he seemed quite preoccupied, which of course he was. Hovagim's thoughts of the boy persisted while he rather mechanically placed one brick atop another on the wall. Repeatedly he saw before him the small, dying child, and when the images became almost lifelike, his eyes filled with tears, and he turned away to hide his grief from the others. Hovagim too was reminded of a passage from the Gospels which he had heard in church and kept hearing in his mind: "The one who cares for such a child in My name, cares for Me."* That, he thought, had to be true. It seemed his free will and Christian conscience were in agreement.

Yet were there not practical difficulties? And what would his family think? Hovagim, after all, was unmarried and would need his brother's wife to care for the child, and it was difficult to say whether she would bond with the boy and love him. If only the child were beautiful and healthy she would probably accept him gladly. On the other hand, the notion of adopting a child had often enough been discussed in the household as the only practical solution to the tragic misfortune which plagued his brother's marriage.†

Several years had passed already since Hovagim procured a wife for his younger brother, Hagob. The eldest brother had already married when their father was alive and had moved into a separate room in the family house. He maintained an independent household but continued to work alongside his younger brothers who had gradually matured and joined the family trade.

Then it came time for Hovagim to marry, but he, who seemed the most prominent of the brothers, did not feel it was opportune to do so. His father, who had already been ailing for years, subsequently died, leaving Hovagim with three younger brothers and two sisters to care for.

---

* Mark 9:37.

† Jeppe is referring to the couple's loss of their own children.

I cannot marry, he thought, while I already have a family to care for. Instead, he indicated to Hagob that it was time for him to get engaged. Hagob had long wished to get married but had remained silent about it since Hovagim was not yet engaged and had not previously discussed the matter. He therefore felt he could not accept Hovagim's proposal and claimed he was in no rush to marry. Hagob pointed out that their sisters also needed to find spouses and that the family was already burdened by enough expenses. Yet Hovagim was quick to decipher his brother's evasions. He consulted their mother and a few other older women, and they decided upon Chanum of the Tatarenk family as a future wife for Hagob. Though the Tatarenks were one of the richest and most respected families in Urfa, it was rightly expected that the union would be approved as Hagob's family, the Biredjiklians,* also was reputable.

The women opened the negotiations and met with Chanum, a mere girl who they knew well from the public baths and weddings. When an agreement was reached, a priest and a couple of men from the family came to formally propose to Chanum. She received jewelry from Hagob's mother, the acceptance of which symbolized that she was betrothed. Hagob, on the other hand, now carefully avoided passing through the street where Chanum lived in order to avoid seeing her which would be highly improper.

On two or three occasions a year during the major festivals, Hovagim provided Hagob with money so he could buy jewelry for Chanum. All other funds Hovagim administered as the head of household for the general benefit of the entire family. However, the jewelry that Hagob bought, which for the time represented a considerable sum, was his private property. Other family expenses included the dowries for the two sisters who were married off during those years. Yet Hovagim was a good administrator who made sure the family funds were adequate for all needs.

When the sisters had left the household, Hovagim told his mother that he thought the marriage to Chanum could be planned for the fall. She was then fourteen, which was a mature enough age to get married.

* The family originated from Biredjik, a town on the Euphrates and about fifty miles to the west of Urfa.

It was a grand wedding. Hovagim spared no expense as it was a matter of the family's honor. He presided over the ceremony as the family patriarch and escorted Hagob to the bridal room. Each night the family parlor was converted into the couple's bedroom but reverted back to its collective, social function during the day. The satin sheets were neatly folded, stored in a linen closet, and periodically shown to visitors. The new dual use of the parlor lent a certain luster to the room.

Chanum looked so delicate and pretty in her gold-embroidered dress and wearing a long and heavy gold chain around her neck. She was a great beauty, but the brothers neither saw her face nor heard her voice. According to custom she remained veiled and silent. It would be improper for her to speak to any of them except, of course, Hagob when they were alone. Even her mother-in-law she answered only with gestures. A year passed in this manner until she gave birth to her first child, a boy whose arrival elicited great joy in the family.

Hovagim held the newborn in his arms as if it were his own. He did this openly as he was the family patriarch, but Hagob had to show his affection in secret as doing so overtly was frowned upon. Similarly, Chanum should not behave as if the child were hers alone. The boy belonged to the whole family but mainly to the mother-in-law who was responsible for the child and cared for him. Chanum only nursed the child. That was the custom, and no one thought it should be different or that the mother was treated unfairly.

In essence, everyone was happy. But the joy did not last long as the child died after just six months. However, the death was not, as one might assume, considered a tragedy. It was accepted as a part of life in the Orient that more than half of all infants died. The closest friends of the family visited to offer condolences and declared: "May the parents survive." They did, and within a year Hagob and Chanum had another child. It was *only* a girl but the family was equally happy after Hovagim declared that "she also was God's gift." Yet she too died in infancy.

The second death was more serious. The grandmother cried, and the female friends of the family stayed longer to console her. These women felt they needed to share in the grief and they did so genuinely. They needed only to recall their feelings when they buried their own small children; then the tears came quite naturally.

Chanum also grew ever more depressed, and Hagob did not ease her pain as he in a sense blamed her for their misfortune. Hovagim sensed this tension and one day, when the whole family was assembled, he resolved the matter by saying: "The Lord gave, the Lord has taken away. Blessed be the name of the Lord."

Hovagim frequently attended church where every Sunday a Bible passage was recited without any added interpretation or embellishments. The passage was simply read aloud. Hovagim then retained the words in his heart and contemplated their meaning throughout the week. Therefore, he always knew what needed to be said and done, and once he had spoken to the family, everyone agreed to no longer discuss the issue.

Yet when Chanum had her third child, she and the whole family feared from the outset that the child would die. They were ever vigilant of the baby's health and consulted healers at the slightest indication of illness, which in turn meant that the child still died within a short time. Now everyone was at a loss to explain what had happened. There had to be something wrong with the family. In fact, it was likely that either the evil eye or other witchcraft was involved. Everyone sought to advise the family. They might consult a gypsy who could track down the source of the witchcraft, maybe accompany Chanum to a holy spring, or perhaps even make a pledge to a saint. All the advice was enlivened with tales of others who had faced similar misfortune and had been helped by such actions.

Hovagim, however, found little value in these suggestions and instead favored other advice which many claimed was far superior. It called for them to adopt an orphan. Many had done so with good results when they either could not conceive or their children died. And when even the local priest endorsed the idea, Hovagim became fully committed to it. The rest of the family also supported the idea, though they naturally preferred finding a healthy child whose origins were known. They were unlikely to embrace Misael,* but Hovagim was sure that the little boy was destined for their family. The more he thought about it, the more he became convinced that God had led him to Misael and had tied a promise to the

* The spelling of the boy's name changes slightly from this point forward, with a "k" replacing the "s." This is most likely a simple typo in the original text, so the "Misael" spelling is continued in this translated version of Jeppe's account.

adoption of the child, a pledge to lift the curse that apparently hovered over the family and restore their ability to conceive their own children.

Once Hovagim had finally come to this decision, it was already past noon and he suddenly became fearful that the child might have died during the intervening hours and thereby leave his family's curse forever unchanged. He quickly put down the trowel in his hand and told the others he had a matter to attend to and that they should just continue on with their work. Hovagim then set off for the church determined to collect Misael. Yet the boy wasn't in his usual spot at the gate and Hovagim's heart momentarily skipped a beat. Maybe Misael was dead! But in the next instance he turned to ask the other beggars about the boy's fate.

"Yes," they said, "it could be that he had already died, as he probably did not have long to live."

Yet, Hovagim did not abandon his mission quite so quickly. He had to find the boy; it had become for him a matter of vital importance.

After much searching, he finally spotted Misael lying curled up in a cozy nook, taking in the warm winter sun. In Mesopotamia, the sun is always an important source of heat and, when it is at its lowest point in the sky, it is the same as the high point of the October sun in Denmark. "He is dead," thought Hovagim, seeing the boy lying completely still with his eyes closed. But grief soon turned to joy when Misael suddenly opened his eyes and looked up at him. Hovagim immediately placed the emaciated figure on his lap despite the infestation and the smell. To him it was like the discovery of a coveted treasure. Misael almost instinctively sensed the genuine warmth and a small, boney, and dirty arm gradually wrapped around Hovagim's neck as the scab-covered child's head rested on his chest. Without uttering a word, Hovagim wrapped the boy in his cloak and carried him to the family house.

At home Hovagim's mother sat sewing by the window. They did not have glass panes, so when it was really cold, they closed the wooden shutters and were limited to light from a small window located just below the ceiling. But on this day, the sun was shining and filled the whole living room with pleasant warmth. His mother saw Hovagim arrive and was a little curious about what he was carrying. She did not immediately ask him, and he came in and sat down without revealing the item he had brought.

"Well, mother," he said tentatively and pensively, "I have brought us a child so that misfortune can be purged from our house."

"You are probably right to have done so, my son," replied his mother. "There is most likely no other option for us. Hopefully we will not face too many difficulties with this decision."

"We will," answered Hovagim, "but otherwise there won't also be joy." And subsequently he removed the cloak to show her Misael.

"Lord, have mercy!" exclaimed his mother, "could you not find a more wretched child? One dares not touch him and look how the lice are now crawling on you. Return the boy immediately to where you found him and come home again for a change of clothes."

"No, we must keep this child," insisted Hovagim sternly. "Misfortune must be driven off by misfortune; there will be no blessing forthcoming for taking one of the attractive children that everyone wants."

"Chanum!" he called, "go and boil some water and I'll clean the boy myself."

Chanum, who no longer kept herself veiled in the house and even occasionally voiced her opinion, had stood by silently observing the child. She agreed with Hovagim, but felt it was improper for her to openly oppose her mother-in-law. So Chanum wisely kept silent even as the tears that trickled down her cheeks revealed her true sentiments.

Soon a lively fire was burning in the kitchen and shortly thereafter Chanum brought in the warm water in a large copper basin and the hot coals in a brazier. She then motioned to take the boy in order to wash him, but Hovagim objected. Over the persistent protests of the household's women, he assumed the task of washing Misael and made his mother realize that she had hurt his feelings and needed to do something to make amends. She quickly brought a towel and some clothes for the boy, and she sent Chanum into the kitchen for a bowl of soup which they kept warm on the brazier.

Chanum, wishing to immediately embrace the boy, brought out her bedding as a sign that if he was to be "her child," he should sleep together with her. This the grandmother opposed, but, despite her disapproval, she still gestured for Chanum to make up the bed. However, when

Hovagim saw the linens, he simply said, “No, use mine.” The women again objected, but Hovagim was determined and soon after little Misael was lying clean, full, warmly clothed, and wrapped comfortably in Hovagim’s bedding. It was now clear to everyone that Misael was actually a handsome child.

The boy’s little blue cloak had long since been discarded. Hovagim’s mother, using a pair of fire tongs, threw it in the garbage where such disgusting things belonged. She also asked her son to change so she could clean his dirtied work clothes. Hovagim then left the house for about an hour and returned with fabrics for the boy’s clothes and carrying a pair of new red shoes. Misael’s eyes lid up momentarily when he saw the shoes, but his demeanor was soon replaced by a grave, pensive expression.

“My aunt will only take them away from me and sell them. You should not give me those shoes.”

“But you are not going back to your aunt,” Hovagim said reassuringly. “You’re to be our child. Would you not like that?”

Did he? Yes, of that there was no doubt. But he continued to fear his aunt until Hovagim assured him that he would resolve everything with her. His pledge also reminded Hovagim that he needed to discuss the affair with Misael’s uncle. This man was unemployed and, as an outsider in Urfa, he could not easily

find work during the winter. He idled away the days sitting in the sun and lived off his wife’s and Misael’s earnings from begging. However, the uncle was a good-natured man who was genuinely happy to know that Misael had found a good home. He even admitted that he had always felt guilty about his brother’s child living in such squalor.

The aunt felt otherwise and severely chastised her husband when she returned home in the evening.

“May you be blinded in both eyes! I wish you were dead, you loafer! How could you give Misael away when he collects money for us every day? Do you think I have cared for him all this time just to end up with nothing?”

She continued to rail against her husband until his pride awoke him from his sluggish state.

“You damned woman!” he shouted. “How dare you scold me who has authority over you!”

He then began hitting her, but she continued to rant and rave until he had given her a severe beating. The aunt finally begged for a truce, they reconciled, and then sat down together to eat what she had collected during the day.

Hovagim's brothers were very surprised when they returned home that evening. But when they learned how he had reacted toward the women's initial skepticism about Misael, they voiced no objections and instead assured him that he had acted correctly. That, of course, was easy for them to say, because the child did not cause them any inconvenience like he did for the women and especially Hovagim. Misael stayed with him at night and Hovagim had to get up several times to wash him and change his bedding. It was a difficult few weeks before the worst was over and Misael began to show signs that he would survive his illness. His health was highly precarious, so he only recovered gradually.

In addition to matters of cleanliness and Misael's physical condition, there were other issues of concern. The boy was irritable, as was common with neglected children, and he had never enjoyed a structured upbringing. He had lived his life only amongst the lowest classes, had played with street kids on the main church square, and had been the constant victim of his aunt's tough and arbitrary abuse and insults. The women of the household were shocked over the torrent of crude words that Misael unleashed during his bouts of anger. Hovagim, who was only home in the evenings, rarely witnessed these temper tantrums, and the women were left unsure how exactly to deal with the matter. After all, the whole manner in which Hovagim had handled the adoption made them uneasy. They were sure that he would probably be angered if the boy was punished and would think that the women were doing it because they disapproved of having him in the house. They therefore felt quite powerless, and Misael's considerable temper, which was fuelled by his illness, often came to dominate the boy's mood.

But, of course, Misael had to endure much discomfort. It was not until the summer that he recovered somewhat normal digestive function, and for years to come he continued to experience strong intermittent abdominal pains. But otherwise he became well enough to eat the same food as everyone else.

Yet, soon enough another difficulty arose as Misael's eyes again began to ache. He suffered from trachoma, also known as the Egyptian eye disease. It plagues the entire Orient and continues to spread due to the prevailing conditions of uncleanliness and lack of proper care. Misael had to sit the entire day with bandaged eyes and endure the ongoing pain. It was a lot to take for such a little boy.

Every morning, before he went to work, Hovagim lifted Misael onto his back and carried him to see a natural healer who was experienced in treating such ailments. The old woman flipped Misael's eyelids and rubbed them with her thimble until they bled and then applied powder and other mysterious ingredients to the eyes. This rubbing technique was actually not entirely misguided because the infection is located just below the skin in a series of small abscesses. Yet it was a primitive and drastic remedy and one shudders to think how much filth entered the eyes through this method. Some were entirely blinded by this treatment while others recovered fully. Luckily, Misael was one of the latter.

Over a long period of time Hovagim brought Misael for daily treatments. And rather than forsake his work, Hovagim used the time he would usually have spent attending mass to accompany the boy. He felt his hours with Misael were as beneficial as church services. Even when his mother offered to bring the child to the healer, Hovagim would hear none of it. He insisted that he would attend to all matters concerning the boy.

Once Misael's eyes had recovered, the next area of focus was his scalp. After all, he would not be completely healthy as long as it was covered with favus scabs, but ridding him of that ailment presented an even more difficult task than curing the eye infection. This type of favus is a condition which attaches itself to the roots of the hair. If one is vigilant, it is possible in the beginning, when the first oozing abscess appears, to treat the problem by immediately cleaning the scalp and carefully removing all the pus. But when the condition has gone untreated for years then such a remedy is useless. The only remaining option is to pull out every hair by its root despite the terrible pain.

The method used is to cover the scalp with a mixture of pitch and another substance and wait until it hardens. Then one rips everything off in one quick motion. It is a radical approach, but if one is careful to clean and bandage the affected area afterwards, then the condition is cured. Yet it is a regimen that seems akin to medieval torture and, when applied to children, is even worse.

But there was no alternative, and Hovagim decided with a heavy heart to have Misael undergo the treatment. In the meantime, the procedure had been discussed and the boy, being old enough to understand what was about to happen, now also had to deal with his fear. To relieve his anxiety, the family decided to promise him a pet lamb if he agreed to go to the healer. However, Misael was cautious. He wanted the lamb beforehand, and that is how it unfolded. He also insisted on bringing the animal along, which the family similarly accepted. In the end, Misael sat on Hovagim's lap with the lamb held tightly to his body and his face buried the animal's coat as the old woman ripped out his hair. But it was still an ordeal, and Hovagim was almost as drained as the boy by the experience. Needless to say, both were happy when it was over.

Once the wounds were healed and new hair appeared, Misael began to look like other children. And between Misael and Hovagim there flourished an affection rarely seen even between fathers and sons. Every evening Hovagim took the boy in his arms and held him close throughout the night. Misael was his first thought when he came home in the evenings and his last before he left in the mornings. All the tenderness which he had kept bottled up inside, he now showered on Misael who had never experienced parental love or any other tenderness, and he, in turn, embraced Hovagim as the focal point in his life. In fact, Misael always had countless things to tell and show his friend when he came home in the evenings. He also often ran to meet Hovagim when he was walking home so he could hold his hand or ride on his shoulders.

But one evening when Misael came to meet him, it was clear to Hovagim that something unusual had happened. Misael was pale, appeared upset, and his eyes were red and swollen from crying.

"Don't let me leave you! Don't let me leave you!" he almost screamed as he fell to the ground and clasped Hovagim's legs.

"But why would I?" exclaimed Hovagim. "I would never let that happen," he said to console the boy. But Hovagim too grew uneasy when he learned what had transpired. Misael's uncle and aunt had visited the home while he had been at work. They told the family they planned to return to their native region and intended to bring Misael along. Yet it was obvious that they had no moral right to the boy after they had almost allowed him to die. It was instead thanks to Hovagim's efforts that Misael was still alive. However, the uncle and aunt could claim the boy with the support of the law. The uncle had allowed Hovagim to take Misael but he had never received anything in writing, so they had the right to take him back.

It had been an oversight by Hovagim and he soon felt as distraught as Misael. He now entered the house, discussed the matter with the family, and concluded that the situation was grave. Hovagim then met with the uncle and aunt who gave numerous justifications for their demand.

"We certainly can't let our brother's child stay with strangers," they declared. "It would not be right and our hearts could not bear it. He is, after all, as if one with us and we cannot part with him."

Hovagim was soon agitated by their statements and dismissed their blatant lies by pointing out that Misael had been severely neglected and near death. But the aunt, in particular, vehemently held her ground.

"Well, this is the same as always," she railed, "the poor are accused of having limited feelings. We have shared our meager means with the boy, and we dare say that our own children would not have lived a better life. And yet, we are slandered. No, the child is absolutely ours."

Now, good advice was what was needed. After having carefully considered what to do next, Hovagim set off the following morning to visit the old Bishop Choren who lived in the Armenian monastery west of the city. The bishop was a peculiar man who for years had been Urfa's "leader." This position is always occupied by a member of the high-ranking clergy who, unlike those of lower rank, are unmarried and well-educated in theology and often also other fields. He who holds this office serves as the chairman of both the religious and secular Armenian councils and resolves through mediation such communal disputes that become matters of public concern. In addition, he represents the Armenian people and protects their interests in dealings with the Turkish [Ottoman] government.*

* The Ottoman Empire organized its people into separate groups according to religion. Known as the *millet* or "nation" system, it allowed each community to administer its own social and religious affairs in accordance with scripture and tradition.

Members of the clergy must hold at least the title of *vartabed*[*] to be eligible for the office of communal leader, though at times bishops also served. Both are academic ranks whose varying nuances are difficult to discern for the uninformed person. Yet the differences are, of course, rather insignificant, because as "leader" either rank-holder has the same authority.

Bishop Choren had since grown too old to occupy the position and, following some tensions with Urfa's elite, he had retired to the monastery after passing the post to Anania Vartabed. However, despite officially being the new leader, he was often overshadowed by the more prominent bishop. The common people generally preferred to consult him and he frequently agreed to intervene. This led to frequent divisions between the two men, which certainly did not benefit the Armenian cause. Yet the customary practice of retiring the departing "leader" to Jerusalem as a pensioner could not be applied in this instance as Bishop Choren was too notable a man. In fact, he had forged a personal relationship with the empire's supreme ruler, Abdülhamid,[†] who bestowed an imperial order on the bishop and reportedly held him in high regard. It seems that fact alone was reason enough to treat the bishop with care.

But, in addition, the bishop was a very wise and supposedly quite virtuous man who was so greatly respected by the common man that some had begun to attribute to him saintly qualities. Many stories also circulated about the esoteric answers he might have given on occasion. Best known of these was the tale about the European who once asked him why his people, the Armenians, who were related ethnically to Europeans, had developed a servile nature which was generally foreign to Europeans.

---

* This designates a priest or church scholar; essentially a teacher of religious doctrine.

† Sultan Abdülhamid II (1842-1918) reigned from 1876 until 1909 when he was unseated by the Committee of Union and Progress, also known popularly as the Young Turks. He worked tirelessly to modernize the Ottoman Empire through economic and educational reforms, and he sought to unify his Muslim subjects through an emphasis on Pan-Islam. However, he was also repressive and controlling, and in Europe he was often referred to as the Red or Bloody Sultan in the wake of the 1890s persecution of the Armenian population.

"Well," said the old man, "once upon a time a lion met a cat. The lion observed the cat carefully and asked, 'Why is it that you who are so similar to me in build is yet so different in spirit? I strike and seize my prey in the open hunt while you lie in wait and ambush it."

"Lord knows," answered the cat, "every word you speak is true, but you forget that for millennia I have lived among humans."*

It was to this man, Bishop Choren, rather than the "leader" that Hovagim now turned for advice. The bishop listened to the whole affair and regretted that the law sided with the uncle, but he still promised to do what he could to help. After all, it was likely that the aunt and uncle wanted only to extort money, and Hovagim was prepared to pay as long as he could just keep the boy. The bishop therefore dispatched his servant to summon the couple. When they eventually appeared before him, they were compelled to be humble and composed unlike when Hovagim spoke with them. They too were soon happy to agree to surrender all rights to the boy for a sum of three hundred piastres.†

Towards evening the uncle, aunt, Hovagim and Misael met with the bishop to draw up a document which assigned Misael to Hovagim as his son. The uncle, who could not write his name, dipped his thumb in ink and, before witnesses, pressed it onto the paper where the signature should be. Then Hovagim paid the agreed three hundred piastres, they all kissed the bishop's hand, and the uncle left content with his treasure.

The fee paid by Hovagim was considerable. Even though it is true that three hundred piasters is only about forty crowns,‡ it represented a lot of money for Hovagim who struggled to earn that amount over a two-month period of hard work. On the other hand, it also meant that one could purchase a lot for that amount of money. It was not too long ago when a man could go to the market with twenty øre** and buy dinner for

* The gist of this short story is a classic example of Orientalism. Jeppe is conveying the notion that the Armenians had surrendered elements of their European Christian identity through centuries of Ottoman domination and had been compelled to compromise and adapt in order to survive.

† The piaster or *kurus* was a subunit of Ottoman Turkish currency equal to one hundredth of a gold pound.

‡ Denmark's currency. In the 1890s one crown or *krone* equaled about $.20.

** One fifth of a Danish crown.

the whole family, or another man could be heard complaining, "God save us! It is so expensive that we may soon have to strip the land," when he got only three eggs for one øre. Prices had changed a little since then, but forty crowns was still a significant sum. Hovagim's family naturally found that the amount paid was much too large but wisely kept silent.

Once Misael was securely tied to the family and his health had generally improved, Hovagim determined it was time for the boy to attend school. Yet at that time school attendance was not considered a matter of course and was instead quite uncommon. However, the news was well-received at the family home where the women were glad to be rid of the boy for most of the day, a fact which was easy to understand.

So one morning, Hovagim took Misael to the school. The main classroom was large and spacious with bare, drab walls. On the floor stood a solitary table and chair for the teacher and there were also a few old, dirty raffia mats used by the children. But the lack of furnishings was contrasted with the abundance of kids, over one hundred of which were gathered around the teacher. She called on each one to come up and read a passage from an assigned book, even though that meant each student was only tested once every seven hours. In the meantime, they had to sit quietly and study. It was, in short, a less than ideal form of schooling, but it was also quite inexpensive as the weekly tuition was at most five øre.

It was in this setting that Misael took a seat. He received a new book and quickly skimmed through it, but for a boy aged five, more was needed to keep him occupied. So he began to look around the room, soon spotting a boy he knew and striking up a conversation with him. However, within moments the boys heard the teacher's voice:

"Levon! Misael! Be quiet!"

Misael now felt rather puzzled about how he should pass the time. He started to pick at a hole in the raffia mat until the boy next to him called out to the teacher:

"Miss, Misael is damaging the mat."

What followed was a smack across the fingers and a stern warning to sit still. But Misael instead became angry and when the teacher looked away momentarily, he took a stone from his pocket and struck the boy who had told on him with a well-directed blow to the head. Screams and upheaval replaced the quiet of the classroom and this time Misael received a thorough beating.

However, this treatment only angered Misael further. Once his punishment was over, he sprang out the window, which in Oriental fashion was low to the ground, and proceeded to hurl stones into the classroom and shower the assembled children and teacher with swearwords. This commotion summoned the church verger who seized Misael and inflicted another beating on him, enough to convince him to temper his anger and sit down. But at the first recess he left the school, ran home, and did not return that day.

The following morning, Hovagim brought him back to the school. Misael, however, ran away again but was soon caught and returned by the church verger. Tensions continued during the subsequent days with Misael sometimes being beaten and even tied to a pole in the classroom. Finally, after a time, he was calmed enough to simply sit quietly without doing much of anything. Yet he remained a challenge for the teacher and his education progressed very slowly.

But the pace of learning was generally slow for all the students due to technical challenges. The children in the class had to learn the building blocks of reading which on average took three years. Further, the Armenian language consists of thirty-six letters with difficult names (*aib*, *baen*, *kem*, etc.), and, once learned, one faces the added challenge of spelling. After all, how *ho-aib-hi-re* spells *hajr* is not easily understood. So many students remembered more about their days in school from what they felt across their backs than from anything they learned. In short, the teachers and children were both plagued by an inefficient system of education, and it was only the parents who had few complaints. They were generally happy to be rid of the children for part of the day because most homes had only small courtyards but housed large families with many kids. In their minds it was almost as bad to have the children rummaging through the courtyard as allowing them to roam the streets and commit mischief.

In the fall of 1894, when Misael was about six years old, Chanum gave birth to yet another child, a boy baptized Kevork (George). This was a joyous event because a delay in her renewed pregnancy had raised fears that the prescribed remedy of adopting a child had failed to work. But now everything was in order, bringing joy to the entire family and seeing Misael become Kevork's *kirvae.**

The women brought the infant to the church to have him baptized. His naked body was completely submerged in the baptismal font by the priest according to the rituals of the Gregorian Church. Then he was dressed, wrapped in a cloth, and laid across Misael's outstretched arms. With a lighted candle in each hand, Misael proceeded into the main church carrying Kevork up to the altar. There another priest chanted a – fortunately – short mass over each of the infants assembled that day and took each one in his arms as he circled the altar. To conclude the ritual, the priest put a tiny piece of the host in each baby's mouth. For Misael, it seemed a very lengthy and tiring ceremony, but he endured it with dignity.

Misael often went to church as Hovagim brought him along to attend mass every Sunday. He did not mind because when he was with Hovagim and knelt down beside him, the time passed quickly. After mass, Misael also enjoyed passing out raisins and other sweets to the children who sat begging before the church door. When he passed by them, he always held Hovagim's hand tightly and often had tears in his eyes. Misael could simply not forget how awful life once was for him. And though he loved sweets and Hovagim allowed him to fill his pockets, he never hesitated to give it all away when he saw a poor child.

Misael also cared a great deal for Kevork. As soon as Misael was deemed old enough to handle the baby, his greatest diversion was to play with Kevork. However, this only happened occasionally because Kevork was quite a delicate child. It was clear that he too would lack a strong physical disposition. Yet the family was not particularly worried about Kevork. They were thoroughly convinced that the child would live. After all, they had Misael, and he was their guarantee that Kevork was to survive. And this optimism was not misplaced, for the boy outlived the

* Essentially, he became his big brother, his mentor.

age when the previous children had died. It seemed everything promised a happy life for the family until a terrible calamity all at once crushed their home and their joy.

Chapter Two

Black Clouds

During the summer of 1895 a *vartabed* from Armenia proper passed through Urfa en route to Constantinople. For a few days he stayed in the city as Anania Vartabed's guest and received, as was customary in the Orient, a visit from a delegation of local Armenian elites. Hovagim's deceased father had been a member of that elite and held a position of prominence which the son had since inherited after his brothers unanimously selected him as the male sibling best suited to represent the family at such gatherings. Therefore, once Hovagim received word that the visiting *vartabed* would meet with a city delegation, he stripped off his work clothes, put on finer garments, and headed for Anania Vartabed's residence.

When Hovagim arrived, a crowd had already assembled in the small hall used on such occasions. At the far end of the hall, he saw Anania Vartabed sitting at his official post with Bishop Choren on his right and the visiting *vartabed* on his left, and immediately next to the bishop were Urfa's four priests. Along the walls were cushion-covered benches on which sat the senior and most prominent men of the city, carefully arrayed according to age, wealth, or other distinction. Additional people, mostly the younger men, who had not yet earned a place on the benches, were seated cross-legged on the carpeted floor.

When Hovagim entered the hall, he greeted the assembled men with a "Good day, everyone," which was reciprocated in unison. He next went to kiss the hand of the prelate after which he made his way to the rear and modestly took a seat near the door. Here Hovagim found Krikor, Chanum's brother, who also was one of the younger men in attendance. And once he was seated, the men sitting nearby welcomed him one by one, each moving a hand to the forehead, tilting the upper body slightly forward and uttering the Armenian greeting. Hovagim answered with a similar motion to each of them and responded, "warmly received."

This mutual greeting went smoothly since Hovagim, rather uniquely, had no enemies, which otherwise, in such a gathering, was reflected by the feuding parties not exchanging pleasantries and instead stubbornly looking away. After the greeting, a servant brought Hovagim a small cup of Turkish coffee and, once he drank it, he had finally "arrived."

Hovagim had been one of the last people to arrive at the hall. Soon after, the private conversations ended and Anania Vartabed proclaimed that his brotherly colleague and guest wanted to tell the gathering something about the conditions in Armenia. Many had already heard a great deal from the refugees, but it had all sounded rather unbelievable. Unfortunately, those tales had now been confirmed to Anania Vartabed by his colleague, and he was grateful that everyone present would get an opportunity to hear a true accounting of the plight of their Armenian countrymen.

The visiting *vartabed* then rose to address the gathering. He was a fiery orator whose words came alive before the assembled men, imparting vivid images of the burning villages, the murdered men, the dishonored women, and the orphaned children who now lived like wild animals in the forests. They saw before them everything that he described and it chilled all present to the core. Everyone's mind became focused on the one poignant question: Why?

"We don't know," answered the clergyman and shrugged his shoulders. "There were few disputes between us and the Kurds, and in many regions relations were good until a few years ago when the mullahs* began to incite the people against us. Many of us have heard their speeches in the villages, so we know what they are telling them."

"How long will you tolerate the heathens among you?" they rail. "It is an offense to Allah. Do you not see that all the land's riches will soon belong to them? They deceive and cheat you at every opportunity and come out ahead. Why do you allow that to happen? Don't you know that Allah has decreed that you, the believers, shall rule the earth and enjoy its riches, and that the infidels shall be your humble slaves and lay the fruit of their labor at your feet? You have forgotten Allah's words, and that is why so many of you live in poverty and need, while the infidels sit warm

* A mullah is a local religious leader and teacher.

and content in their homes. It is but Allah's just punishment for your having ignored His will and forged friendships with those who oppose Him and are like a foul odor in His nose. Rise up and end your transgressions before Allah punishes you more severely."

"With such speeches repeated over and over," noted the *vartabed*, "it is no wonder that the Kurds attacked. The government, rather than protect us, ensured that the Kurds were well-supplied with arms while we could hardly procure any. Some villages were able to mount an effective defense but they now live in open hostilities with their Kurdish neighbors. Also our brothers in the towns were subjected to pressures from all sides. Ominous signs abound."

"All that is clear," he continued "but we still don't understand what reason the mullahs had to launch their campaign against us. It is as if someone prodded them to rise up."

Once the *vartabed* had finished speaking, a deep silence descended over the hall. Everyone considered what he had said, and gradually all eyes turned toward the bishop as the only person who could provide an answer to the question on every man's mind. But the old man remained silent for a long time, just staring out across the crowd. Suddenly he sat up in his chair and, with a piercing look in his eyes, he told the assembled men: "He who is surrounded by threatening dogs will eventually have no choice but to throw bread at their feet."

Silence again reigned in the hall. It was a new riddle; who was it that was cornered by dogs? No one dared ask, for it was a time of spies and people did not trust one another. But then the visiting clergyman again rose to speak:

"Rightly and with justification it is said that few men in this country are as wise as Bishop Choren. It is true that our gracious sultan – may God bless him with a long life! – was hard-pressed by the Kurdish chiefs in our region. They were often on the verge of rebellion and openly coveted the fertile lands lying beyond the border."

"That is what our holy book promised us," the *vartabed* continued, "that we should face adversity here on earth. In truth, we are shed like water for the sake of our faith."

Again the hall became quiet until one in the crowd cautiously pointed out that Urfa was situated far from the border and that conditions might therefore be better here. That prompted the bishop to again sit up in his chair and declare: “It is an unwise shepherd who fails to load his musket when he hears the wolf’s howl in the distance.”

After that, no one else had anything to say. And from that day forward, the Armenians in Urfa began to procure weapons.

One by one they stood up, approached to kiss the clergymen’s hands, and exited the hall. They filed out in a dignified and orderly fashion, beginning with the eldest men. Krikor and Hovagim were among the last to head out onto the church square and a bit further down the street they met up again. As they walked together, they struck up a conversation about business, the common and neutral topic for all men in the region. In fact, it never failed that when one walked behind a number of men one would sooner or later hear references to money.

But what else could they talk about on the open street? It was considered improper for men to converse about family affairs outside of the home and to discuss women was downright indecent. Politics and other public matters were also avoided due to fears of spies. And the lack of leisure activities and a relatively unchanging weather further limited the number of viable topics of conversation. That left business as the only real subject for discussion when one was out in public.

On this occasion, as Krikor and Hovagim walked together, they contemplated the current prices on livestock, a topic which particularly concerned Krikor whose livelihood involved buying animals from villagers and reselling them for slaughter in the city. But neither man was entirely focused on the conversation as their thoughts were dominated by quite other matters. So when they reached Hovagim’s street, and their paths were to separate, he asked if Krikor would come home with him.

“The family is at the public bath,” he said, “and my brothers are at work. Come with me to the house and let’s drink a cup of coffee and smoke a cigarette. After all, I’m not going out again this evening.”

“Yes,” answered Krikor, “I have time to stop by as I don’t have anything to do either.”

Once they entered the house and had assured themselves that no one was present to overhear them, they soon forgot about the cigarettes and coffee and turned instead to a discussion of the issue weighing on both their minds. Hovagim had not really understood the bishop’s statement and he now took the opportunity to ask Krikor, who was a few years his junior but very bright. In particular, Hovagim was unclear about who was hounded by the dogs.

"It's the sultan, Abdülhamid," Krikor told him. "In many places there is grave discontent with his rule. I have noticed that frequently while traveling through area villages, especially around Diyarbakir.* The Kurds often suspect that he is to blame for all their poverty and suffering. While amongst them, I heard it told that several chiefs were considering rebellion. So the bishop believes that the sultan has now allowed them to prey on Armenian areas in order to distract them from other concerns."

"He may be right," continued Krikor, "but I also think that many Muslims envy our standard of living. After all, they believe it should be them enjoying all the fruits of the land and that we should be their humble slaves. It will probably remain that way as long as Armenians and Kurds live side by side. We work diligently and therefore we prosper, a fact understood by the Kurds no matter how hard we try to hide it. They detest our success and attempt to deny us our bounty through violence. But, admittedly, there are also a number of very avaricious Armenians who cheat the Kurds terribly. In short, it's a complex situation."

"I just wish these problems were behind us. I no longer dare to travel far from the town to buy animals, because I can assure you that many villages have become rather unfriendly. Something dangerous is stirring out there as well. However, you don't notice that because you only rarely leave Urfa."

"No, you're right," responded Hovagim, "one does not sense any hostility from the men in town, but the boys have started to very frequently shout "*giaur*"† after us. They must have learned that from their parents."

"That's right," nodded Krikor. "That is always the first sign of trouble. The Turks rarely reveal their intentions, so if it were not for the Kurds and the children, we would have difficulty knowing their feelings toward us. In any case, we need to buy weapons but also exercise great caution

* A city located on the Tigris River about 90 miles northeast of Urfa.

† Also spelled *gâvur*, it was a popular Turkish term used to refer to Christians. Its meaning can be loosely translated as "infidel."

since one of our fellow Armenians might carelessly mention it to the Turks."

"Tell me, Hovagim, what type of gun do you have?" Promptly Hovagim fetched his gun and the conversation turned to weapons. They agreed that Krikor should get Hagob a gun, an item he could buy quite cheaply and without raising suspicion when travelling through the countryside. The two also decided not to mention anything at all to the rest of the family. Their relatives would only begin to worry and, besides, "one cannot trust women to keep a secret." If now only the other men who knew about the plans would also keep quiet.

But it was soon evident that such was not the case. The horrible stories from Armenia spread like wildfire from house to house as did rumors that the same was to happen in Urfa and that the men were buying weapons to prevent it.

A few days later, Hovagim, Krikor, and two to three other Armenians decided to head out to their vineyards to see if the grapes had ripened and whether everything was in order. Each driving an ass before him, they descended through the Armenian Quarter's steep and narrow streets and turned at the large soap factory onto the main road which passed from the Samsat Gate into the city center, the bazaar. That part of town was strictly a commercial area where one only saw stalls, such as the coppersmiths who had their workshops in one street, the cobblers in another, and yet a third filled with shops selling manufactured goods.

The bazaar was the customary gathering place for Armenian men. It was mainly they who occupied the stands and workshops while the other ethnic groups mostly frequented the area as customers even though a few Turks and Syrian Arabs and, of course, many Jews, also had shops in the district. However, the Armenian presence was so dominant that during Sundays and other Christian holidays, the bazaar was almost deserted, while one hardly noticed that anyone was absent on Fridays and Saturdays when the Muslims and Jews held their holidays.

When Hovagim, Krikor and the other Armenians reached the main road, the asses naturally turned to follow the familiar path to the bazaar until yells and a few stones from their masters persuaded them to head in the opposite direction. Soon they passed under the arch of the Samsat Gate and drifted on into the countryside. They followed the Aleppo road eastwards for a short time until they rode past the bridge over the Karakoin (the Black Sheep), a seasonal river which now during the dry summer months was reduced to a barely noticeable trickle inching along at the bottom of the deep ravine. But in the winter and, especially in the spring, it looked entirely different with roaring masses of flowing water that sounded like thunder and could be heard as far away as Urfa. The bridges spanning the river had to be built high above the water in order not to be ripped away during the seasonal floods. Many a time the river had transformed the valley west of the city into a small sea, its waters crashing against the rocks.

When the men had passed the Karakoin River, they turned off the Aleppo road and followed a riding trail heading north. It led them through a tiny hamlet where a few impoverished Kurdish and Arab families lived in wretched hovels. Each of them carried a gun and as soon as they had passed the small settlement, they checked to see if their weapons were loaded and in order. They had to be prepared to defend themselves against robbers or any other trouble which might arise.

The trail led them onto the plain where tracts of volcanic soil appeared like widening streams approaching from the north. During the winter and spring this black, fertile earth had yielded lush green wheat fields, but now in August they had long since been harvested. Grayish yellow and drab the fields stretched towards the east and southeast into the endless plain. But westwards there was a sight much more pleasant to the eyes. Here were Urfa's vineyards, spanning like a long, green band as far as one could see towards the northwest in between the mountains that encircled them to the north and west. If one turned southwards, Urfa appeared with its houses, minarets, and picturesque, old walls, and, behind the city, towards the southeast, one could see the beautiful gardens. And to complete the panorama, there was also the old, mountainside castle with the two towering columns.

As one stood there, looking southwards, Urfa, enhance by its surrounding landscape, looked like one of the region's most beautiful towns and made for an impressive sight, especially at that moment, bathed in the rising sun's rays. The men, however, did not pay any attention to the landscape's beauty. They certainly loved their native soil and were attached to it with every fiber of their being, yet they were not consciously aware of it. They could not define what it was that warmed and comforted their hearts and filled them with spontaneous satisfaction, but still they gradually broke into song, singing the hymn "The Dawning Light." It had many verses which they knew by heart, but everybody fell silent after the first one, for they were no longer alone on the road.

Many Kurds from the nearby villages had appeared on the thoroughfare, en route to Urfa to sell wheat. It was the season when all the customers converged on the wheat market to make their purchases. These Kurds must have awoken at dawn because in the Orient people began their day early as society had yet to transform night into day through to use of artificial lighting. Be it winter or summer, they limited their activities to the hours when the Lord provided light and not a moment longer.

The joy the Armenians had felt, as reflected in their song, evaporated as quickly as their voices fell silent when they saw the Kurds. Krikor recognized most of them from his travels to the villages so he greeted them, but several did not return his greetings and their demeanor was quite dark and hostile. This hostility compelled the Armenians to ponder yet again the matters that had weighed on their minds for some time, but since they did not dare voice their concerns, they simply rode on up the mountain in silence.

From the summit the Armenians could look northwards out over a small plain that was throughout dotted with vineyards. Their properties were located there, but in order to reach them, they first had to pass the village of Karaköpry (Black Bridge) lying at the foot of the mountain. It appeared a charming place with lovely gardens watered by a small stream, but the village was very unpleasant to pass by because the people who lived there had always been a disagreeable lot. They were Turks and widely known for their evil deeds. As the Armenians approached, they were, of course, met by a crowd of jeering boys yelling "*giaur*" and, even worse, throwing stones at them. It would have been quite easy for the men to chase the boys away, but they knew that the slightest reaction would only agitate the parents who eagerly awaited such an opportunity to attack the Armenians. And if such a clash occurred and one of the Armenians was wounded or even killed, experience had taught them that the government would ignore the incident. Conversely, they all knew that not one of them would escape alive if any of the Turks were harmed. In short, they had no choice but to patiently tolerate the juvenile antics.

To make better time, the men had dismounted and were driving the donkeys before them. In this manner they soon reached the "café," a small rise under a large tree where a man had spread out a few mats, put up some benches and was selling coffee to passersby. Here a large number of the men from the village sat cross-legged and spent hours smoking cigarettes or the hookah, drinking Turkish coffee, or playing *tavla.** When the Armenians greeted the crowd, the Turks did not respond and instead looked menacingly at the small party of travelers. However, Mustafa Agha, one of Urfa's richest Turks, who spent a good part of the summer on his estate in Karaköpry, was in the crowd sitting on the most honored spot and he did, almost demonstratively, greet the party and especially Hovagim whom he knew. The other Turks looked at him in surprise and then too warmly greeted the Armenians. One man even stood up, chased the boys away and exchanged a few kind words with Krikor before returning to his seat.

The Armenians could now continue their journey unhindered and once out of earshot of the Turks, they immediately began to discuss what had happened. They all agreed that Mustafa Agha was their friend and that there were many like him among the city's rich Turks. That thought gave them some sense of security as they believed that the influence of those men could protect them from assaults by the mob. A calm descended over the group and as they continued along the road, their attention now gradually shifting to the beauty of the vineyards and speculation about the harvest.

However, they would have been far more concerned if they had heard what Mustafa Agha told the villagers after they were far gone.

"Tell me," asked Mustafa Agha, "do you usually make a racket while hunting so the intended prey can run away?" And when the perplexed villagers just looked at him, he continued:

"You, and people like you, are the reason why the Armenians are now armed to the teeth. In them, we will face a tough challenge. But what is critical is to not reveal anything before the time is right."

* Backgammon.

Once the Armenians reached their vineyards, they faced another unsettling situation. The shelters where they lived during the few weeks of the harvest were in ruins and it was clear from the scattering of the stones that it had been done intentionally. Such lodgings were primitive and little more than a row of open-air stalls lacking windows and doors. They were completely open toward the north and each measured a few paces in width and depth, just enough room to store a little bedding and a few utensils. Each "room" could be covered by a makeshift roof using either a tent or branches and turf. And the walls, which stood a little taller than an average man's height, were constructed of unhewn stones. That was the extent of their housing. These were very simple but still somewhat timely to construct and now a group of Muslim boys or young men had amused themselves by humiliating the Armenians through the destruction of their small shelters.

Such incidents frequently made their blood boil and were worsened by the fear of venting those frustrations. The rage was allowed to seethe and left the Armenians aged and careworn at an early age.

But this time the anger was not so intense. The men accepted the vandalism as just another link in the chain of hostilities they faced at nearly every turn, the weight of which had gradually become oppressive. They often tried to dismiss the nightmare and attempted to convince themselves and others that they were simply imagining things. However, that approach failed because whenever they experienced even the faintest trace of joy, it was immediately crushed as soon as it emerged.

So it was with the time spent on the vineyards, those few short weeks when the Armenians escaped the cramped city. They could look forward to nature's splendors and to eating their fill of the most wondrous of fruits, the sweet and nutritious grape. But instead, concerns rather dominated their minds, thinking about those coming weeks. They foresaw being harassed en route and even once they reached their vineyards, and the thought of bringing their wives and children into such an environment made them uneasy. Yet the men needed their families along as everyone's help was required to harvest the crop. Further, grape juice provided the families with their only source of sweetener for the entire year. So the Armenians could not abandon their vineyards. They had plowed and developed much of the land and were determined to harvest the grapes. The stone shelters could be rebuilt but the grapes could not be replaced if stolen.

On some of the Armenian vineyards the locals had made incursions onto the estates despite the presence of a Kurdish guard. Yet he hardly cared when the Armenian owners complained about the thefts.

As time passed, the Armenians became increasingly depressed. They decided to return home via Garmuch.* There all the residents were Armenians, so the travelers would not be harassed and both groups might enjoy and benefit from meeting. However, the visit unfolded quite differently from what the travelers had anticipated. The Armenian villagers had a much more keen sense of the Muslims than did their counterparts in the cities. They were very disheartened and had nothing but gloom to relate, so the travelers returned to Urfa in the evening both depressed and full of dark premonitions.

The time on the vineyards had come and gone but had been unpleasantly eventful. Travel on the roads was difficult, robbers roamed the nights, Armenian children were harassed by Muslim boys, and the Armenians were pressed to protect their women from insults. But they made it back to Urfa unscathed, carrying a good supply of winter stores. The work too had been strenuous as they worked day and night to collect the crop quicker than normally. Time for leisure activities had simply not been available. And once they secured the harvest in large clay pots as was customary, Hovagim became fearful that the crop might be taken from them.

The recent events had made Hovagim silent and pensive. Unlike his brothers, who often drank to console themselves, Hovagim sought comfort in the Church even though his faith was nearing a breaking point. He had always felt that his life and wellbeing was in God's hands, but now he sensed that connection wanting. Instead it seemed his fate was in the hands of the Turks and, when he thought of their hostility and dirty looks, he felt gripped by terror. It was not so much his own experiences, however, as those inherited from his relatives that had implanted such an intense fear in him, which even *his* faith could not defeat.

---

* A village located just to the northeast of Urfa and having a population of about 5,000 residents.

Yet his faith did not abandon him. It could not allay his fears, but it gave him the courage to face death.

Hovagim was convinced that his best experiences lay beyond the grave. In fact, only rarely did his own mortality raise concerns. It was always the others he thought about, especially the two children, Misael and Kevork, who often played on his lap. The very notion that they should be orphaned and abandoned, perhaps die in misery, was almost impossible for Hovagim to endure. It was for them he prayed and for their safety he planned as best he could.

One evening in October the Biredjiklian family had a visit from Krikor. What they spoke about was obvious as all Armenians discussed the same thing when they trusted each other. Krikor, who was quite a weapons expert, inspected their guns closely but otherwise did not say anything out of the ordinary. But as Krikor was leaving, and Hovagim accompanied him into the courtyard to open and then close the main gate, he quietly said: “You all should avoid the Turkish Quarter tomorrow.”

“You don’t think it is safe?” asked Hovagim, who together with his brothers had recently begun a small job in that area of the city.

“No,” answered Krikor, “I don’t think so. I know nothing definite, but tonight, under the cover of darkness, a lot of Kurds and Arabs have entered the city.”

“Why are they here?” Krikor asked probingly without expecting an answer. “I saw them as I came home late from the main square and their presence struck me as strange.”

With their conversation at an end, they parted. That night Hovagim hardly slept. Several times he went up on the roof and, through the stillness of the night, thought he heard suspicious sounds coming from the Turkish Quarter. However, it could also just as well be his racing imagination that clouded his senses.

But the next morning, Hovagim suggested to his brothers that it would be best to stay home on this particular day. He told them of the rumors and said that it might well be unsafe to move about the city. So they stayed in the house and courtyard, busying themselves with various chores. And Hovagim positioned himself on the stairs, just at the height of the flat roof, a vantage point from which he was shielded from the outside by the wall but could still observe the surrounding neighborhood.

Suddenly Hovagim saw something surprising. In front of the gate to the monastery where Bishop Choren lived, there stood four Turkish soldiers, bayonets fixed to their rifles. He could not understand why they were there. Was it to protect the bishop from some danger, or was he a prisoner?

It was also clear that the roads were full of people. Hovagim could see many groups of Arabs carrying lances and approaching from the south along the Harran road and from the east on the Mosul road. Similarly, crowds of Kurds appeared on the Karaköpry road, but Hovagim could not see if they were well-armed. However, in the city itself there did not seem to be more activity than on any other morning.

But then the quiet of the morning was shattered by musket shots coming from the bazaar. And, as Hovagim momentarily sat motionless, listening to the sound of shouts and screams, he saw people come across the heights to the west. Urfa, as commonly known, is built on the eastern face of a ridge which drops off steeply to the west but slopes gently down toward the east and the plain. Up on the heights lies the Armenian Quarter, while the Turkish homes, bazaar, and administrative buildings are situated on the plain. It was then on the western ridge which peaks above the Armenian Quarter that Hovagim saw the first people, a grouping which soon grew into a large crowd. It consisted of the dregs of Urfa's Turkish population augmented by many Kurds and Arabs. Hovagim could see them clearly because his house was close to the western wall. They were armed with muskets, lances, axes, knives, and whatever was at hand, and it was clear that the crowd was utterly unorganized and without leadership.

As soon as a large group had gathered just below the summit, they began firing down into the Armenian Quarter. A lot of the residents, mostly women but also some men, had shortly before gone up on their roofs to find out what all the shooting and commotion in the bazaar was about. It was this very group of Armenians that the mob above the city was shooting at. On one roof near Hovagim a woman was hit in the abdomen and collapsed. The other Armenians quickly scattered down into their houses, leaving only the gravely wounded woman to suffer where she fell. Almost simultaneously shots were also heard coming from the southern part of the quarter. Another crowd of Muslims had appeared on the mountain beneath the old fort and was attempting under heavy fire to come across Abraham's Dam and thereby enter the quarter near the large church.

By now the Armenians had rapidly organized their defenses. From the windows in the houses of the western and southern areas one could hear the sound of well-directed rifle fire that struck many in the front ranks. The remaining attackers cried out wildly and continued advancing and, through the ongoing shooting, an additional sound was heard, a piercing "li, li, li, li, li, li." It came from the Muslim women who had climbed onto the roof tops to observe the fighting and through their cheers voiced their approval and incited the men to double their efforts.

As the mob reached the entrances to the Armenian Quarter, they were met by musket fire and swinging axes as a confused melée ensued. The fighting ebbed and flowed with the Turks advancing farthest from the direction of the bazaar. But by noon many had died on both sides, and the attackers began to waver.

The Armenians had triumphed. Now it was the turn of the Armenian women to cheer. It sounded as if there was a wedding in every house in the quarter. A heady emotion gripped the Armenians and all intracommunal disputes and family feuds evaporated from memory.

However, the Armenians had also suffered losses. Many had died in the bazaar and all the Armenian stalls were gutted. Those who lived outside the quarter had, of course, been struck down and many bodies were strewn along the streets.

But what was the significance of the Armenians, who had been oppressed for centuries, meeting their archenemies with weapons in hand and being victorious? That mob, whose insults they had always had to endure without protest, and which so often had made them feel inferior, had fled before the raised Armenian hand. The Armenians had stood tall and looked into the eyes of the Turks as equals rather than bowing or groveling before them.

Certainly, on this day there was no need to serve up wine to celebrate the victory. But no one was simply sober-minded anymore either. Instead, the Armenians straightened their backs and took deep breaths of relief like their people had not done for centuries. The men also looked at their wives and children and wondered about their possible fate if events had unfolded differently. Some caressed their muskets while others went to the church to express their gratitude. The many heartfelt prayers they had uttered during the foregone, unsettling weeks had been heard after all. And the offerings that the women had promised the saints were now delivered joyously. Many a rooster ended its life that night to honor the holy Kevork or Johannes and, later, to feed the families of the poor. Some people even dipped their bread in the ashes and ate it happily as they had pledged to do. The dead were also buried but few shed a tear over their passing. They were heroes and people felt they must have been grateful to die on this day.

That evening many celebrated inside their homes while others stood guard. Many even wished the enemy would reappear so they could shoot them down. But no one came. Only quiet reigned over the Muslim Quarter. They too had posted guards in fearful anticipation that the Armenians would attack and avenge the ills they had faced for decades. Yes, that day and that night were almost worth a whole lifetime.

But during the following morning reality began to sink in, first for a few of the older Armenians, then for some others and finally it spread to everyone else.

"What now?" the Armenians asked themselves.

After all, behind the disorganized mob there existed a society which through the ages had crushed Armenian rights under foot and slowly but surely clipped their wings and subjugated them. This society had fostered a fear that penetrated the very core of every Armenian. They felt like school children who had defied their teacher and through rash action had made matters worse rather than better. What could they now do to rebuild tolerable relations with the Turks? There seemed no other option than to try to bribe the Muslim communal leaders and then gradually restore the old societal norms.

Further, the Urfa Armenians were, for now, cut off from the rest of the world. They had their own quarter and were masters in their own homes, but they were essentially trapped. However, the Armenians were not pressed to make hasty decisions as it was the fall, and they had plenty of provisions. But these supplies would naturally dissipate eventually.

The Armenians regretted not being able to consult the bishop, but he was under Turkish guard in the monastery. They did not even know whether he was dead or alive. Yet the Turks were not comfortable with the situation either. Without the Armenians, daily life simply did not function well. There were no bakers in Urfa who were not Armenian, so the Muslims would have been without bread had not a few men with foresight rescued a couple of bakers when the mob stormed the bazaar. They converted them to Islam, wrapped a white scarf around their turban as a sign of their new faith, and carefully guarded them to prevent their murder or attempted escaped back into the Armenian Quarter. In this manner, the Muslims overcame their most pressing need, but, of course, people cannot live on bread alone. Many other things were also absent without the Armenians.

Urfa's Turkish elite had not participated in the mob attack mainly because they knew that the Armenians were armed. They could not see why they should have risked being killed by the Armenians. It seemed to them that there were other, far less dangerous, ways to exploit the Christian population. In fact, many of the Turks had quietly opposed the incitement by the mullahs. They believed it was a grave mistake to indiscriminately kill the Armenians. After all, it was well-known that life's comforts were partly attributable to Armenian labor. It struck the Turkish elite as glaringly ignorant to kill one's own slaves; one might as well also put down one's donkeys. But they also acknowledged that there were differences. One would, after all, never see a donkey forget its place as it happened with the Armenians. It was that fact and its consequence which now had to be considered.

Fundamentally, the Turks feared the Armenians. They did not imagine that they would suffer an armed insurrection, but they could not see how to overcome the Armenians either. One could consistently oppress them and treat them unfairly without provoking their outright resistance. But, in response, they simply adapted and persevered. It was as revealed in the anecdote:

An Armenian was attacked on the road by a Muslim robber who not only took his money but also stole his clothes. Once naked, the Armenian turned to the thief and said: "But you still haven't taken my gold bracelet!"

"What?" the puzzled robber asked as he started to again search through the stolen clothes.

"I can't see any bracelet," he exclaimed.

"Well, that's because my bracelet is my profession," answered the Armenian.

"With my skill I can reacquire all that you have stolen from me and more still, but once you have worn out my clothes, you will once again be dressed in rags."

Yes, that was a true story. The Turk had only his sword. In contrast, the Armenian had his industrious hands, his good sense, and his varied range of skills, but above all, he had an indomitable energy and an iron will to succeed. And the Turk knew instinctively that Armenian strength was greater than his own, and it was that force which would inherit the earth. After all, was the Turk not already under pressure from all sides? What else could it be that made the Europeans so frightening and pushed them to slowly but surely drive the Turk back? They would one day conquer his Orient and expel the Turk from his Paradise, this *dolce far niente* or *kef* in Turkish.* It seemed there was only one way to escape destruction and that was to stand up and fight them with their own weapon, the work ethic. Yet, of course, that entailed surrendering the very joys in life.

But now, in the Turk's own land, this same force, which he so feared, was gaining strength and becoming a menace. If he chopped off a head, seven new ones immediately sprang forth. It was the spirit of the Aryan race which the Turk hopelessly fought against, a spirit he labeled as Christianity since in his mind the two were inextricably linked. And precisely because he felt the struggle was futile, the Turk fought so confoundedly. Actually, the Turk did not know whether to hate the Armenian, fear him, or even despise him, for there was also reason to do that. The Armenian's nature had over the ages of oppression become subservient and groveling before those whom he feared. In contrast, the master population possessed a certain dignity and considered the servile groups with disgust. So the Turk was always ready to restrict the activities of the Armenians but not to exterminate them.

* A life of idleness.

The masses, on the other hand, along with the Kurds and Arabs, did not think so far ahead. The prospect of plundering the Armenian homes was enough for them, and it was with that motivation that the unorganized and failed attack on the Armenian Quarter had come to pass. Now the Turks saw dangers from two sides. They feared the mob might raid their homes to satisfy their unfulfilled expectations, and they also feared the Armenians, that they should realize their strength and advance beyond the Armenian Quarter in pursuit of revenge. As a precaution, the Turks alerted the army to be prepared for all eventualities.

But nothing happened. The rural population left Urfa again, and after a few days, the Turks sensed that they had nothing to fear from the Armenians either. Quite the opposite, the Armenians wished to restore relations with the Muslims. However, the mullahs reacted forcefully to this development.

"Just look! How long will you continue to be masters in your own homes?" they railed. "Next time it will be the unbelievers who will attack your quarter."

Yes, action had to be taken, but as long as the Armenians were well-armed, it was unlikely the Turks could be victorious. So messages were secretly passed between the homes of the most respected Armenians and notable Turks until one day, a couple of weeks after the calamity, a meeting was arranged between them. The gathering occurred in the home of one of the most influential Turks and was entirely unofficial as neither a representative from the government nor the Armenian *vartabed* was present. The Turks had arrived first, and one of them had gone to personally escort the Armenian representatives to assure them of complete safety outside their quarter. When they arrived, the assembled Turks greeted them warmly, but also formally and somberly, much as was the custom if someone had died.

Once seated comfortably and having exchanged pleasantries, the Turks began by asking about the Armenian losses. Some of the Armenians who had been killed in the bazaar were well-known to the assembled Turks and should have been present among the representatives at such a meeting. As their names were revealed, the Turks addressed the survivors with the common greeting always used when death was discussed:

"May you all stay alive!"

Afterwards they sat quietly for a time, some even shielding their faces in a gesture of grief for the deceased.

Then one of the most senior Turks began to speak on the gathering's behalf, his voice faintly shaking with emotion:

"May God punish the guilty! Their eyes shall be blinded and their hearths shattered! By Allah! The death of Bedros Agha* hurts me as if it were one of my own relatives that God had taken away. What tragedy haven't they brought down on our city when they sowed mistrust between you and us and destroyed our flourishing bazaar. But perhaps that is not the worst consequence. What transpired has been reported to Constantinople, and these 'foreigners,' who understand nothing of our lives in these parts, must have framed the reports in such a manner as to make you, the Armenians, the guilty party and the ones toward whom the Sultan's anger will be directed."

"We were astounded when we heard the news," declared the elderly Turk, "because we knew better than anyone that you had every right to defend yourselves. What else could you have done? We were so overjoyed when you repulsed these 'animals' to lick their wounds. Who knows, perhaps we were next after they had finished with you, and we too feared for our lives. In any case, you have bravely repelled an attack which threatened us both."

"We are also very thankful that you recognized our upright disposition and turned to us so we can jointly reestablish tolerable conditions again. After all, we must stick together to form a common front against two forces. Against the Kurds and Arabs, these donkeys in human form, who are only distinguished from the farm animals by language, and against the 'foreigners' who only seek to enrich themselves without any care for how it affects us."

"Indeed, we speak to you in confidence. If the 'foreigners' heard what we have said today, we know they would cut our throats. However, the truth must be told no matter what. We firmly believe, based on our mutual friendship forged through the years, that we are your natural

* Another commonly used title of honor for civil or military leaders. It is unclear how this Armenian, Bedros, acquired his title, but it is probable that it was bestowed in recognition of his local prominence.

guardians, and we have initiated negotiations with the 'foreigners' on your behalf. The money you sent to us we have passed on to them; such people as they only care to fill their pockets and exploit the area. Once they received the money, they agreed that if you surrender your weapons, they will inform Constantinople that all is in order and will dispatch more soldiers to protect us all from the mob. We objected to the demand about the weapons because we will lose half our strength once you are disarmed. However, they would not compromise on that demand. So we made them swear on the Quran that they would uphold their guarantees once the arms were collected."

"That was the extent of our dealings with them, and these are the conditions we have negotiated and will now discuss further with you."

Silence descended on the gathering once the Turkish elder finished his statement, and the Armenians quietly considered the situation. They found parts of the Turk's speech were sensible much as other parts indulged their vanity. It pleased them that the Turkish elite had finally acknowledged the value of the Armenians and had determined that an alliance with them was better than one with the Muslim mob. It made sense that Turkish interests would drive them to such a conclusion.

In dealings with the rural population, both the Armenians and the Turkish elite exploited those people in various ways. The Turks used the corrupt state system to forcibly rob the population at every opportunity, and the Armenians took advantage of the people's inexperience in business and their chronic lack of money. Clearly, it was equally urgent for the Turkish elite and the Armenians to suppress the people by all means possible.

Further, they needed to form a common front against the "foreigners," meaning the city's *mutassarif*, police chief, and commander of the gendarmerie. These three posts were the only ones that required a government education and were occupied by people from outside the city, while Urfa's citizens filled all other positions. The men who held those three important jobs had, in order to secure them, "greased the wheels" in Constantinople and therefore did their utmost to enrich themselves while in office. To make matters worse, they usually only stayed a short time, often transferring to another area after just a year. Hence, they never became acquainted with their region of administration and, had a local citizen secured their favor through considerable bribes from which he hoped to benefit, such a person would have to start all over with another official once the former one was reassigned.

Such a state of affairs was certainly a great bother for everyone, but it was still surprising how bluntly the elderly Turk had voiced his opinion. His life could be in danger if his views became widely known, and the trust he put in the Armenians was not lost on them. It was a clear sign of his genuine friendship and his intention to stand with them through thick and thin.

However, with regard to the money, the Armenians were sure the Turks had not bribed the *mutassarif*.

Rather, they had probably kept it for themselves. So the Armenians sensed that the Turks were seeking additional funds since they had already "spent" what was earlier handed over, but they had yet to be "paid for their efforts and inconvenience." But that they openly acknowledged having received any money at all was a clear indication that they intended to resolve the matter amicably.

In the Orient the matter of bribery followed fixed but unwritten rules. A bribe was like a salary paid before a job was completed. If one accepted such a payment, it meant one also accepted the job. But if it turned out the project exceeded the person's abilities, the money was repaid. It was in essence a means of doing business. So, what the elderly Turk had said was in actual fact that they would restore order but that the payment received was insufficient.

Now, for the Armenians a greater fee was not a problem. A few thousand piastres more or less was immaterial as there were stashes of both gold and silver coins in the Armenian Quarter. What mattered was whether they could trust the Turks, and that was an awkward issue. Their kind words and forthcoming manner had flattered the Armenians and deflected their suspicions. It would also have been most unwise to doubt the Turkish pledge as that might have caused the entire effort to founder. But the Armenians did believe that they could raise a neutral point. They could ask the Turks whether the government was trustworthy and thereby also question them indirectly.

After a period of quiet, the most notable Armenian turned to address the gathering. He first thanked the Turks for the friendship they had shown by willingly helping to resolve the difficult situation and for speaking candidly. The Armenians hoped they should prove worthy of that trust. Next, he acknowledged it would constitute a weakening for both parties if they surrendered their arms, and asked whether the Turks did not believe that the *mutassarif* would accept more money in exchange for dropping that demand.

Before the senior Turk answered this question, he searched out the host who rose to demonstratively check all the windows, doors, and closets before retaking his seat and sending the old man a reassuring gesture.

"I am sure he would if it was up to him," answered the Turk in a soft voice, "but he has told me that there are spies observing him. If he gives you assurances without collecting your weapons, it may cost him his life as it will immediately be suggested in Constantinople that he has accepted money and is in collusion with you."

The Armenians now accepted that this demand was non-negotiable. What remained was to make the Turks swear, something to which both parties attributed a great deal of significance.

"And you believe," asked the leading Armenian, "that one can trust the *mutassarif*'s word?"

"He swore on the Quran," responded the elder Turk, "and we cannot imagine that a Muslim would do that without being sure. It would be terrible to invite upon oneself Allah's wrath in this life and the next.

We all heard his pledge, and I will no longer enter my harem," he continued," if this is not the honest truth."

That latter statement constituted a profound and fearsome oath, one considered almost weightier than a promise based on the Quran. The gathered Turks paled upon hearing the pledge and the Armenians hurried to seal the agreement by stretching out their hands.

"Why did you swear, Mahmud Bey?" inquired the Armenians.* "Your word is already more than sufficient for us." But in reality they were happy with the result. They again thanked the Turks for their kindness and said they now needed to consult with their people. The Armenian delegation found the offer most acceptable but still needed to fully

* Bey was a title carried by senior Ottoman officials in government service.

inform the community as all individuals should be responsible for their own fate. Hence, the meeting ended and one of the Turks again accompanied the Armenians back to their quarter's various points of entry. Shortly thereafter, the Turks also departed for home.

Mahmud Bey was glum and sullen faced when he made it home that evening. He had his bed prepared in his own quarters and his wives waited in vain for him both that night and those that followed. The women wondered about his absence but none of them could explain the reasons. It was simply known that the bey was very annoyed and should be left alone. A few days later, at the public baths, his wives mentioned the situation to Mustapha Agha's wife, and the following night she discussed it with her husband.

That news gave Mustapha Agha something to think about. "Ah, these women! They truly were a liability. After all, how long would it take before this news made its way by some secret channel into the Armenian Quarter and thereby revealed everything?" As a result, Mustapha Agha dispatched the city's foremost mullah to call on Mahmud Bey one day. During the course of his visit, the mullah focused their conversation on religious issues and the weight of various directives in scripture. "The most important of all," he said among other things, "is holy war, the war against infidels. If that cause is helped by breaking one's oaths, then one is released from honoring them." That same evening Mahmud Bey returned to his harem.

The day following the meeting with the Turks, a large number of Armenians again assembled in the small hall for a deliberation. Both Hovagim and Krikor were notified of the gathering and opted to attend. At the meeting, the communal representatives reported what they had achieved in their negotiations with the Turks, but in the absence of the same atmosphere colored by the Turkish attendance at the discussions, the benefits of the prospective agreement appeared meager. The only tangible guarantees were that the Turks had accepted the bribes and that Mahmud Bey had taken an oath. And on that basis should they now give up their weapons? They could with good reason question such an arrangement.

Anania Vartabed therefore criticized rather sharply the agreement and was quite clear that if he had been present at the negotiations, a better deal would have been secured. A few others, who had expected to be part of the delegation and therefore felt slighted, echoed his objection. This criticism annoyed the representatives, and they asserted that it was obvious that these men only opposed the agreement because they were excluded from the process and now were attacking them personally. They were acting, it was asserted, like children who couldn't evaluate whether an offer was acceptable or not. In contrast, the representatives said they would never have presented the deal unless they believed it was the only possible solution. And they wondered whether the critics thought the Turks would ever accept having an armed Armenian Quarter which could engage them in street battles. They should rather thank the Lord and the delegation for the ability to negotiate with the Turks. In fact, everyone knew that it was only due to their personal favors and years of friendship that the Turks even considered dealing with the Armenians and were offering to support them against their fellow Muslims. If one now insulted the Turks, they argued, through mistrust and suspicion then the Armenians would drive them to side with the government, and the day when soldiers were to enter the quarter would not be far off. Urfa's garrison was certainly small and the Armenian community could probably defend itself against that force, but behind it stood the whole empire. What could possibly be gained by opposing an entire country?

But perhaps the most frightening development, stressed the representatives, was that the critics considered nothing but their own narrow self-interests. Out of spite because they had failed to win the community's trust and had not been chosen to speak for the people, the critics now opposed the only possible solution and did not for a moment hesitate to hurl the entire population toward assured destruction. They sought only to satisfy their own personal ambitions, including their drive for revenge and to discredit the delegates. But what else, they concluded, could one expect from such men?

What followed was an exchange of personal attacks and for a time the hall reverberated with verbal strife. The gathering eventually broke up without reaching any consensus decision, and the groups quietly moved to organize themselves into factions. Positions hardened, and if the delegates had earlier harbored some slight suspicions about the Turks, those doubts now vanished. The criticism by their opponents and their own words in reply had certainly also served to convince them. It was absolutely clear that the door to salvation should be used now; otherwise, it would close and doom the whole quarter to destruction. They saw it as their simple duty to open their people's eyes to that reality. It was incomprehensible to them that not everyone could see that their critics were driven by the basest of personal motivations. What a tragedy it would be, now that everyone's lives and welfare were at stake, to let oneself be misled by such motives. They had to be resisted by all means for the sake of the unwitting people, who under the guidance of the critics would blindly march toward their ruin. And resisted with vigor they were.

The members of the delegation were the city's most influential Armenians. They had many supporters who wholeheartedly endorsed everything they said and did, and every one of the delegates now felt like a messenger who had to win as many converts as possible. Arguments were made that advantages of one type or another could be arranged if one sided with the right party. But one's friends were, of course, not forgotten. The delegates also felt a holy duty toward the "uninformed" who otherwise might allow themselves to be led into temptation and danger by these few independents.

These independents, these critics, were untrustworthy men, whose lives unfortunately left much to be desired. Their past actions could adversely affect the current debate because, as everyone knows, a person's actions reflect his nature. Therefore, it was worthwhile to evaluate the men who stood on the side of the opposition. However, it was clear to anyone that they were lesser individuals when compared with the delegates.

Praise be to God, the community knew to whom they should throw their support. Why else would they have elected them? It would indeed be an odd system of politics to first vote for them and then afterwards, once they had negotiated *such* good conditions, to abandon them.

"That's why things always go awry for us," said the delegates, "because we choose a middle path and never know which way to turn. This is our national flaw."

Meanwhile, the opposition was also active. They agitated tirelessly and even received strong support for their position from a quite unexpected source. One day an Arab woman approached one of the guards posted at the main entrance to the Armenian Quarter and asked to speak with Anania Vartabed. She was brought to see him and reported that while gathering twigs behind the Armenian monastery, an old man atop the wall had motioned for her to approach. After she complied, the man asked her to deliver a letter to Anania Vartabed and paid her sixty piastres to do so. She found that most agreeable and had immediately set about completing her errand.

On the note were words that unmistakably originated from the bishop's hand: "The dog may well wag its tail when it sees the wooden staff, but it might also bite if you put down the staff."

It was clear the bishop sought to warn the community against surrendering the weapons, and his note was a great support for Anania Vartabed. Yet still he was overruled. The faction supporting the delegates was simply too strong. They argued that the bishop was insufficiently informed about events because he was cut off from the outside. If he only knew what they knew, so the reasoning went, he too would endorse the turnover.

The majority of the older generation also supported the delegates. They were used to putting their confidence in money's influence on the Turks. "A golden key," they believed, "opens all doors." In fact, they had yet to see how anything lasting could be achieved through an Armenian use of arms. The wisest action was to yield and move to reaffirm by different means that which would otherwise be lost.

In contrast, it was the young people who supported Anania Vartabed, but it would defy tradition if youth carried the day. After all, what did they know about life? They first had to learn about life from the older generation, and they were in addition entirely unused to asserting their will. Gradually they just yielded to the pressure. And without conducting another vote, the community simply began to deliver its arms to a set building on the church square where one of the delegates took possession of them. The other delegates took on the greater challenge of visiting the homes of the most ardent opponents in the hopes of convincing them on a more individual basis.

Hovagim and Krikor belonged to the *vartabed*'s faction, Krikor by conviction, Hovagim because Krikor did so. So the day soon arrived when one of the delegates came calling along with the local priest to try and persuade Hovagim to change his mind. But that was no easy task because he too had read the bishop's note, and he firmly believed the religious leader was wiser than all the others put together. The priest, however, relied on scripture to convince Hovagim that one needed to obey the religious authorities because ultimately authority is derived from God, so they alone could sanction the use of force. He therefore accepted his duty meekly and surrendered his two muskets.

The two visitors, however, knew such arguments would not convince Krikor, and feared, due to his infamous temper, that he might become incensed and throw them out of his house. They were consequently careful to call on his home only when he was out. And with his elderly mother alone at the house, they managed to deceive her into believing that the whole family would be alienated from the community unless they gave up their weapons. The poor woman became so concerned about "what others might say" that she agreed despite knowing full-well that her son would be angry. She reluctantly allowed them to collect the weapons which were hung on the wall and then sat down to await the consequences of her actions once Krikor returned.

Immediately upon entering the living room Krikor noticed the empty spaces on the wall. "Where are the muskets?" he shouted angrily while directing a menacing look toward his mother. The old woman burst into tears and told him who had come to the house and that they had frightened her into turning over the weapons. Krikor lunged forward and was about to hit her, but he came to his senses and recognized that it was after all his mother who stood before him. His hand, already raised, was quickly lowered again and, without uttering another word, he stormed out of the house to confront those men who had been in his home. Once Krikor tracked down one of them, he showered him with insults and would have assaulted him despite his age unless other men had not intervened to prevent it.

But Krikor failed to recover his muskets because they were now under secure guard near the church square. So in an effort to console himself, he went to visit Hovagim, but was instead horrified to learn that his friend had also surrendered his weapons. Krikor now felt as if all his plans were unraveling. He returned home, locked himself in the upstairs living room, and remained there alone for the rest of the day without eating or drinking anything. Not until that night, once everyone else had gone to bed, did his family hear him emerge from the room, pick up a lantern, and descend into the cellar where they stored straw for the asses, firewood, and such. His mother, driven by curiosity, snuck out to follow him downstairs. Krikor, however, hearing the steps behind him, cut her off at the entrance to the cellar.

"Go away!" he yelled threateningly. "I will hit anyone who comes down here."

His mother stumbled backwards in fear, and Krikor's brothers, who now emerged, also heeded his warning. They could hear him rummaging around downstairs, but over the following days he did not speak to any of them, and they were careful not to disturb him or enter the cellar. After three to four days, Krikor's temper improved, so, on a day while he was away from the house, one of the brothers went down to investigate the cellar. However, he discovered nothing of note even after a thorough search, so what Krikor had been doing down there remained a mystery.

Hovagim, his friend, also grew concerned about the unfolding events. One day he summoned Chanum to the kitchen and told her: "Bring me your jewelry. It's worth a lot of money and can provide for the children's future if something should happen to us."

"But let's keep this a secret," he added pensively as he removed a brick from the wall, revealing a small hiding space. Chanum handed him the valuable jewels which he wrapped in a scarf before placing it inside the wall. And once Hovagim put the brick back into position it was impossible to detect that anything was amiss.

"Count the bricks, Chanum," said Hovagim, "and remember the exact spot."

That night, Hagob, her husband, asked, "Where are your jewels, Chanum?"

"In my chest," she replied. "I'm rather depressed these days and have no desire to wear them." And so it came to pass, here as in many homes, that small secrets sprouted and evolved.

In time all the Armenian community's arms were collected. Some had been confiscated by force, but most were turned over voluntarily. And only very few continued to hide their weapons or claimed they never had any. So in late November, word was sent to Mahmud Bey that the arms were ready for official collection, and he was asked to notify the government. The following day the gendarmes arrived and transferred the weapons to their garrison where they would be stored temporarily. At the same time Mahmud Bey was also awarded a gift for his role in furthering communal peace.

It genuinely appeared as if the government was committed to the restoration of relations. The official security forces were expanded, helping to persuade the Armenians to lower their vigilance and begin to slowly return to the bazaar. But the initial days were difficult as they cleaned up their looted stalls and considered the challenges of rebuilding. Tensions also arose with their renewed interaction with the mob, many of whom coveted revenge for their relatives killed in their failed assault on the Armenian Quarter. It gnawed at them that they had been repulsed, so the Armenians had to endure an ongoing stream of condemnations and threats.

Further, it could not be hidden from the Armenians that all the Turks were heavily armed, and it seemed to them at times that they recognized in their hands some of the very same arms confiscated from their homes. They therefore inquired with their "friends" whether it would not be possible to also disarm these dangerous elements. "If only we could!" the Turks responded obligingly. "It would also be very reassuring for us, but unfortunately there are no laws that permit us to disarm true believers. What a shame that you all do not share our religion because then the situation would be entirely different. But as it stands, you do not need to fear the mob, as we are also very well armed."

However, the Armenians did not exactly feel reassured. It seemed their lives were in the balance and that caution was warranted. Hovagim, for example, had not resumed working on that building project he had taken over down in the Turkish Quarter. The owner sent for him repeatedly, but Hovagim kept making up excuses: the weather was bad or he felt poorly. He did not feel safe down there, and Krikor kept telling him to stay away from the area at all costs.

Oftentimes the delegates were told that they had probably been too hasty in surrendering the weapons. Yet they always replied with assurances, claiming their friends were trustworthy, and told people that they shouldn't be afraid. Unruly seas, they suggested, did not become tranquil all at once, but little by little quiet would be restored. The Armenians simply needed to remain calm.

But many instead felt uneasy and were plagued by troublesome dreams. This kept the soothsayers busy and brought many things to light; one could sense that ominous times were approaching. It was not just the year that neared its close and the days that became darker; it was also people's hearts that darkened evermore.

Chapter Three

The Tempest Breaks

It was now the last week of 1895. The year was at its darkest, but it was not yet Christmas. That holiday is first celebrated by Armenians around the middle of January, so the late December days provided little immediate joy.

Hovagim, who was returning from morning Mass just as dawn broke, entered his home to witness a typical domestic scene. Misael was insisting on wearing his new boots to school, but his grandmother would not let him. She said they should be saved for Christmas. But Hovagim sided with Misael: "Let him have them, Mom. Who knows if we'll even survive until Christmas?"

Yes, who knew? The ominous shadow loomed seemingly ever closer with these words.

In the meantime, the mother-in-law served Misael his breakfast so he could eat and head to school and then set herself down with little Kevork on her lap. The men, who sat in the corner of the living room smoking cigarettes, also yearned to spend time with the children. Their carefree games were almost the only thing that brightened the day and occasionally even helped the adults forget the darkening skies.

But it was not customary for the men to be at home and inside at that time of day. Normally they would have left hours earlier and be happily hard at work. However, now they did not dare enter the Turkish Quarter, and no Armenians were contracting to have anything built in these uncertain times. After all, who knew if they would even be able to continue living in their homes?

The forced inactivity increased the men's discomfort as they became sluggish and bored. They often spoke about improving the barn now that they had the time, but it never moved beyond talk, and they instead just stayed seated in their customary corner day after day. For hours they remained there in silence or sometimes they argued over insignificant things that before had never troubled them. On this day, however, they were momentarily entertained by Misael, who was seated next to Hovagim, and was telling them a story about the family donkey. The men had almost forgotten their concerns when they were startled by a woman's piercing scream coming from a neighboring courtyard.

In a flash they leapt to their feet and rushed outside. There they saw the woman, standing on the rooftop next door, screaming and motioning and pointing toward the hillcrest west of the city. Moments later, a bullet whistled across the rooftops and almost struck the woman. Hovagim immediately headed for his observation spot and the others could see that his facial expression became sullen and completely altered. They did not even have to ask, as they understood the situation even before he came back down. The Armenian Quarter was again under attack and this time they were unarmed. It meant certain death.

What now?

The youngest brother was the first to make a decision. "I'm heading to the church," he said, "there I'll feel most secure."

"That's up to you, brother," replied Hovagim. "I prefer to die in my home, but you must all do what you think is best."

"Brothers! Come along with me," pleaded the younger sibling. "I'm also sure that Krikor has something planned, as his house has so many nooks and crannies and he thinks of everything."

But Hovagim absolutely refused. He was convinced that it was hopeless, and he could not make himself leave home. So the youngest brother ran off alone while everyone else followed Hovagim into the living room. For a few moments they sat there staring at each other. The women and children cried while the men were confused and knew neither what to say or do.

Meanwhile shots rang out from all sides, and horrible screams from the west indicated that the attackers had entered the outlying houses and had begun their bloody work. Next the screams came from just outside their door. A moment later, it was ripped open and a woman rushed in carrying a child in her arms. Her hair was disheveled and blood was dripping from her ears. She was Hovagim's sister.

"Flee, brothers, flee!" she screamed. "My husband has been murdered; they slit open his belly with a knife. Then they took my jewelry from my hair and ripped the earrings from my ears, and next proceeded to loot our house. That was when I saw my chance to escape. You all must get away! They will soon be here!"

Exhausted, she sank to the floor and sobbed uncontrollably. The brothers looked at each other in a collective state of shock. But whereto could they run? There was no hiding place in the house; they simply had to await their fate. This utter inability to do anything to prevent the ongoing horror was almost unbearable. Then Hovagim stood up and began reciting a prayer for the dead, and soon a sense of calm enveloped the family. The familiar words briefly recreated the solemn atmosphere they experienced when attending a funeral. Yet it only lasted a moment, as the shots and screams reminded them that it was their own lives that hung in the balance, and the terror gripped them with renewed intensity.

Only Hovagim remained calm. He had so often and so intensely envisioned in his mind the coming heavenly magnificence that he now, suddenly, saw it so clearly and near that he could almost touch it with his outstretched hands. Of course, he also saw the dark gate through which he first had to pass, but it almost didn't frighten him at all. Hovagim simply sat back quietly and said his goodbyes to this household which he had cared for and kept united for so many years, where every spot and object reminded him of past joys or the simple, virtuous life. And it now seemed to him that the renunciation of excesses had been one of life's best decisions.

Hovagim also bid farewell to the individuals around him, in essence his relatives, who had been his entire world and whom he had always kept in his thoughts no matter his activities. Lastly, he turned to Misael, who sat by his side with his head buried in Hovagim's chest as if to escape the horror. And as they embraced, Hovagim suddenly became indignant over what was happening.

"Why should this boy again have to experience misery?" he asked himself. "Has he not already suffered enough?"

Hovagim sought desperately, to the very core of his soul, to pray for the boy, and he suddenly sensed that through all the noise he heard a faint voice which spoke to him:

"Do you believe that you love him more than I, or that you know best what suits him? What do you know about the joy I have prepared for him, or what plans I have for him?"

With that, Hovagim felt triumphant and reassured, and he was filled with a deep calm. But that peace of mind came none too soon, as the shouting, firing, and the cacophony of chaotic sounds came ever nearer. It was clear that the culprits had now entered their street. Hovagim's brothers surrendered to their survival instincts and retreated deeper inside the house, towards the back room, to seek out hiding spots under the stack of brushwood and behind the linens where they would not be immediately visible. There they stayed with beating hearts, feeling maddened by fear. The women helped to hide them before they also made themselves scarce. Only Chanum walked over and sat down next to Hovagim with Kevork on her lap.

By now the killers had reached the neighboring courtyard. The gate was ripped open and a series of screams from the women, coupled with Turkish shouting, sounded clearly across the wall. The Turks were looking for the men, but were apparently also looting the house at the same time. Then they found one of the men. Hovagim recognized his voice and could hear how he begged for mercy. What followed were the sounds of a swift ax blow and then a wail which gradually dissipated. Next they discovered another victim, and the events were repeated. Other attackers focused on the women, and they could hear them scream and run around frantically. It was an almost indescribable uproar.

Those were terrible moments, and Hovagim actually felt relieved when their own gate was forced open. He bent down and kissed Misael and then handed him to Chanum. For a second they looked deep into each others' eyes before she put her arm around the boy and pulled him close, and Hovagim marched determinedly out the door to confront the onrushing mob. They were startled initially when they saw him approaching with such calm and determination, and for a moment they fell silent and became uncertain, almost to the point of taking a step back. But in the next instant, a young lad stormed forward and crushed

Hovagim's skull with a single merciless ax blow. He fell forward without a sound, and the killers rushed on over his body and into the house.

The invading group consisted of about ten young Turks from the city's better families, even Mustapha Agha's nephew was among them. Those who had earlier seen these men, when they walked quietly and leisurely through the streets or sat at a café, could not possibly recognize them now. Their clothes were dirty and blood spattered, and their faces altered. Some were pale, almost a yellowish-gray color, while others, whose blood had rushed to their heads, had livid eyes and contorted facial expressions. They acted as if they were drunk though only few of them were.

If they had only stopped and asked themselves what it was they were actually doing, they might have been astonished. But there was no talk of ceasing, as they were as if possessed by something stronger than themselves. It was after all the will of Allah that the unbelievers should be wiped out.

In fact, the night before was when the unrest first began in the city. The word spread from house to house that the hour had arrived, and by morning everyone carried a weapon with him as he went to the mosque to pray. What followed was the mullah's fiery call for the believers to perform Allah's will. He stood before them with his dagger drawn and everyone followed his example as people could hardly contain themselves.

From every street the mobs emerged. They riled each other up en route as they approached the Armenian Quarter. Shots were fired, a few thugs broke into the first house, they saw the blood flow, and thusly everyone was worked into a state of frenzy. They went forth as if in a haze, striking people down without reflection, robbing, and even raping those women whose beauty caught their fancy.

The gang now in the Biredjiklian house had participated in the bloody affair for several hours. For a moment something had stirred in them when confronted with Hovagim's pride; they had almost been shaken out of their intoxication. But once he was struck down, the spell once again took hold of them and they charged on into the living room. Inside they found Chanum sitting with the two children held tightly to her body. Fear had paralyzed her, so she could not stand up, scream nor even cover her face. However, initially no one paid much attention to her, because the killers were mainly interested in finding the men and the money. They pressed on into the back room, and soon Chanum recognized Hagob's voice. The poor fellow was discovered, and she heard him plead for his life.

"First, tell us where you all have hidden the money, you dog!" the men railed at him.

He told them he did not know since his older brother hid such valuables, but a hefty beating soon changed his mind. They led him out of the back room and he retrieved the money from a small space within the cabinet. Chanum could hardly recognize him, as he was like an old man tottering across the living room.

Once the killers found the money, they pulled Hagob out into the courtyard, and a man with a drawn knife guarded him as the others continued searching the house. Soon after, his two other brothers were also discovered and herded out to join him. Their sister, who also hid, suffered a similar fate. But their enraged mother then charged the Turk holding her daughter and, once he realized – despite the darkness in the back room – that they were only women, he released her and instead began searching for valuables.

Meanwhile, another man interrogated Chanum about her jewelry but stopped once Mustapha Agha's nephew burst into the room. The nephew looked straight at the young woman with eyes that made her shiver from head to toe. He then gestured a clear command to the other man and, from that moment, no one paid much attention to Chanum. The group instead ransacked the house, seized a few rugs and collected other valuables. And just as they were leaving, the sound of three ax blows was heard, much as when a slaughtered animal is chopped up. Then the killers were gone.

What lingered were groans in the courtyard that soon faded, replaced by the death rattle. The old mother rushed outside screaming and collapsed by the bodies of her sons. But God was merciful on this day, as the old woman never got up again. She had a weak heart and slowly her desperate weeping was supplanted by labored breathing. Her face turned blue and she died beside her sons.

It was then that Kevork's wailing ended Chanum's state of shock. The child had been paralyzed by fear, but now that the tension had lessened, he began to cry. That sound also loosened the restraints that had bound Chanum. She instinctively pulled the child to her breast, but he found little comfort and would not nurse. "Perhaps the milk is bitter," she thought. She then got up to look through the upended rooms and their scattered possessions for something that he could eat. Misael now also came to his feet. He had been sitting with his head buried in Chanum's lap but next felt drawn to walk outside only to witness the horrible sight in the courtyard. Gripped by terror, he fled into the stable. The ass was gone, but he ran over to a pile of chaff, lying behind a large chest, with the aim of hiding there from all the madness. However, he suddenly felt something moving. It was the eldest brother's two little boys who had already sought refuge there. They both screamed in fear when Misael touched them because they thought the Turks were still searching for them. But they soon recognized him, and the three subsequently pulled close to each other as they awaited death.

The setting sun sent its last rays into the destroyed home and illuminated the three sisters-in-law who sat with their children pressed up against them and crying in bewilderment. What had happened, and what was to follow? All they could hear was the sound of mania across the city, the shootings, the slashes, the blows, the piercing screams, and the brutal yells. At times it seemed close, then further away, and sometimes people ran quickly past on the street. Just outside their door it seemed someone was struck down because after the sound of footsteps faded away, they heard moaning and groaning for a long time, but no one dared look. Later, they saw a group of screaming women fleeing across the rooftops. Who were they, and where were they headed? Yet they didn't ask them; their senses were numb.

With darkness came the cold, so the women gathered themselves and arose to bundle up their children. Fortunately the young ones were already asleep, however uneasily, as their exhaustion demanded they rest. But then the women suddenly remembered the little boys. They didn't dare call out to them, so after searching for them without success, they mourned their deaths as well.

In turn, as nightfall descended, the city also fell quiet. The crowds of executioners headed for the mosques to perform the evening prayer. There the mullahs pronounced Allah's satisfaction with what the men had done and called on them to resume the task in the morning. Everybody then went home and ate dinner, but as they were all too excited to sleep, they instead met up again afterwards to divide the spoils, discuss the day's events, and to drink. In several instances the gatherings became sheer orgies of celebration.

Once the Armenians realized during the night that the Turks were gone, they began to stir and moved to investigate the extent of the damage and whether there were any possibilities for salvation. In those areas where the men had been killed, the women were reluctant to remain among the bodies, and sought instead to find shelter elsewhere. That led large crowds to seek refuge in the main church while whole individual families went to move in with relatives. But it was terrible to pass through the streets, which were strewn with corpses and household items that had been pulled from the homes and dumped. People stumbled over the human and material debris in the dark, but no one dared to even light a match.

However, the women of the Biredjiklian family opted to stay in their home, even as they sat numb and in silence with their sleeping children. And as the night progressed, hunger lured the young boys out of the barn. They made their way into the living room, found a few pieces of bread, and crept under a blanket to keep warm. Soon after, they too were asleep.

Then suddenly around midnight a man snuck into the courtyard. It was the youngest brother; he was coming back from Krikor's house. Once the calamity broke over the city, it became apparent what Krikor had been doing down in the cellar. He had built a hiding place, essentially a cave beneath the house with an entrance so well hidden that no one could detect it. There he and his brothers hid; Hovagim's brother had been invited to join them. "Had I only been able to contact Hovagim," Krikor lamented when he entered the cave as the last man, "but it's unfortunately no longer possible to reach him." There the men remained hunched over in the cramped space for the entire day as they listened to the Turks ravaging through the home above.

For Chanum, it was like a beacon in the night to learn that her brothers were still alive. She had wanted to join them, but her brother-in-law had actually believed she would be safer at home.

The next morning it was hardly yet dawn when the Turks again charged into the Armenian Quarter. Many of them were now drunk and therefore more brutal than the day before, and they had also been reinforced as large numbers of people from the countryside had streamed into the city during the night. They had brought along whole caravans of animals to carry off to their villages the items to be seized because this day the focus would be on looting.

Many marched, with the mullahs in the lead, into the areas they had not reached the day before. Here they dragged the men into the streets, killed them, and then assaulted the women. One mullah even pledged to strike down by his own hand one hundred Armenian boys. The unfortunates were dragged into a small square, where he set about murdering them one by one with his knife. But by the time he got to the last one, the mullah's strength was exhausted and he declared:

"Allah must surely forgive that I cannot do more."

Another group of Muslims set about ransacking those districts where the Armenian men had been killed the day before. The killers had mainly limited themselves to money, jewelry, and other such valuables, so the crowds now turned to what remained. Quality linens, copper basins, sweets from the vineyards, rugs, clothes – all was seized and loaded onto the pack animals, and soon one could see the caravans descend down from the Armenian Quarter. Everything that industrious hands had assembled was now passed off to those who had been unwilling to work.

Hovagim's house was also looted, resulting in an additional horror for the women. They could now either face starvation or join Turkish households and serve their husbands' killers. Both options were horrible.

Around noon a solitary Turk strolled into their courtyard; it was Mustapha Agha's nephew. He was drunk and went straight for Chanum, who resisted his advances and managed to break free.

"Well, well," he said, "you'll soon enough change your mind, and then I'll return to fetch you."

So, shortly after he was gone, Chanum grabbed her young sons and fled to her brother's house, and the other women in the household similarly sought out places to hide. When the Turk came back in the evening, he found the nest empty.

As the third day dawned, a Sunday, the Turks were about finished murdering the men they had captured. Yet, the looting continued, and the hunt for women was ongoing as some were dragged away to the harems while others were summarily raped. Other Turks busied themselves with destroying what they could not haul away. The remaining rags and bits of clothing were dumped in the courtyards; window frames and doors were piled on top, and all set alight. Even stores of food, which they did not want, were destroyed by drenching them in kerosene.

But the culminating action was the grand autodafé at the cathedral. Here hundreds of women, children, and a few men had sought refuge. As the Turks closed in on the main square, the Armenians fled into the church and crowded up into the spacious gallery. However, the Turks followed them inside and, as the main door was just beneath the gallery, they immediately set about placing all sorts of flammable items by the entrance, doused them in kerosene and set it all on fire. A collective scream of despair from the hundreds of Armenians greeted this criminal act. Everyone knew it invariably meant death.

Outside the cathedral, the bestial mob waited to strike down anyone who attempted to escape. Meanwhile, choking smoke filled the building and the flames slowly engulfed the Armenians, at last setting the gallery afire....*

Gradually the screams subsided and a frightful stench of burnt flesh reeked through the windows and doors, driving back the crowd. Throughout the rest of the afternoon and during the whole following night, the church continued to burn, yet the building did not collapse. It was built of hewed stones and they remained in place. But all of the beautiful interior ornamentation was lost, eliminating the finery that a pious and gifted population of industrious artisans had contributed over

* The massacre at Urfa's cathedral was the most ghastly event that unfolded over the hellish hours lasting from Sunday to Monday, 28-29 December 1895. It is estimated that as many as three thousand people died within the confines of the would-be sanctuary.

a century. One had donated an elaborately printed protective covering used for the main altar during the fast, others had decorated the altars with carvings and metal work, and the women had donated their most valuable embroideries.

All these treasures were now gone, and they could never be replaced because all the masters who had performed those tasks were dead and there was no one to teach the young. The ancient, artistic crafts were all but extinguished during the massacres.

That Sunday night the Armenian Quarter was a frightful sight. Through the streets and inside the courtyards bodies and bits of clothing were strewn about. In the houses the surviving women sat half-naked, mostly even without linens to cover themselves, and in many places lacking the windows and doors necessary to keep out the winter cold. Many also lacked even a little bread to eat or a bucket to collect water. The children clutched their mothers tightly and sobbed out of fear, hunger, and cold, but the women knew not what to do. How were they to feed their children or provide them with warmth? And what new horrors would the next day bring?

Several were driven mad during the night, while others contracted ailments that would plague them for the rest of their lives.

When the mobs again descended upon the Armenian Quarter on Monday morning, they found Turkish troops posted at the entrances, and they were turned away. The rural peoples then had no choice but to return home to their villages. But events had whetted their appetites, so many decided to head for Garmuch, the only Armenian hamlet in this region. The Armenians there, it was assumed, certainly also owned many items that the peasants coveted. However, the residents were prepared for such an onslaught, and they confronted the crowds at the edge of the village and sent them away bloodied.

The raiders retreated, but thoughts of Garmuch kept egging them on. Just a few days passed before the villagers again saw a large mass of people approaching across the plain. That sight prompted them to prepare for death because they realized the attackers were too numerous. But as the mob neared Garmuch, the unexpected occurred as a torrential downpour, such as happens in southern lands, suddenly broke from the sky and forced the entire mass of humanity to flee. And they did not return because their passions had cooled by the time the rainy season ended. Garmuch simply remained untouched like a sanctuary in the midst of the destruction.

Chapter Four

Atop the Ruins

Once the military had reestablished order in the town, the Turkish government dispatched forces to the Armenian Quarter to ensure that at least the women and children did not starve and that some semblance of stability was restored. They gathered up the survivors and evacuated them to various mosques or one of the large khans outside the Samsat Gate. Among those who were transferred were Chanum and her two sons, Misael and Kevork. She had few clothes to wear but had found an old piece of fabric to cover her head, and almost treasured it more than any other possession because she still feared that Mustapha Agha's nephew might see her and seize her. Chanum also placed Misael with a different group of people so he would not be recognizable because he stood out as having been in hiding by still wearing all his clothes. Even his new boots shone gaily amidst all the suffering and it occurred to him how fortunate it was that he had kept them on that fateful morning.

Well, when was that anyway? It all seemed so long ago! At that time he had been sitting on Hovagim's knee – Oh, where was Hovagim now? He had just lain there with his head split open. What had since happened to him? Just then the multitude passed the family's house and Misael was tempted to rush in and check on him. No, he decided, that would be too frightening. And besides, the sheep and the ass were now gone, also.

How in the world had all this come to pass?

Suddenly Misael jumped at the sound of something unfamiliar behind him. It was a man dragging a cadaver. He had tied a rope around the dead person's ankles and was pulling it along in just the same manner as when Misael had once seen a dead ass being removed from the quarter. The clothes had mostly been stripped from the body and the throat was slashed so the head just dangled and was being bounced back and forth as it passed across the cobblestones. One of the women in the crowd just stood there staring at the corpse with terror in her eyes. Then suddenly, she screamed and ran off as if possessed. She had recognized her husband.

As the crowd continued on and turned into the main street toward the Samsat Gate, they joined a whole train of such corpses. Some showed signs of having been burned, either partially or in some cases even completely blackened. The city's Jews were the ones dragging the bodies. They had been ordered by the local government to perform this menial task and had to be grateful that they were not meeting the same fate. Fanaticism was in full bloom, putting all unbelievers in serious danger.

On the main thoroughfare stood a number of young Turks just looking at the women with lustful eyes as they passed by. But the Turkish soldiers were there too and strict directives had been issued. No man dared put his hands on any of the women. In contrast, the Turkish women were not so restrained, and they had turned out in large numbers to take pleasure in the misfortune of others. The women shouted slanderous accusations at the Armenians and the Turkish children threw stones, both actions that the soldiers ignored.

It was an arduous descent to the Samsat Gate, and just beyond it, they witnessed a scene which made their hair stand on end. Here the murdered Armenians were piled up, one atop another, and the mound kept growing as new corpses were added in a steady stream upon exiting through the archway. There were so many and they kept coming down the road in incalculable numbers.

Once the women reached the khan, they made their way into the guest rooms until they were filled and then filed on into the stables. Subsequently portions of bread, cooked grains with meat, and other food stuffs were distributed to the assembled people. A quantity of old clothes and some linens of the poorest quality were also made available, but, however meager, it was better than going without. It was thanks to the government together with the rich Turks that this was done because they did not want to see the survivors starve.

After all, there was now no need to fear that these doomed and for decades abused people should retain any dreams of independence, especially since similar events had unfolded in every town with resident Armenians. These brutalized remnants should be preserved as they would forever be like subservient slaves from whom the Turks could only benefit. Yet it was not this consideration alone which prompted the Turks to be merciful. They were also fearful about what they had done, and this emerged slowly as the impassioned intoxication wore off.

They feared Allah's anger. Despite the assurances of the mullahs, most knew very well that their actions were wrong. They expected that God's punishment would befall them. If a plague or some such calamity occurred, they would have seen it as well-deserved and simply accepted it. But as nothing happened, the people gradually reassured themselves that the mullahs had been correct; Allah was satisfied with their handiwork.

However, they also harbored a fear that the Europeans would avenge their fellow Christians. They expected nothing short of a declaration of war from a united Europe and were concerned about what would result from such a development. But that didn't happen either. The European governments even hesitated in applying any real pressure on the Turks to protect the surviving Armenians. Once the Turks realized this fact, the Armenians lost all rights. They were abandoned by both God and man, and against them every transgression would hence be permissible.

But fortunately, Christian people were not as unconcerned as their governments. Deep down they felt partly responsible for what had occurred and, since they lacked the power to influence foreign policy, they chose the only route that remained open to them. They organized large fund drives and collections to assist the survivors. And so committed was public opinion in Europe that the Turks dared not seriously block the charitable efforts.

In Urfa, Christendom had a worthy representative in Miss Shattuck, the director of the American mission. She pioneered the local aid work and led it with such a spirit that she was respected as much by the Turks as the Americans. In fact, a conversation between two Turks of that era has been preserved. One of them remarked that it was a pity that during the fire at the cathedral, the Armenian community had lost a magnificent portrait of the Madonna which had hung above the main altar.

"Oh, it doesn't matter," the other answered, "they have Miss Shattuck, after all."

During the massacre she provided shelter for hundreds of Armenian men and women in the American mission compound. She accepted all with open arms who could reach the mission, and her noted standing in the community, also among the Muslims, served to protect them in the midst of a sea of human upheaval.

But now that the fourth day had passed, and the horrors were at an end, Miss Shattuck was one of the first who emerged to meet with the Armenians. Just the sight of her was for the frightened and broken-hearted women a boundless comfort and relief. They knelt down at her feet, hugged her, and showered her with prayers for help and with questions. Hundreds of times the same query was heard: "What shall become of us?"

She consoled them, attempted to provide new hope, calmed them with assurances that the killings and outrages were at an end, and distributed food to the full extent of her supplies. But her main responsibility was to care for the wounded who were left behind in the quarter after everyone else was led away. She was a trained nurse and soon every available room in the mission was converted into an aid station. There she cared for the injured, and she saved more than two hundred people who would otherwise have died.

During the night, when everything was quiet, knocking could often be heard at the main gate through which pale, hunched over, and terrified souls snuck onto the mission grounds. They were mostly men who now dared to emerge from their hiding places and who knew of nowhere else to turn to save themselves. And even though it had long been overcrowded inside the compound, room was made to accommodate them as well.

For a few days, the women stayed in the khan and mosques while the quarter was cleared of corpses. By the time they were almost all removed, the rains came and thoroughly cleaned the area. The water streamed through the gutters of the steep streets, carrying with it all the filth. In the beginning the water was red, but gradually it assumed the usual grayish-yellow color. Once the rainfall tapered off, the women were sent back to their homes.

But what a homecoming! When they saw their homes again, they fully realized what had been lost. It was hardest on the women from affluent households, who were at their wit's end since they had never performed anything but domestic duties. How would they now fend for themselves? There they sat in empty rooms with their children in the middle of winter, with inadequate clothes, little food or firewood, no providers, and without hope for the future.

However, much was done to meet the community's immediate needs. Large sums from Europe and America made their way to Urfa, and Miss

Shattuck organized the local relief effort. But it provided little lasting comfort because it was charity. Every time the women collected their monthly handouts, they did so with the ominous sense that it would be the final time. That feeling humiliated them.

It was during this time of crisis that Miss Shattuck conceived her great vision. She believed these women had skills around which they could build an existence. They could all embroider, a talent learned in childhood. Their entire wardrobes had been embroidered, featuring both gold and silver threads as well as silk. In contrast, the men had always worn modest clothes to avoid awakening Turkish jealousies. But the women, who were never seen by the Turks, could dress elaborately, reflecting their wealth.

Women did not buy their fineries from shopkeepers; they were sewn and embroidered at home. Some beautiful pieces had even been passed from mother to daughter over several generations. But now such items were lost, and the Turkish women, who never mastered that art form, were the ones wearing the stolen adornments.

Yet the Armenian women had retained their skills and would thereby be able to support their children. The artistry that had served to beautify their married lives – as no expense was spared – they now needed to sustain their physical lives. The most talented women met with Miss Shattuck and developed the patterns from which items were made that could be sold in Europe and America. And other women overseas then made sure those goods were marketed.

The calming satisfaction the work imparted colored the women's hearts. They could now feed their children based on their own labor. No longer were they dependent on the charity of strangers, nor did they have to simply accept being married off by their families in order to be cared for. They were now self-supporting. A unique type of woman began to emerge in Urfa, and she was by no means any lesser than the woman of old.

The manner in which Miss Shattuck initially managed this women's industry was not entirely successful. She failed to generate enough turnover of the varied embroideries to put a sufficient number of women to work. But she probably did not appreciate the actual character of Oriental art. It is in fact a decorative art as it follows a set, stylized base-pattern with small changes in form and colorization added intermittently according to the nature and tastes of the individual seamstress. It is precisely in such personal attentions to intimate detail that the art form's charm lies. These were lost under Miss Shattuck's management and with them the full splendor of the embroideries.

But she was otherwise successful all the same. Little by little, she started an additional industry making finely embroidered handkerchiefs which also turned out well for her. In that production the emphasis was only on accuracy and clean lines rather than an appreciation for art. And it became an industry which expanded to employ thousands of women.

Miss Shattuck possessed the unshakeable will and steadfast endurance required to introduce a new business and have it take firm roots. The new industry became the property of Urfa's people, and it survived Miss Shattuck's passing.

Meanwhile, her mission was far from exhausted with the caring for women. The conditions of the men also made demands on her as there were still Armenian men in Urfa – they soon appeared from all sides. The American mission had sheltered many of them, and more still had successfully remained hidden in their own homes, either, like Krikor, in a prepared room or one like it offered to them at the critical moment. Still others had received refuge in Turkish homes.

There were friendships that had shown themselves to be strong enough to overcome fanaticism. But it was offered by Turks from whom the Armenians had generally not expected to receive protection. It was rather those who were uneasy about everyday lives, the gamblers, the drunks, and the hooligans who stood by the Armenians in their time of need. And it seemed as if they had no real connection with their own people or their religion and simply acted based on human instinct.

Other Armenians had simply adopted Islam during those terrible incidents and had been led as "converts" to the mosques. Eventually most returned to their own church over the next few years, since one of the few things that the Great Powers demanded of Abdülhamid was that these forced conversions be deemed invalid. A Muslim who rejects his religion is customarily condemned to death, but an exception was apparently made with respect to the "converted" Armenians.

Miss Shattuck cared for the surviving men in every possible manner. She supported them with money and assisted them by word and deed as far as her abilities and energy stretched.

Chapter Five

Fresh Seedlings

Above all else, Miss Shattuck never forgot the children. She loved them the most and experienced her greatest joy when interacting with them. Their current distress therefore touched her deeply as the children's fate, in truth, seemed harsh. Many of them, who at birth were laid in silk-lined cribs, now sat on the bare stone floor, and they, for whom large jars were once filled with raisins and sweets in the fall, now found hardly even a dried piece of bread. They often had to even go to bed hungry. Yes, to bed indeed! For what had become of their sturdy beds? Could one even use that word to refer to the rags with which they now had to cover themselves?

Conditions were certainly tough! Yet for many, a sun still shone in the sky: motherly love watched over them. There was always someone who was content with the worst place under the tattered sheets, if only it meant the little ones could keep somewhat warm; one who could forego yet another portion of her meager rations when hunger tormented one of the children; one who put aside all concerns for herself to provide for her children; and one who never considered her actions as remarkable when she had sacrificed everything.

Yes, those who had a mother still enjoyed a little sunshine that could warm them. But there were also children who had no mother.

When Miss Shattuck's made her rounds from house to house to console and assist the abandoned women, it often happened that she encountered a child who was tragically without parents. Some were children whose parents had died before the massacres, and, with the high rates of mortality in the Orient, that had happened far more frequently than one should otherwise have assumed. But at that time, orphans did not represent a significant challenge. There were always uncles and aunts or grandparents who were obligated to care for them, as it would shame the family if the children of relatives were neglected. And if there were kids whose relations were too poor to care for them, then the church stepped in.

The child would be presented to the assembled congregation after mass, and the gathering would be sufficiently devout that at least several individuals would come forward and volunteer to take the child. The notion of compensation was never discussed. Only a fear of losing one's own children could excuse a failure to assume one's duty in this matter.

Yes, that indeed was how things used to be. Then everyone had enough to eat and to feed their fires, enough to wear, and enough to sleep and to sit on. At that time it did not matter whether one had a child more or less. But now the poor rations were hardly sufficient for one's own children and, even though one feared God and gave the child a little food, one still longed for that small, donated piece of bread. And it seemed as if the gaze of that child's eyes, growing larger with hunger, made the available portions appear even smaller.

The ragged linens were also inadequate to cope with the nights. The orphaned children often had the misfortune to bed down on the bare floor where they lay catching a chill.

Miss Shattuck took such a child by the hand and found him a permanent place at her home. A plate was also provided, and it was filled three times daily. It was as simple as that, but so many small slots were needed that the crowd within the walls of the mission continued to grow. There were just so many children in distress.

Those who had lost both their parents during the massacres were even worse off. They had no idea where to turn. Some hid quietly in a nook just awaiting death while others roamed the streets in tears.

"Dear God! That's Mariam's child," said a sympathetic neighbor wife and took in the child. "Why are you running about by yourself?"

"Because my father was murdered," answered the distraught child.

Those words were almost unutterable, but there was also no need to speak them because everyone knew. The question that remained was what had happened to Mariam. A Turk had dragged her away and the screaming child that clamored to her was simply pushed aside. Or perhaps the child did not even know what happened. Maybe the boy hid out of fear, and when he emerged his mother and little sister were gone. Mariam, in fact, was never seen again. Yes, she probably fled into the church from which no one would ever return. Well, in truth, one old woman did escape from there alive. She had ended up lying beneath a pile of bodies and they had shielded her from the flames. Oddly, the smoke had not choked her either, and she had recovered after being pulled from the ruins. But she seemed rather affected by the experience, so it was difficult to be sure whether everything had happened as she described.

Yet, she did claim to have seen Mariam. She described how Mariam had stood in the front row of the church gallery with her child pulled close. And once the flames flared up and started to ignite the wood-work, she went quite mad, screamed uncontrollably, and threw first the child and then herself into the inferno. However, the old woman told that same story about so many Mariams, Ichsas, and Chanums. She probably saw some woman do exactly that, yet she no longer remembered who it actually was.

Meanwhile, Mariam never did return, and the neighbor wife already had her hands full with three children of her own. She had long ago come to regret her willingness to care for the orphan because "one cannot do more than one can do."

"No, of course not," Miss Shattuck replied. She could not do more either, but she knew who was the Father of all orphans and was absolutely sure that He would find a way to help this one child as well. She continued to take the little ones by the hand and lead them home and, if she was handed a child that was too young to walk, she carried him in her arms. Home they were all sure to come.

In the meantime, Miss Shattuck repeatedly sent out calls for further assistance. Some made their way from behind closed doors all the way to God's throne, while others passed along hidden paths to the Turkish borders and from there by mail to Europe and America. The two types of messages worked jointly so that so many people felt their hearts and consciences touched. They were moved to ask themselves:

"What have I done to deserve that my children have a good, warm bed and eat their fill every day, while another people's children have to lie on cold stone floors and have nothing to ease their hunger?"

Some donated sums of money. Others contributed more; they volunteered themselves.

In Germany the call summoned one man whose name became tied to the Armenian cause. It evolved for him into a matter of vital importance and he worked tirelessly in its interest. That man was Dr. Lepsius.

In the spring of 1896, his representative, Mr. Eckart, arrived in Urfa with the aim of establishing an orphanage. He was greeted warmly by Miss Shattuck, who helped familiarize him with the alien environment and assisted him in all matters. The two were happy to share a mutual understanding. From their first meeting, Mr. Eckart accepted that he should yield to Miss Shattuck's greater experience and learn from her. And so it unfolded that through the many years that followed, tensions never developed between the German and American missions. They were active in the same city, focused on the same issues, without the notions of competition or envy ever emerging between them. In fact, they both had pure intentions and only wanted to help, rather than being concerned about propaganda or self-promotion.

The time was certainly ripe for Miss Shattuck to receive greater assistance. More than two hundred children were by then assembled within the walls of the mission and many more were waiting to be admitted. And it was not just Urfa's Armenians who sought Miss Shattuck's aid; from the surrounding, smaller towns like Biredjik, Adiaman and Severek, she also received heart-wrenching letters with tales of abandoned children.

There were a great many needs to address, and Mr. Eckart immediately focused on finding lodgings and having them outfitted to house children. It was possible to lease a few buildings located close to each other and not too far from the American mission. Five courtyards were converted into orphanages, two for boys and three for girls. Miss Shattuck helped him to find suitable house fathers and women to perform the more subordinate tasks, and eventually the day arrived when the "German" children were separated from the "American" ones and left for their new homes, which collectively became known as the "Lepsius Home."

One fine spring day, Ohannes Effendi,* the house father in one of the German orphanages for boys, was sitting at a table in the inner courtyard

* It was a title of respect and courtesy, essentially meaning gentleman or sir.

of the American mission station. Before him, lined up against a wall, stood a row of fifty boys arranged according to height. Their names needed to be recorded, so as each child stepped forward, he was assigned a number, more or less in sequence with age. Number one was perhaps twelve or thirteen years old, while number fifty was not even able to stand, lying instead in a cradle and was simply counted. When Ohannes Effendi reached the number thirty, he saw standing before him a boy aged maybe seven or eight years old with darting eyes, but who was clearly quite captivated by the proceedings. He answered promptly that his name was Misak* and that his father's name was Hagob, who had been a mason. But when asked his age, Misak became quite puzzled. He didn't know how old he was, but then most everyone else did not know their age either. Ohannes Effendi subsequently looked him in the mouth, as if he was buying a horse or a cow, and thereafter wrote down: "eight years old."

But the final question Misak answered with ease, as he was well-aware that he belonged to "the great church" and was a Gregorian. Once all the boys had been registered, they paired up holding hands, and Ohannes Effendi led the procession to their new home. The two female assistants, known as *mairik*,† followed, each with a small child in her arms, and bringing up the rear were the oldest boys carrying the cradles. All the children's eyes beamed with anticipation, and they were certainly not disappointed when they finally reached their destination and the heavy iron gate, which hid the trappings of their new home, was opened before them. Yet what was it that captivated the boys most about the unfolding scene? Was it the newly washed, tiled courtyard under the vine-covered roof, with a reflecting pool and little garden in the center, or was it the figure of Tuma Chanum, the attractive, friendly, and youthful wife of Ohannes Effendi, who stood with her little daughter, Rachel, and greeted them?

---

* This is still Misael but now under a new name, the title name of the story. The change is a bit abrupt in the narrative, but Jeppe soon reveals how and why this alteration was made.

† An Armenian word meaning "mother"; these women were acting as house mothers for the orphans.

They felt an almost irrepressible urge to rush about and take in all the sights and explore every room in the two-storied wings of the building that partially enclosed the courtyard on three sides. But such behavior was now a thing of the past. Now one remained standing in place until instructed by someone to go elsewhere. And on this day, the first place they were allowed to enter was the wash house. They all needed to be thoroughly cleaned and given a change of clothes before they could be admitted to the tidy sitting rooms.

Misak received a vigorous scrubbing and the soapy lather streamed down his body. He even got it in his eyes, but he hardly felt it, because the anticipation for what was to follow was so great. And what unfolded certainly did not disappoint. He got brand-new underwear, a blue coat, a red shirt with a wonderful woven design in rich colors, and a fine pair of red shoes. Next, Mariam Mairik helped him to get dressed.

"Be still, Misak!" she admonished.

Well, that was easy for her to say. He had had to stand and later sit still for such an awfully long time, and everything was simply too exciting. What he really wanted to do was to run into the street and show the other boys his finery, but that was, of course, out of the question. Instead, he hoped to at least walk across the courtyard on his hands. And as he did so, he let out a spontaneous shout of joy just before entering the room on the other side of the courtyard.

But then Ohannes Effendi appeared in the doorway. "How is it that you're behaving, Misak? Come inside and sit down properly!"

Fortunately there was so much to see in the room that it tempered Misak's disappointment over having to yet again remain still for so long. Everything was so nice in there with bright red and blue striped rugs on the floor for seating, a grand picture on the wall, and in one corner stood a small brown crate on carved legs. Yet the day was rapidly coming to a close, and Misak was about to fall asleep when suddenly something new unfolded. They were led into another room where rows of shiny, polished tin plates with equally polished spoons were arrayed on neat, blue-checkered tablecloths. And from the kitchen came a wonderful aroma.

To the boys it seemed to last forever before they were shown to their seats. But they needed to remain patient for just a little while longer. Ohannes Effendi went to stand in one end of the dining hall, removed his fez, and said grace at length. Would that "amen" never come? – Finally! It was as if a collective sigh of relief passed through the gathering. And what a soup they now were served. It was greeted with loud cheers.

"Silence at the table!" boomed Ohannes Effendi's voice.

Oh! The boys were about to explode with pent-up satisfaction. Thankfully they were about to eat, so they fell silent again quite willingly. Their mouths would now be busy with other matters.

After the meal, the boys milled out into the courtyard and began to play games. Ohannes Effendi came out a few times to shush them, but that did not help much. Then one of the boys was pushed and fell so awkwardly that he hit his head against the courtyard pool. Blood flowed down the side of his face, and everyone was summoned back inside. The questioning that followed began and remained futile, as no one would admit to the deed. Ohannes Effendi grew angry and proceeded to scold the boys. But then Tuma Chanum entered the room, bringing along with her little Rachel, and she declared that they wished for peace and quiet to prevail on this first night, and with that the poor atmosphere subsided.

Later, a brown, crate-like box was brought out. Ohannes Effendi sat down in front of it and suddenly the most wonderful melodies sprang forth. Misak was so moved that he became quite teary-eyed. Everyone joined in, singing along with the music and it was a beautiful moment. But after the song Ohannes Effendi took out a thick book and began to read something aloud which did not interest Misak in the least. It was lengthy and difficult to fully comprehend, and worse yet was to follow when Ohannes Effendi stood up, removed his fez, folded his hands together and with closed eyes gave a long, long sermon. Misak began to doze off before the liberating "amen" was uttered.

He then suddenly became wide-awake again because now they were about to see the sleeping quarters. The boys almost forgot about everything else when they saw the blue-checkered bedspreads with delightful red stripes and the snow white sheets. For a short while they stood quietly and were engrossed in the displayed finery. Then each one was shown his place to sleep.

Ohannes Effendi next made the rounds and showed each of them how they should fold their shirts and coats before they went to bed. Once under the covers, and when all the small dark heads were arrayed neatly on the white pillows, he exhorted them to thank God for everything He had bestowed on them.

"And, in addition, children, it is strictly forbidden to talk once you're in bed. Now is the time for you to sleep. Good night!"

Alas, one could never find the time to finish a conversation.

Misak shared a bed with a little boy of the same age. His name was Asadus and was from Biredjik. They had had so much to tell each other but would now have to save the rest for another time. The comfortable bed also gave Misak something else to ponder, as he had not rested so softly since he slept in Hovagim's arms. A lump formed in his throat and seemed to almost choke him as he thought longingly of Hovagim. If only he could see him again and hear his voice one more time, just one last time!

But then suddenly he saw Hovagim before him with a large gash in his head. He lay sprawled in a pile of bodies, and blood flowed everywhere. What in the world was this sight? Misak was about to scream, but then he awoke, realized where he was, and simply lay staring into the glare of the bedside lamp until all the corpses faded from his mind. Soon other images appeared. He saw Chanum walking down the street with Kevork in one arm and holding himself by the hand. But it was such a frightful scene. Almost every door facing the street was open and the courtyards beyond were strewn with dirt, rags and charred wood, but not a living soul was in sight. Then they reached their own gate and entered the courtyard. But was it really their house? Yes, the well was where it should be, as was the stable and the various doorways, but the space was so empty that one could become quite frightened.

Chanum put Kevork down beside Misael* and instructed them to play together for a moment while she entered the house. Misael did as he was told, but then he noticed a large, dark-brown spot and suddenly realized from where it had come. He swiftly lifted Kevork into his arms and ran in to rejoin Chanum. He dared not remain out there for even one minute longer. Chanum was not in the living room, but he soon found her in a dark corner of the kitchen. She was removing something from a hole in

* The narrative now temporarily reintroduces Misak as Misael, as the boy recalled the recent past and related how his identity was to symbolically change. (see also note no. 49)

the wall, something that glimmered and which she quickly hid under her clothes. Then she picked up a brick from the floor and placed it back in the hole. Next, as she turned around, she was quite startled to see Misael and Kevork. Yet she also understood that they had been scared out there because she too felt very uneasy in the empty, ransacked house. She therefore quickly gathered up the children, having every intention to quickly leave that place.

But by the gate to the street they met the eldest brother's wife, who came creeping along the outer wall, sobbing and with her six children in tow.

"Well, I'm sure you're headed for Krikor's, Chanum," she said. "Alas, oh God! My brothers are dead. What shall become of me with these children? If only the Turks had also killed us."

Soon after, they arrived in Krikor's home. They didn't get to see him straight away as he still stayed hidden during the day, but the two sisters-in-law were there along with the grandmother, Chanum's mother. She greeted her daughter lovingly as did Krikor's wife who was a very young and kind creature. The older brother's wife, however, mumbled something along the lines that they themselves already were short of bedding and lacked enough food to eat.

It would have meant a little more food for them and a few more rags with which to cover themselves. But Chanum and Krikor had always made sure that Misael was included and cared for. Otherwise it would have looked dire for him because that woman, the sister-in-law, was so prone to push him away and even kick him. All that she could grab for herself, she fed to her own children.

One day the ongoing tension led to serious strife between the women, and strong words were exchanged. But then Krikor had intervened to assert his position:

"Chanum is my only sister. My home is her home, and you two," as he directed a sharp look at the sisters-in-law, "must listen to her."

Well, that was all well and good, but Krikor's brother sided with his own wife, and besides, the men were at work during the day, so the women could then quarrel undisturbed.

Krikor was one of the very first who ventured out of the Armenian Quarter and showed himself again on the main square. Ignoring the women's tears and prayers, he had simply set off one morning. A day so long had probably never passed before, as in the house hardly a word was uttered and fear was etched in everybody's faces. How could he, they all wondered, freely go out to face those executioners!? Naturally, they would never see him again. But as evening descended, he reappeared, and he brought food with him.

A few days later the second brother had accompanied him, and now their home was probably one of the best provisioned on their street. The women also weaved and embroidered, so they could all have eaten their fill, but it was not enough when tensions persisted over sharing the food. Misael was and remained a thorn in the side of the others. Kevork was still little and was, of course, Chanum's biological child, but Misael was not, so why should they continue to care for the orphan? After all, Chanum could just turn him over to the orphanage.

But Chanum refused. She remembered well the look in Hovagim's eyes and his body language when he handed her Misael, and it seemed clear to her that Kevork would die if she ever parted with the older boy. In fact, Kevork already looked quite unwell. He was so thin and pale, and he could at times sit rather passively for a long time beside Chanum, just staring at a fly or a tangled rag.

Why shouldn't she then also keep Misael with her? She had given Krikor her jewelry, and it was with that money that he had reopened his business. She quite simply had a right to stay at the house with both her two children. Yet still she tired of the unrelenting pressure and started to speak with Misael about the orphanage. All that good food and fine, new clothes he would receive there made an impression on him, and his thoughts gradually came to accept that some day he might have to leave. However, he was still unprepared when one spring day she climbed up to him on the roof and said that now was the time. Misael had simply not found the time to truly listen to her about this possibility. That morning, he had also been busy gathering grass and flowers that grew up there on the roof. Those ingredients were now boiling in a damaged pot, so he thought there couldn't be any question of leaving, certainly not until after the grass soup was finished. It was not until she lured him with a baked treat that he agreed to come along.

Soon they reached the American mission compound. Crowds of women and children milled about inside and it did not seem as if there could be room for even one more person. However, up in one of the rooms Miss Shattuck greeted them all the same. They both approached to kiss her hand, but she declined it and instead motioned for Chanum to take a seat. The young mother then told the whole story about Misael and finally asked if he could be admitted to the orphanage.

"Of course," said Miss Shattuck, "such a child without absolutely any family is a natural candidate."

What happened after that moment remained unclear for Misael. A woman had recorded his name, but she had told him that he should instead be called Misak. "Misael" was simply deemed improper. Then Chanum kissed him and left, while he was led into another room to join a group of assembled boys. It seemed almost as if it wasn't happening to him but rather to someone else.

That single utterance of Miss Shattuck had changed his entire world, so he found it quite natural that he also received a new name. Misael, who had played in Hovagim's arms, who had been Chanum's son, and who had a whole crowd of uncles, aunts, and cousins – a whole family – he, was now dead. Misak, in contrast, lived, but he was only a number in a large community where he could be forgotten at any moment. No one was truly responsible for him since he had "no relatives." Even Miss Shattuck, who was the wisest and best person imaginable, yes, perhaps even related to the good Lord, had said that, so it had to be true.

Already the next day, Miss Shattuck had led all the boys out onto the Aleppo road to greet a foreigner. They were told that the tall, young man who had arrived was named Mr. Eckart and that he had come to design new homes for them. Everyone looked forward to that event, because there was such a terrible overcrowding within the mission walls that it was quite difficult to ensure that everyone was fed let alone well provided for.

Confusion dominated Misak's mind when he thought about all the days preceding his arrival at the German orphanage. Figures danced strangely intertwined before him even as they became ever more unclear. But just as he was about to slip off to a deep sleep, a loud sniffling very near his bed brought him back to reality. He turned around and saw Asadur sobbing.

He probably has no relatives either, Misak thought, and moved to give him a loving hug. For some time they lay there together, each crying until their eyes grew heavy and they both fell asleep, their heads resting on the wet pillow and their arms locked in an embrace.

Misak was not, however, the only one that night whose thoughts were focused on the past. There were many who felt, consciously or not, that they were beginning a new chapter in their lives, and therefore sought to come to terms with what lay behind them. The one who did so most intently was probably Ohannes Effendi, and that was hardly surprising, because he had taken on a major responsibility and it weighed on him. But he was equally convinced that it was God who had guided him to this point in his life. Just as it was He who had freed him from the hands of his enemies that day when he lay beneath the stack of kindling sticks and could so clearly see the man who stood before him, axe in hand, and ready to strike him down as soon as he found him. Ohannes Effendi had prayed for salvation with every ounce of his soul and had pledged that if he were to be spared in this time of desperation, he would dedicate the rest of his life to the orphans. After all, he understood well, based on the screams and wails filling the air, that there would soon be many such unfortunates.

Indeed, it was then that a wondrous thing happened, as the Turk opted not to clear aside the bundles of kindling and instead went back outside to the courtyard where he told the others that the shed was empty. Ohannes Effendi did not for one moment doubt that it was God's hand that had intervened and had shielded him from his enemy's sight. This realization immediately filled him with an immense sense of joy. Not only had he been saved from certain death, but it had also revealed that his faith was not futile. His father too had been spared, and once the storm had passed, the family finally reunited in the empty house.

"Are you all here?" the old man asked in an emotionally-charged voice as he looked over the gathering.

"Yes," came the response, "we are all present, no one is missing." Upon hearing the news, he fell to his knees and praised God in a loud voice, expressing a sentiment shared by all present. It truly was one of life's greatest days. It was as if blood had been painted on the doorpost, and the Angel of Death had simply passed them by.*

Ohannes Effendi had once worked as a government bureaucrat and retained from that time friends among the Turks. They quickly sent food and clothes to the family once some normalcy was restored, and the family house was also one of the first that Miss Shattuck visited. The father was one of the leading men within the small Protestant congregation and a personal friend of Miss Shattuck. She was happy and moved when she learned that both he and his two sons were alive. Ohannes Effendi, remembering his pledge, became one of Miss Shattuck's assistants, and when the orphanages were established it was self-evident that he would be employed as a house-father in one of them. After all, there were few men left in Urfa who were as well-educated as he.

The next morning, with the sun already up and life stirring in the orphanage, Misak remained sound asleep despite the persistent ringing of the morning bell just outside the dormitory windows. A captivating dream busied his mind's attention and kept him fast asleep. He was convinced that he was walking along with a caravan of donkeys and that it was all the donkey bells that caused the ringing. But then suddenly the donkeys began to crowd around him and he had to hit out to make his way through the herd. Unfortunately for Misak, however, a group of the orphans had quickly gathered around the bed and they now all laughed out loud at the sight of his antics. And only slowly did he realize that he was actually lying in bed. The donkeys vanished but the bell was real enough and it was ringing just next to his headboard. It was Ohannes Effendi's little daughter who swung the bell, and all the boys still resting sat up in their beds and enjoyed the moment. What a delightful way to be woken up, and joyfully the boys got out of their beds and went down for their morning wash. In the orphanage everyone was required to wash each morning, and not just the face, but also the neck and arms. Such a routine was unfamiliar for the children because that was not common practice in Armenian homes. People were considered clean as long as they bathed once a week. And if they also splashed a little water on their faces

* This reference is to the Book of Exodus account of the Jewish exile in Egypt, when God spared the first-born children of the Jews from being struck down by plague.

and wiped their noses in the morning, then they had met the standards for cleanliness.

The boys, however, soon found the morning wash delightful, while the girls remained more inclined to believe that one contracted poor eyesight and many other ailments when one washed and combed one's hair every day. Their female relatives in the city reinforced those misperceptions at every opportunity, suggesting that all such *à la franca* * attitudes were actually harmful to the community.

But within the orphanage, either protest or consent was really irrelevant, as one simply had to follow the rules. These regulations included a stipulation that half an hour after the first bell rang, the ringing resumed. This time it sounded for morning prayers, which in every practical respect were like those in the evening. And hardly were these over and everyone milled into the courtyard, when the most anticipated and most agreeable bell rang. It summoned everyone "to take their meal."

On the table was another bell, placed next to Ohannes Effendi, and it was rung before the boys were seated, before they said grace, before they began to eat, and finally before they again rose from the table.

Everything unfolded like clockwork.

The boys had to hurry with the washing up, because soon the ringing resumed again. They lined up against the brick wall and, as they stood there quietly, they could hear how the air was filled with a chorus of bells. Soon they learned how to distinguish between the sounds of the various bells. There went the one from Hrumian's house for boys, then another from one of the homes for girls, and next rang the one from Miss Shattuck's. She had kept on about one hundred boys, so she continued to run an orphanage.

The sound of the many children's voices which had just filled the entire street soon subsided and another chiming commenced. Now it was the bell from the great Gregorian church that tolled and summoned all the school children in the Armenian Quarter to congregate. They all lacked clocks in their homes and instead they looked to the sun to tell

* The note and italics are original to the Danish text. Jeppe defined the phrase as "European," or literally acting Frankish.

time or otherwise listened for the great bell that could be heard now and again.

But the Armenians were now saddened when they heard it as it was almost a symbol of their condition.

Before the massacres the bell had been without equal, having such a full and clear voice that seemingly encompassed the emotions of the people, and expressed to them that they were a community where individuals could find solace and relief when they needed it. After all, the church meant so much to the Armenians, not just religiously but also for their entire culture which revolved around it. And the tolling of the great bell emphasized that central significance.

Furthermore, just as the calamity had struck and affected the entire Armenian community, so too the bell had endured its part. It had sustained a debilitating crack during the fire and now its voice was labored. However, the bell would not give up. It continued to sound with its pitiful, broken voice, and, those who listened closest understood what it said:

"We may well be broken, but we are still alive, and we have a Lord who does not forsake the broken reeds. Let us not abandon hope."

And gradually more and more people began to listen to the bell's message. Initially the tears flowed at the sound of its broken voice, but as they came to better understand its meaning, people raised their heads and tackled the work of communal recovery with greater energy and confidence. Soon even their enemies sensed that the Armenians were alive and yet again prepared to resume their struggles for survival.

In fact, on this day the bell's voice conveyed something hopeful. It was as if it had a reason to be thankful and reverberated with happiness. And this atmosphere so affected all the Armenians who lived in the upper reaches of the quarter that they came out to stand in their doorways to the streets or climbed to the roofs to survey the scene. It was after all the very day when all the orphans would for the first time attend school. Certainly the orphanages were a tragic reminder of the misfortune that had descended on the community, but the children also represented their hope for the future. These kids, who were so thoroughly raised by their foreign caregivers, should one day....

Well, what would actually be their role? No one seemed able to articulate exactly what people expected of the children, but perhaps for that very reason expectations were so high.

By now Ohannes Effendi's boys were ready. He moved to the front of the group and then they set off, leaving only the youngest children behind to stay in the homes with the women. And once out on the street, they spotted Hrumian's boys filing out through their gate further up the road. Miss Shattuck's gate was now also visible at the far end of the thoroughfare. Yes indeed, her boys were coming out and joining up as well.

Soon the column passed one of the orphanages for girls. Just inside the open gate the house father was visible and behind him stood all the girls wearing large, bright shawls with which they covered their heads.

And immediately after the boys had passed by, the girls headed out to join the procession. Everyone was clean and well-dressed, and conscious that they were going to school to become skilled people who would show the Turks what it meant to be Armenian. Yes, the event was a celebration, one of those days in life one never forgets. The joyous children who ventured to participate in the march felt at that moment as if chosen by fate. And the other children, those who stood watching the procession from the doorways or the flat rooftops were captivated by the scene. Many would soon thereafter plead with their mothers to allow them to likewise join an orphanage.

Chapter Six

The Second Temple

Urfa's Armenians did have schools before the massacres. The intellectual influences of the West had seeped into the community through many channels and had, among other things, resulted in the Armenians coming to see their children as independent persons. In the back of their minds, the notion lingered that their children were not born only to serve their parents, to care for them in their old age, or to carry on the family name, but rather that the parents too had a responsibility toward their children. And even though those sentiments were still in their infancy, once joined with the strong Armenian drive to learn, it had led to the belief that their children should attend school.

But then the terrible catastrophe had destroyed everything and an entirely new school system now needed to be established. However, the population was for the time unable to shoulder the associated costs. Subsequently, the Americans stepped in and a school was opened in various rooms located in the vicinity of the "grand" church.* It was towards those facilities that all the orphans were now headed. Misak had not been inside the building since the frightful event. The fire had been so horrifying and dreadful that he had not dared come near to the place, but now he again entered through the gate around which his life had seemingly come to revolve. Suddenly it all felt so overwhelming to him. An intense longing for Hovagim and everything else that lay in the past weighed on his heart and brought tears to his eyes. He quickly wiped them away and put on a brave face.

Just then they passed by the church. The large door was wide open, and he could see far inside the building. But was it the same beautiful church? All the wall decorations and carpets were gone, leaving only a large, empty and smoke-blackened room. That image would long plague his dreams.

---

* Quotation marks are original to the text.

Inside the building, craftsmen were hard at work. Some were scraping the soot off the stone walls; others were placing iron supports around the columns. The limestone, the material used for the entire construction, was no longer as sturdy as before the fire. In addition, another group of men were working on the new gallery. The Armenians were restoring their church, the gathering place of their people. They were determined to again have a place that could be the center of their lives and where they could sing their hymns anew.

But it came to pass with this church as with Jerusalem's Second Temple. It remained only a faint reflection of its predecessor's grandeur because the Armenians in Urfa never became as wealthy as they had been before the massacres and could therefore not adorn their church as beautifully.* Instead, it seemingly came to house a richer spiritual life because the mindset that had begun to influence the Protestants also affected the Gregorians. The waves from the West swept over them and implanted some elements of change with both good and bad interspersed. In fact, the age that had faded away so quietly was the age when one not only assumed a father's role but also shared his outlook and adopted almost unchanged his intellectual nature; the age when the word from the Gospels, the one heard on Sunday, was really the week's only new spiritual inspiration. That age, which gave rise to simple yet deep and pious characters like Hovagim, was over.

And was it not precisely this new age that accompanied the kids as they marched into the church square?

Steadily the crowd grew and grew. Alone from the orphanages there were over three hundred and many more came from all across the town. The newly hired teachers were also present as were the housefathers and the missionaries. What followed was a joint effort to shape, arrange, and plan the curriculum. There were, in short, plenty of tasks to occupy one's time.

The evaluation process was in a sense the least complicated because it was soon determined how few among the kids already had some learning.

* Jeppe's point is well-intentioned in conveying a historic parallel between Jewish and Armenian persecution. However, during the final years of the Second Temple's existence, under the direction of King Herod (r. 37-4 BCE), the temple complex was greatly expanded and beautified.

Most had to enroll in the beginning classes. And they were thereafter generally divided according to age, including classes with twelve to fourteen-year-old students, who not only had never been in school, but among whose parents none were literate. It was in truth virgin land in need of cultivation.

Soon the school plans were finalized and the leadership determined that since it was considered wise and beneficial to let European and American children attend classes for six hours daily, so too would it be suitable for the Armenian children. And so, there the new students now sat, but whether it was ideal for them was an entirely separate question. Conversely, had they been set to work in a workshop and trained to use their hands, it would all have been in order. Through the generations it was established that when sons were aged ten, their fathers took them along to work to begin teaching them a trade. That had now become a set custom, ensuring that at the traditional age they were prepared to assume their responsibilities.

But these educational changes, the kids thought, were unbearable. Most of the time, they had to sit still and stare into space, only occasionally being asked to focus their minds on something that, in turn, was most unfamiliar. It soon became apparent that this state of affairs could only be maintained through the strictest of discipline. And if conditions were difficult at school, it hardly improved in the orphanages after classes let out. The boys craved a release and the freedom to use their energy and hands after feeling pent up. It too followed that if there was nothing sensible and purposeful prepared for them to do, they would soon get into mischief.

Ohannes Effendi was probably the one who most clearly recognized the existing flaws. After all, he was among those who came to suffer the consequences. He had to deal with the misbehavior, and he could not ignore that the unnatural conditions provided fertile soil for all sorts of unbecoming conduct among the boys. In time, he proposed the establishment of half-days at school for the older boys so that they could receive training at artisan workshops in the afternoons. The missionaries generally favored this idea, but it encountered much resistance from the Armenians among whom there were many with a voice in the running of the school. They had become very attentive to the superiority of Europe and Europeans, and they now believed it was all due to their system of education. If they could only harness such a system, it could become the sword in their hands to finally defeat their age-old enemy. Hence the ever-constant mantra of their arguments was as follows: "As much schooling as possible for our children." That attitude and conviction meant that Ohannes Effendi was always outvoted by a large majority.

In any case, he was actually one of the great supporters of schooling and believed that the main role of the orphanage was to produce students. He also viewed vocational training as only a fallback for the least gifted pupils. Instead, his key interest was focused on the brightest boys in school. They were the ones who could bestow a reputation on his orphanage and on him, while the other boys remained only a challenging burden. Misak, in fact, now benefited from having struggled to learn during his former studies with the petit school teacher. He seemed bright for his age, did not need to attend the introductory classes, and immediately was placed among those who showed promise. In addition, he was a personable and quick-witted boy, and now, as he began to act accordingly, it became clear that he was very gifted at interacting with other people. He was, indeed, well-liked by both young and old at the orphanage. Tuma Chanum was especially fond of him because he was so good about interacting and playing with her small children. But for Misak, it was truly a pleasure to spend time with them, embracing their imaginings and partaking in both their childish joys and disappointments. He was a natural with them and always took their hearts by storm.

Indeed, Misak felt at home at the orphanage. He sensed a strong attraction to the loving and harmonious ambiance that Ohannes Effendi and Tuma Chanum knew well how to create around them. Everything they touched became beautiful. Not only did order reign throughout, such as order with everyone's wardrobe and such things, and order as regarded time and in work, but they also knew how to decorate with flowers or a rug in just such a way as to please one's eyes. Further, Ohannes Effendi played music so beautifully and Tuma Chanum would sing along. On such occasions all the boys just forgot their concerns and would either sit quietly and listen or even join in. He would also on occasion invite the boys to his private quarters and serve them tea and cakes. Then after the younger children were put to bed and with the older boys seated all around, he would take out his handwritten book of songs. That constituted an act of bravery for it contained Armenia's songs, those songs which their oppressors had prohibited them to sing. But Ohannes Effendi was determined that the children entrusted to him should know them despite the Turkish ban. He believed that they could not become true Armenians if the history of their people, their great writers, and their national melodies were a closed book to them.

Quietly he played the melodies and Tuma Chanum sang along with a faint voice. In breathless anticipation, with glowing faces and shining eyes, all the boys listened intently. Armenia's old kings and heroes danced into their minds, they fought and triumphed alongside with them, and their chests heaved with pride. They also felt the bitterness of their defeats and all the misfortunes that followed. Armenia's songs of grief gripped their hearts and brought forth tears. During those sessions their senses of national consciousness were stirred and intensified, and their lives were given an ideal and a goal. They felt their purpose was to restore their people from its tragedies. And for days thereafter they walked around in a near-daze, humming the melodies under their breath.

Additional joyous activities at the orphanage included walks outside the city. A German woman, who for a time was attached to the mission, came by a few days a week and led them all out, because during the first few years after the massacres, the Armenians did not really feel safe enough to venture outside the city's walls alone, as they could be severely harassed with ease. In contrast, the presence of a European provided significantly more security, as generally the Muslims kept their distance from the mission children who belonged to the foreigners. After all, it was rather uncertain what consequences one might invite if the children were approached. So the orphans generally escaped the terrible oppression that other Armenian kids endured during the years after the massacres. Those latter children were utterly defenseless against the brutal Muslim youths, and they became accustomed to accepting every humiliation and offense that the local hoodlums chose to inflict upon them. Their sense of fear and subservience soon knew no bounds; it had become second nature at far too early an age.

The young people from the orphanages were far braver and dauntless, having at times even inflicted a good beating on the Turkish boys. Certainly, they eventually also learned life's realities once they left the orphanages, but they were by then not nearly so soft and impressionable.

Chapter Seven

Lonely

On November 2nd, 1903, Misak stood alongside the orphanage's other boys at the entrance to the sunken road,* waiting in anticipation for the one in whom he would now put a great deal of faith. Some time earlier the rumor had reached the orphanage that a woman from Europe was to arrive and that she would become a mother to them all. But simultaneously it was said that she already had a son among them, one to whom she had long been a foster mother. No one knew the fortunate boy's identity, but there were many who hoped that they were him. Perhaps no one's thoughts were as preoccupied as Misak's with this question. As time passed, he had found it ever more difficult to be alone in the world. Often his thoughts were of his distant foster mother, who was so good to him, and he wished longingly for her to not be so far away.

When he now heard about the woman who was coming, he felt strangely confident that she had to be *his* mother. That wish had become like a prayer for him, and he soon convinced himself that it had finally been answered. Now, as the procession appeared up on the road, he could pick out the foreign woman, riding amidst the crowd on a white donkey. The train of people then halted just in front of the gathered children – he now saw her face and heard her voice for the first time. Yes, that had to be her, Misak thought, it was simply impossible that she wasn't his mother. His heart simply rushed to embrace the woman from the moment his eyes caught sight of her.

The assembled children broke into song for her, but Misak was too anxious to utter a sound. Then Mr. Eckart got down from his horse and walked along the row of kids, seemingly intent on leading "her boy"

* Sunken roads are a common feature in many underdeveloped areas. They are essentially unpaved roads which cut through and down into the landscape, leaving earthen embankments on either side and creating the impression of passing along an uncovered tunnel.

forward to meet her. But no, Misak thought, there had to be a mistake as Mr. Eckart walked right past him. Instead, the German brought forward another boy, one of the orphanage's least gifted, who had a large, unshapely head, and was, in all regards, a rather dumb and unattractive child. The woman clearly appeared disappointed as an altered expression momentarily descended across her face, but she soon smiled again and patted the boy on the cheek.

Misak, on the other hand, could not smile because for him the sun had disappeared, and it would not shine again for days. He felt that what had happened was unfair. The other boy already had a mother, be she unkempt and without schooling, but still a mother, and she suited him well. But why should he have one more when Misak was alone? And though Mr. Eckart pledged she would be a mother for them all, there were after all three hundred children. No, Misak was convinced he would derive little solace from her. He felt, in fact, an intense disappointment that would not easily be overcome.

The months passed, and the following summer, Misak sat for his exit exams at Urfa's school. Asadur, the little boy with whom he shared a bed on his first night at the orphanage, stood alongside him when Miss Shattuck, following the ceremonies in the church, handed them each their diplomas. Now the question was whether they should continue their studies and enroll in the American college in Aintab* or simply learn a trade. Ohannes Effendi wanted them both to attend college, but the orphanage had funds to send only one of them, so in the end it was Asadur alone who went. Misak favored this outcome as he wanted to become an artisan and felt unable physically to pursue academic study. He chose, instead, to become a cobbler and subsequently began subsequently his training in the orphanage workshop.

Misak now entered the ranks of the older apprentice boys, who to some degree were in conflict with Ohannes Effendi. When the five original orphanages were united under two house fathers and were moved into a large khan outside the Samsat Gate, he had assumed responsibility

* The college, officially known as the Central Turkey College, was founded during the 1870s by the U.S. missionaries of the ABCFM. It continued to operate at its Aintab location until the Great War, during which the missionaries resolved to transfer the campus to Aleppo in present-day Syria.

for Hrumian's boys as well as his own. That had become too much of a challenge for him, as he could not manage so many children, and the older boys were naturally the most difficult. Among them was Misak who was keen to make trouble, as he felt tired and unsettled by too much school work. Adversity made him testy and quick-tempered, and since Ohannes Effendi did not tread carefully, Misak soon bristled with defiance. At times, those feelings so intensified that Misak's emotions were left quite in tatters, even though, after a little contemplation, he should have realized that he needed to be careful since he could not as yet support himself through his work nor be sure to find a cot in Krikor's house.

Then one day things came to a head. Misak had so lost his temper, not only with Ohannes Effendi as happened frequently, but also with the Danish lady who visited the orphanage daily. Yes, he had quite openly defied her. And though she left that evening without saying a word, there could be little doubt that the next day he would be expelled, for such behavior was quite unheard of at the institution. "Misak must be out of his mind!" declared the other boys. "And what harm," they asked, "has she done to him?" "Well, regardless," the boys concluded, "he'll be gone by tonight." They therefore all made sure to say their goodbyes; his fate was seemingly sealed.

Misak spent much of the subsequent day in anticipation. Naturally he regretted his conduct; there was no good reason for his outburst and he knew it could have serious consequences. But he still refused to admit fault, favoring rather to leave without a word or even face starvation now that the struggle had ensued. He was, in short, itching for a fight. And he wished that things would soon come to a head as his nerves were ever strained under the tense circumstances.

Finally, in the early evening hours one of the boys rushed into the workshop, announcing through the doorway, "She's arrived!"

Misak immediately dropped the shoe in his hand; the anticipation was now unbearable. Within ten minutes he was summoned: "Misak is to report to the upstairs office." He subsequently bid farewell to the head craftsman as he was sure a return to the workshop was unlikely.

But it was indeed a challenge to stand alone before her in the office. She refrained from yelling and just looked at him intently; it was as if his appetite for a confrontation vanished without a trace.

"Are you ill, Misak," she asked, "or are you otherwise unwell since you are carrying on in such a manner? You really ought to tell me what's wrong. After all, I want to help you if I can."

The words quite swirled around him, and they so surprised him that he hardly understood their meaning. But her voice was warm and gentle. It was namely the tone which touched him to the core. However, what could one say? He found it impossible to explain all that ailed him. Not a word could he utter, not even the obligatory "forgive me" that all the boys were so well-mannered to declare when needed. But in this instance it was unnecessary as she seemed to understand his feelings quite well without him uttering a word.

"Yes, yes, Misak," she said reassuringly, "you're excused but always remember that I am your friend."

Overwhelmed by these words he just managed to kiss her hand before he stood, once again, outside her door, feeling embarrassed and confused. The older boys had gathered downstairs in the workshop to discuss the situation; they were, in fact, so preoccupied that they failed to notice Misak when he returned. He came in and quietly sat down with a peculiar expression on his face. And when the others learned how things had turned out, they too fell silent and went their separate ways. But Misak now felt it was difficult to remain agitated; for much as he was still filled with spiteful feelings, just a tender smile sent his way could make them all dissipate.

In the spring of 1905, when the Danish lady was in Lebanon to recuperate, Misak left the orphanage, initiating for him a time of troubles. During those days Krikor was away from home, and Chanum was on bad terms with her sisters-in-law. She struggled to cope, living with them under the same roof, and now, as Misak rejoined the household, their collective burden grew. Ideally she would have taken Kevork and Misak with her and moved elsewhere, but how were they then to survive? That persisted as a key question now that times had changed significantly since the massacres. Urfa had entered a period when prices on the necessities of life rose while salaries were about the only area that did not keep pace with everything else. Hardest hit by these events were the Armenians, for they depended on their physical labor, making them particularly vulnerable. The Turks, in contrast, had all the advantages on their side. The law in no way protected the Armenians against abuses and, now after the massacres, when almost all capital and real property were in Turkish hands, they could exploit and further disadvantage the Armenians at will. Armenians had even to kiss the hand of the Turk and just be content if their lives were spared! And as everything they needed to survive was simultaneously getting more and more expensive, life in the Armenian Quarter became almost unbearable; everyone was plunged into hopeless poverty. Even master artisans could barely make ends meet, and apprentices and youths were pressed and exploited in the extreme.

Misak was at his wit's end as none of the cobblers needed his services. Ultimately he did find employment with an Armenian dry-goods dealer, but it earned him only fifty øre* a week and his daily supper. He had no choice but to stay with Chanum despite feeling terribly humiliated over being ordered around by her sisters-in-law. After all, he needed a roof over his head. And that was just about all which he received. In the beginning, he had taken a piece of bread before leaving for work every morning, but one day he found the cupboard bare. The bread was gone, and one of the women stood there laughing at his expression of disappointment. Soon his already fragile health fell victim to those conditions; he started to cough up blood and could only just make his way in the mornings to his job at the merchant's stall.

Then one day, as Misak was at the store, one of his friends turned up. The latter's good mood really surprised Misak who failed to see any reason to be joyful. "Misak," said his friend as soon as he stepped inside, "she's come home and asks that you visit her on Sunday." The "she" in question was the Danish woman, as everyone knew in their circle, and in her they placed all their hopes when something troubled them. Now Misak's spirits too soared; he felt as if he could already see a way out of the misery.

* Half a Danish crown.

When Sunday finally came, he made his way to her house as early as seemed appropriate. Upon seeing him, however, her face took on a curious expression. He understood well that words were unnecessary; his friends had clearly told her all about him.

"Times have surely been tough for you, Misak," she observed, "and it is high time for a change. I have found a finishing-school for you, namely at the home of Nerses, where you can stay. I'll be sure to cover the costs."

Nerses, the man in charge of procurement for the orphanage, already cared for another boy that she had placed with him and paid for. In this new home, Misak's condition soon improved, and he stayed there a year during which he simultaneously served as an apprentice to the merchant. His particular business, to which Misak now became exposed, was one of significant dimensions. The brothers Kullahoghlian presided over one of the few well-established Armenian merchant houses in Urfa. The eldest brother, Hagob Effendi, was a handsome man who looked dapper in European clothes and knew well how to carry himself at formal gatherings. At times he also traveled to Aleppo to oversee their procurements in the area. The other sibling, Nasar, was a bit of a ruffian, but his responsibility was to deal with the Kurds and Arabs with whom he did good business.

It was a motley clientele who frequented the store. And for Misak there was much to experience and learn. Armenians were, of course, among the customers. They were experienced and understood well the true value of the merchandise; they simply asked the store owner what he had paid for the goods, and it never occurred to him to deceive them. He quoted them the wholesale price and subsequently they jointly negotiated an appropriate markup until an agreement was reached.

Rich Turks also frequented the store. Their presence always put the merchant on his toes, being sure to always offer them a chair, coffee, and his utmost attentions. Only at the end did they broach the subject of business. He charged about twice what he wanted for the goods; the Turks haggled and gradually the price went down. When the Armenian refused to go any lower, the Turks turned and feigned to leave. But once stopped at the door, an agreeable price was reached, one which the merchant had already set for himself at the outset. He then did not neglect to stress that he was actually losing money on the deal, but was ultimately quite unconcerned in view of their special friendship.

Immediate payment would, of course, have been better for the merchant, but instead a credit was issued and it then became an art to find the opportune moment when he could ask for the money without insulting the Turk. Much begging and buttering up was required in this endeavor. For that reason Hagob Effendi joined the Turks at the café to carefully await the opportune moment, and he always had to pretend that it was a particular favor when he received any money. But much of it was, of course, never forthcoming.

Transactions with the rural population followed a different pattern. From them they demanded without batting an eye four times the value and would eventually settle for half that. The amount was then credited as the farmers never had payment on hand. But during the harvest or in the spring, when the sheep's butter was ready, Nasar could be found in the villages securing one shipment of butter or grain after the other. In town each was sold for at least twice the assessed value in the village, and thereafter Hagob Effendi moved to pay his bills with the trading houses in Aleppo, where he too had purchased everything on credit.

This trade with the rural communities was profitable but, at times, when Nasar arrived in a village to collect the butter or wheat, he might find it deserted. A hostile tribe would have destroyed everything. He too risked being attacked personally, having his goods stolen in transit, or simply finding that the farmers would refuse to pay.

Over time, the longer Misak was part of this business, the more he came to loathe it. On such terms, he thought, he wouldn't want to be a merchant; he'd feel compelled to compromise both his soul and sense of honor in order to conduct business in this manner. Yet what alternative path he should follow remained unclear, and he acquiesced in the status quo until a new development forced him to act.

Chapter Eight

An Unexpected Joy

On a beautiful Sunday morning in May, Misak strolled along casually to make his usual weekend visit with her.* Normally several other people were already there when he arrived, and Misak tended to take a seat in one of the spots nearest the door. There he would sit politely with a slight smile on his face and talk only whenever someone spoke to him, so he would not otherwise join the conversation in the room and would eventually leave as quietly as he had arrived.

But on this day as he motioned to leave, she held him back; he would need to stay until all the others had left. Misak now reviewed pensively all that had passed during the foregone week, but he failed to pinpoint anything that he had done to raise concerns. Yet doubts persisted in his mind. These Europeans, after all, were so peculiar and at times took serious issue with things that wouldn't trouble others. Eventually, after everyone had left, she turned to him.

"Misak," she asked, "will you accompany me on a trip? I'll be gone for most of the summer."

This question was entirely unexpected, but his enthusiasm was hardly wanting.

"Misak," she continued, "you should think carefully about this because it won't be easy. My health is poor and I require much assistance."

"Do you believe you can take on that responsibility? After all, you're not really familiar with my ways and needs."

Her words embarrassed him and he even felt a little hurt by the notion that he might not be up for the task. In fact, he felt desperate to prove himself. And what did such a trip not mean for a young person who was otherwise confined to the same, limiting town? He therefore pledged assuredly that he'd do his best.

---

* "Her" is Jeppe and the year is 1906.

Over the next few days, Misak felt as if he were floating on air, as he so looked forward to what was about to unfold. The merchant [his employer] was, in contrast, less pleased. It was not every day that he hired as trustworthy and talented a person as Misak, but discussing the issue was rather pointless. Misak in no way considered returning to work as his head was filling with plans of adventure. The trip's destination was Kharput,* a town deep in the heartland of Armenia proper. And naturally, he thought, that should be near Musch,† possibly giving him an opportunity to visit his birthplace and track down some relatives.

So preparations began apace. Mr. Künzler accompanied Misak to the passport bureau, and his presence was indeed fortunate because on his own the boy wouldn't have gotten his papers in order for months. In fact, his name did not even appear in the government's registry. Yet this was quite common as recorded names were subject to the military tax since birth, so no one frequented government offices unless to address a pressing need. And when the name was then belatedly added to the official records, one needed to "warm" the hand of the particular bureaucrat to secure his discretion. Mr. Künzler, of course, understood all these formalities and was also good friends with Khalil Effendi, head of the local registry office. Jointly, these factors smoothed the process, and a passport was issued.

Meanwhile, a few other Armenians had also secured passports and they now sought to accompany the travelers and enjoy the protections of a European. As word spread, a small, impromptu caravan soon assembled, the services of a caravan guide were secured, and, with preparations finalized, the designated, mounted gendarme appeared. He was supposed to escort the European lady and serve as the government's guarantee of protection. Misak felt privileged by the escort, but the gendarme's presence was also an added burden; the boy's responsibilities would include preparing the officer's food, adding to his already quite

* Also commonly spelled Kharpert, Harpoot, or Harput; it is an ancient Armenian town, today known as Elazig, and located about one hundred miles north of Urfa.

† A town about one hundred and fifty miles to the northeast of Urfa and approximately thirty miles to the west of Lake Van in the heartland of historic Armenia.

numerous other duties. In fact, he was rather taken aback by just how many items such a lady needed on a trip. And much preparation and running around to make purchases and finish packing nearly compromised Misak's mood before they finally set off.

But once underway the joys of the countryside took center stage, his eyes seeing far into the distance and no longer confined by dreary urban walls. Nearest the town were pretty vineyards and gardens as well as many people on the roads. Misak now sat relaxed on his mount after the many tasks tied to their departure and gladly took in the natural scenery and the hustle and bustle. Gradually the landscape changed, the trails became more deserted, and they passed through torched villages. At the store, he had often heard tales of robberies and attacks, but it was something else to actually see the destruction.

In time, they came upon a party of Kurds who asked them if they had encountered anything suspicious in the valleys just traversed. These men expressed concerns about traveling that way as only the day before a whole caravan disappeared in the area. This news unsettled everyone in Misak's caravan. The gendarme and the Kurdish caravan guide rechecked their guns, and the Armenians nervously fidgeted with their pistols tucked into their belts and, as they rode on, they began to tell each other tall tales about outlaws, one more hair-raising than the next. Soon, they thought, their eyes saw a rifle barrel poking out from behind every rock.

The tales painted a fearful picture of one man in particular, a Kurdish chief, who from his village on the plain spread death and destruction across the region through his band of fighters. Misak had certainly heard mention of the name "Ibrahim Pasha"* and taken in the often conflicting stories about him, but those stories had at the time seemed more like tales from a distant land. Now, however, myth was being replaced by a frightful reality creeping ever closer. The boy felt he needed answers about this man, as it seemed strange that a robber commanded disciplined fighters whom he dispatched on raids, and stranger still that their escorting gendarme feared the chief. And those fears were very real,

* "Pasha" was the senior most title bestowed on Ottoman civilian and military officials. The Kurdish chief was by the early twentieth century a powerful local leader and a sultan loyalist. He generally remained faithful to the Ottoman central government until the Revolution of 1908.

as Misak soon discovered when he mentioned Ibrahim Pasha's name to the officer, prompting jittery body language and nervous assurances that the pasha was a man loyal to the sultan.

"If only he were blind in both eyes," uttered the caravan guide. "I once had fifty beasts of burden that his men stole from me. But now I'm but a poor man traveling the trails behind the few animals that remain."

In contrast, one of the Armenians in the caravan had served for a few years as a village priest in Garmuch. He took Misak aside and impressed on him the need to choose his words carefully. One could never be sure how others would react to a slip of the tongue, and "Ibrahim Pasha" was a dangerous subject. Incidentally, he continued, the Armenians of Garmuch liked the Kurd as nowhere else did they enjoy such security as in "his lands." On one occasion, he recounted, some Kurds had attacked and robbed an Armenian who had arrived in one of the villages to trade. And upon his complaint to the pasha, the guilty men were beaten severely and all the stolen goods restored to the merchant.

These conflicting stories confused Misak ever more as he contemplated the matter, but he was soon jolted from his thoughts by calls from the lady. "Look, Misak," she gestured, "there's a flock of goats up on that hill. See if you can get me a little milk."

Misak thought this an odd request, but he had after all pledged to do her bidding, so off he went to get the milk. The caravan halted and everyone gathered to confer. When the shepherd saw the people down below gesturing in his direction, he became quite afraid and motioned to flee with his flock. This prompted the gendarme to give chase in the hopes of earning greater *bakhshish** through his favors towards Chanum Effendi [Jeppe]. Within moments the shepherd was made to stop and he felt greatly relieved to learn that the strangers wanted nothing more from him than a bowl of milk.

Misak next helped the lady off her horse, as she wanted a bit of a stroll with him at her side. She also wanted to know what everyone had been discussing previously with such avid interest, so soon the two of them were exploring this same subject further.

* It essentially refers to a gift, tip, bribe, or payment made for services.

"Isn't it strange," she mused, "that the sultan is so determined to destroy his own lands? The Kurds are after all capable enough as brigands without him needing to give them arms to enhance their efforts."

"Yes," Misak agreed, "you're absolutely right. But Abdülhamid is not just an evil man, he is also reputed to be sly as a fox, so he must be up to something. I just cannot put my finger on his exact designs."

"I don't know either," she agreed, "I have after all only been here in the region for a couple of years and it takes time to familiarize oneself with all the particular circumstances. But I've heard wise people say that the Kurds wanted to revolt, so the sultan opted to align some of the most capable chiefs to his side by giving them certain privileges in exchange for suppressing other Kurds and keeping his coffers filled. One advantage they received was command over the Kurdish soldiers. The Kurds generally avoided military service with all their might, but it was easier getting them to serve in the Hamidiyen regiments that were now established and commanded by these chiefs. Service in such units suited the Kurds far better. It pleased them to raid while in uniform, not to mention the privilege of being handed new weapons to carry out their duties."

"In this region," she continued, "it was Ibrahim Pasha who sensed the winds of change and in a timely fashion sought to join the sultan's cause."

"All right," the boy wondered, "but why does he sometimes torch villages while at other times he moves heaven and earth to recover just a solitary stolen chicken?"

"Well, that isn't something he does at different times but rather in different locations," she answered. "The lands down around Veranscherir* belong to him and are populated by the Milli Kurds,† who of course are his fellow tribesmen. In that region he is a good lord who cares like a father for his subjects."

"Then it must be good to live there," remarked the boy.

* Also spelled Viransehir; it was the reputed home base of Ibrahim Pasha and located some fifty-five miles east of Urfa.

† The Milli Kurds were a confederation of Kurdish tribes. They were generally resident in today's southeastern Turkey and northern Syria.

"Yes, it is nowadays," answered the European, "however, in the past it was anything but good, when they were dominated by the Karagetchili Kurds who habitually pillaged and burned the area so it almost became a desert. But now Ibrahim Pasha is clearly ascendant since he commands the soldiers while the Karagetchili chief is the sultan's enemy and must fend for himself as best he can. At present, it is his tribal members who must flee from their villages."

"Is this region," asked Misak, "Karagetchili land?"

"No, it isn't," she shot back, "this area is even worse off as it lies between the rival tribes who quarrel over its control."

"How is it that the Kurdish tribes," the boy continued, "are so torn by infighting and motivated to devastate?"

"Well," she replied, "what can I say? They are in an age of development when peoples act in this manner. After all, youths also always feud with each other."

"Age?" Misak asked probingly. "But they seem to get just as old as everyone else."

"Yes, the individuals do," the lady affirmed, "that is indeed true." But their race as a whole is another matter. Besides, I'm not even sure if age is the main factor because in Europe people carried on in a similar manner just a few centuries ago. However, they are not much wiser now, as tribes have just grown into nations, that's the main difference. The pillaging of the past is now termed war, which is more infrequent since so much needs to be mobilized, but then each conflict causes greater destruction when it ensues."

"But in Europe the land is surely not similarly made a desert?" Misak asked.

"No, not in that way," she replied. "They instead compete bitterly over land and for a free hand to expand."

"But in that case," the boy continued, "why don't they come and occupy these vast lands? Just think how much appetite could be satisfied."

"'They', you say," remarked the lady. "Who are 'they'? The representatives of the Great Powers sit in Constantinople, keeping watch on each other, careful to deny any one an advantage, and the sultan understands this dynamic well."

"Do you know his motto?" she asked the boy.

"No, surely not," he replied.

"He says," the lady observed, "that it's all about setting the dogs on each other, leaving the bone to oneself."

Misak laughed. The Oriental expression clarified things for him much more so than any longwinded explanation. He imagined the two Kurdish chiefs as a couple of dogs fighting, and the sultan sitting on the sidelines and enriching himself, because it was clear to the boy that a share of the pillaged riches went directly into the ruler's coffers. But Misak's mood then darkened as he considered all the suffering that these conditions inflicted on the land, and his thoughts turned to his people who were tormented and being crushed by the infernal machine of oppression. They couldn't offer any resistance and were simply trampled upon.

"How heavy a burden," he finally lamented, "to be an Armenian here in Turkey."

"Yes, that is so true, Misak, but let's not dwell on that as nothing good will come of it," the lady answered. "I suggest we get back on our mounts as I'm tired of walking. Let's then sing a little, that'll surely lift our spirits."

Towards evening they reached the inn, but it was in such a poor state that they prepared to camp under the stars. Misak was soon quite busy as there was so much to do before dinner. He needed to put up the lady's travel bed, make tea, and otherwise attend to her as she was weak, tired, and required much assistance. So, when she told him, just before going to bed: "Thanks so much for today, Misak. You have seen well to my needs," he was as happy as if someone had given him a gift. What a great feeling, he thought, to care for such a person; if only things were always so.

The following morning, Misak straggled a little behind his fellow travelers. Suddenly he sensed a certain nervousness creep over the caravan, and only the lady seemed to ride on in the lead without a care. Misak soon discovered why the mood was shifting as two Hamideyen officers appeared from a side trail with a small troop of their soldiers following not far behind.

The officers proceeded to follow the caravan and, as Misak rushed to join it, he quickly closed the distance to the two men. However, they ignored the boy's proximity and calmly continued to converse with each other in Kurdish. Misak had learned the language quite well during his time in the merchant's service and was rather frightened by their words, as one suggested to the other nothing less than to kidnap his mistress.

"It'll be the simplest of actions," he said confidently. "The others will naturally all run away, and if not we'll easily wipe them out."

"That's true," agreed his fellow officer, "but what about afterwards when her people set out to search for her?" Then we can look forward to rotting in prison if they don't hang us right away."

"Don't worry! Who," the first one asked dismissively, "should capture us? We are the pasha's men after all, and I know that he can certainly protect us."

"But he won't," the other officer shot back. "Don't you know that he has many friends among the foreigners, so he'll be among the first to search for her. Let's forget this foolhardy ploy as there are many other girls we can seize, and all without anyone lifting a finger against us."

"Other girls!" the scheming Kurd protested. "Haven't you noticed her white skin and rosy cheeks? It isn't everyday such a girl comes along."*

But the second officer held his ground and prevailed on his companion to turn off the road and thereby abandon the dangerous venture. For Misak it was as if he'd been awoken from a nightmare. Fear had gripped him so tightly since he hadn't been able, despite his best efforts, to sense even the faintest hope of preventing the frightening plot. And so for some time afterwards he remained out of sight until his composure was restored. He didn't want her to know the danger she'd faced because such news would only undermine her feelings of safety and happiness as they rode on, and that atmosphere, Misak believed, was imperative if the trip was to benefit her at all.

The next day, Diyarbakir's jagged city walls appeared before them in the distance across the plain. In Urfa they referred to it as the "Black City" because "the stones were black, the stray dogs were black, and the people were black." This seemed accurate as regarded the stones since the whole region was dominated by volcanic flats and the buildings were constructed using a type of very hardened, black basalt. Also the strays, essentially the city's cleaning service and concentrated in packs along

---

* Jeppe, born in 1876, would have been about thirty at this time, so hardly a "girl" but still young.

every street and alleyway, were without exception all black. The people, however, were not any darker than in Urfa, but it was, of course, their souls that were deemed black; that blackness had just not as yet rubbed off on their bodies.

In addition, there was an obvious difference between the two cities. Everything in Diyarbakir had an aura of prosperity, reflected unmistakably in both the houses and the people, whereas in Urfa all one ever saw was stark poverty. These conditions were much as Misak expected, as he had always thought of Diyarbakir as a rich town since the silk fabrics they sold in the store back in Urfa originated from here.

Silks had always attracted Misak's attention, often imagining how the valuable material came about right from the day when the silkworm first emerged from its tiny egg. Those involved in this trade, he thought, must get rich since they need do no more than their own work and not depend on others. If only people in Urfa could do the same, they probably wouldn't have been so poor. After all, what future was there in cotton weaving upon which their lives depended? Cotton, cultivated all around Urfa, was cheap enough, but the spinning was done elsewhere, resulting in the needed, imported thread being almost as expensive as the finished cloth. Thoughts of the poor pay that weavers received for toiling all day saddened Misak a great deal. And despite being so young, his thinking was quite mature, having been shaped by witnessing the suffering all around. His ongoing ties to the missions and their efforts to improve the conditions of the Armenian people by opening new and improved fields of work similarly influenced him, and he enthusiastically supported those programs and hoped to contribute to their success.

Soon after having helped his mistress settle in at the mission house, and having cleaned himself up after the long journey, Misak was ready to head out around town and explore it thoroughly and especially learn all he could about the silk weaving trade. Soon he came upon the bazaar, the place where real men in the Orient preferred to spend their time. But no one, of course, took any notice of him, as all the people rushed about focused on their own affairs and business. Misak felt rather out of place and even quite puzzled by the fervent activity.

Suddenly a voice called out to him and, when he looked around, he saw that it was one of his friends from the orphanage who had found employment in a shop in Diyarbakir. This encounter set things in motion as the boy had family and knew friends of friends in the local silk trade, so during the next few days of rest in Diyarbakir, Misak accomplished his wish, getting to see examples of both silk spinning and weaving. He now knew without question what he wanted most in life: to learn this industry and transfer those skills to Urfa. His enthusiasm fed his lively imagination, and he speculated about how all the poor families of his adopted home town would prosper through the trade. And the factory owner, who was, of course, Misak himself, would diligently develop the business and care well for his workers. However, such thoughts were all well and good, for how was he to learn the trade? It would be both time-consuming and costly.

But only momentarily did he allow the dream to fade in the face of grim reality. Whether or not things were to work out, he thought, the vision persisted in captivating him. At the very least, he needed to confide in the lady, his friend. And what a friend she'd become; it was striking how well she understood his deepest thoughts and how freely he could speak to her after overcoming his shyness. She too was much interested in the silk industry, and when she wasn't too tired, she trekked along with him from one workshop to the next. In her company, everything went more smoothly, as the master artisans felt honored by her visits and were eager to explain their business affairs. She also bought quite a large quantity of fabric, which helped to give Misak a certain status since the merchants came to see him as somebody of note. However, despite this benefit, he remained distant from the coveted goal of realizing his dreams.

After a few days, they set off once again, this time in the company of the Dr. Vischer,[*] the Swiss doctor from Urfa's hospital. They were to vacation together near a small lake high in the Taurus range.[†] Their journey took them through the spectacular mountains, along a path with rushing streams and intermittent rest stops under the cooling shade of

* Dr. Andreas Vischer (1877-1930) was a Swiss national who served as director of the German missionary hospital in Urfa for a decade before the war (1903-1914) and again for one year afterwards (1919-1920).

† This highland plain region is still today a popular destination for rest and recreation.

great trees. Misak hardly knew where to look as there was so much beauty to take in and, when they finally reached the lake, he became so enchanted that tears of joy streamed from his eyes. In a wonderful grove at the water's edge, they pitched their tents, and it was here that Misak would come to experience some of his life's most joyous hours.

In fact, he never lacked for companionship either, since the missionaries from nearby Mesereh[*] had brought along with them numerous young Armenians, and they all enthusiastically sought him out. His mistress had also rented him a boat for the duration of their lakeside stay, and many were eager to join him for trips on the water. Misak was also an entertainer, knowing well how to tell stories and encourage others to share their tales as well, so he soon became the focal point of a small clique. In this setting he listened intently to the stories about the Armenian *fedayi,*[†] those who had left their homes in the villages and had joined together in small bands up in the Armenian mountains from where they now kept up a sustained guerrilla campaign against the Turks and Kurds. Among the young people in the villages there were some who hid pictures of the rebels in their homes and spoke of the men with great enthusiasm. But the majority of people condemned the fighters and their actions and felt that all the community's troubles stemmed from their insurrection. They did not refer to them as brave but rather as dangerously daring, even criminal, so these armed men could, therefore, nowhere publicly discuss their exploits and had always to remain hidden.

Soon Dr. Vischer returned to Urfa, which couldn't cope with his absence any longer, but he'd refused to entertain any talk that the lady should accompany him. She was, after all, yet far from sufficiently rested or strong enough to again assume life's burdens. So the two of them, she and Misak, stayed behind, alone in paradise. One night, as they sat alone

---

* Located near Kharput, the town is also known as Mezreh, Mezire, or Mamüretülaziz. It was at the time an important center of missionary activity, including both German and U.S. missions as well as being home to a U.S. operated hospital.

† An Armenian word derived from the Arabic *fidaiyin* which refers to fighters or those who are prepared to sacrifice themselves for a cause. It is curious to see this term used rather than a strictly Armenian word to describe the irregular forces.

together, he opened up to her. Misak told her his life's story, as best as he could remember, right from the time when he crossed the great waterway* riding in a saddlebag slung over a cow. The lady was captivated and felt intensely how hard it was for him to endure his feelings of loneliness.

"When I stood at the church on Sundays," Misak declared, "and I saw the other children's mothers come and greet them, I so wished that I too had a mother. I felt so terribly abandoned."

For a moment quiet reigned in the tent. Then the lady burst out, "Misak! I love you, and I'll be your mother."

Misak responded with surprise and joy over this unexpected turn of fate that now fell into his lap; a tender kiss on her hand followed. That kiss reflected his very soul, as only Armenians know how to commit themselves to those people who have won their hearts. The pact between the two was now sealed. But what that actually meant neither one saw clearly at that moment; it would take years for them to fully realize exactly what they had promised each other. Through it all, they would face momentous challenges, both from their surroundings and from within their own hearts, but their firm sense of purpose and love for each other helped to overcome every obstacle.

For Misak, the moment was a deep and strengthening life experience. He remembered clearly the day when he had first prayed so fervently that she, who came from afar, would be his mother. On that occasion he had later returned home utterly dejected, but now his prayers had been realized, even far exceeding, he recognized, his wildest expectations. The event served as a cornerstone upon which he would base his future outlook on life, that whatever a person seeks with all his soul's desire and might he shall be granted. Perhaps not at the very moment when he wishes for it, but some day, and maybe differently than expected, it will happen and often in a better and more rewarding manner. That notion gave him great confidence in facing all life's ups and downs.

As autumn approached, the two eventually departed from their beloved Taurus sojourn, leaving behind their many friends as they headed home to Urfa. Their pact, however, did not immediately alter their daily

---

* Jeppe is likely referring to the Euphrates River.

lives, as Misak returned to the home where he'd been residing for some time, and his mother once again settled into her lodgings at the orphanage. Instead, the bond between them would strengthen from within before manifesting itself physically. But together they did set out to plan Misak's future. They resolved that he should learn the silk weaving trade, though it would not prove possible to do so in the near term. After all, if he were to travel to Diyarbakir and live there for several years, it would be impossible for their relationship to ever flourish, something which already seemed challenging. So, they now decided that he should first learn to weave cotton at the orphanage workshops. It would involve many hours of practice to master the trade, but if he learned to weave in one form, it shouldn't be a big leap to the next. Though Misak had to start from the beginning, he harbored so much enthusiasm and such a great ability to befriend both the other apprentices and the master artisans that they all were eager to teach him. Within just a couple of years, he learned the trade and began to think about progressing further in life.

Chapter Nine

Springtime in the Air

The summer of 1908 was a difficult period for Misak. His "mother" had gone on vacation in her faraway home country, leaving him to endure his loneliness more intensely than ever before. Over the past two years, the ties between them had grown ever stronger; it was as if she was part of everything he thought and did, so her absence prompted profound longing. And precisely during this summer something happened that impacted his life significantly, an event which he felt he needed to discuss with her in order to properly understand it.

One day, drummers marched through the streets summoning everybody's attention to announcements by the town criers. The commotion drowned out the clatter of the looms as the voices carried into even the orphanage workshops. People became abruptly attentive and listened. What was relayed was a call for all the town's men to assemble before government house as the *mutassarif* had something new to announce. Immediately the Armenians were gripped by fear since nothing good had ever come their way from that source. Most would have preferred to simply stay home, but perhaps it was best to turn up as then they would at least know their fate. So, at the appointed time, the heads of households made themselves ready, the master craftsmen and their apprentices followed suit, and even Misak rose from his loom and joined the others.

By the time he arrived, a large crowd had already gathered in front of the main government building, and everyone spoke about any random subject other than what was at hand. After all, no one knew if there was a spy right behind them. Finally the doors to the balcony opened and out walked the *mutassarif* holding a large document in his hand. Along with him were a number of notable Turks, a few of the local Europeans, and the various leaders of the religious communities. Together they constituted the town's elite: Mullah, Anania Vartabed and also the Syriac and Catholic leaders. In silence the crowd listened as the curious document was read aloud, and they became progressively more and more stunned over its revealed content. It, in fact, proclaimed nothing less than the end of Abdülhamid's regime of violence and that the empire now had a new constitution.* "The Ottoman Kingdom," as it was now to be known, was turning its back on the barbarism that belonged to the Middle Ages, and aimed to become a modern, civilized state based on freedom, equality, and brotherhood between all nations and religions living within its borders. The new government condemned and specifically distanced itself from Abdülhamid's misdeeds, particularly the terrible oppression of the Armenian people. The document concluded with a call for all nationalities to work jointly toward the new kingdom's prosperity and growth, and for all to embrace it as their true fatherland.

Once the public reading ended, no one seemed to know what to say or do. It felt almost like a dream; one looked at others and had to mentally pinch oneself in the arm to come to one's senses. Then the *mutassarif* spoke up again and started to explain the recent events further. It was the Young Turks,† a name people had only dared whisper out of fear for spies, who had grown so strong, particularly within the army's officer corps, that they had overcome other opponents and through a coup had taken the sultan prisoner. He remained alive and retained his throne, but was now restricted by the constitution and guarantees that he could not breach it. The next step encompassed plans to assemble a parliament to govern the empire, a process under which all nations and religious communities would have equal voting and campaigning rights.

In the intervening time, all powers to screen mail and to censor, whether official or covert, would be ended. The prisons were to be opened and were not to house political prisoners, only those guilty of misdeeds; all those in exile were to be allowed to return to their homes; all should be free citizens in a free country, enjoying equality before the law and security for life and property.

Again, the crowd listened in silence to these unfamiliar words and struggled to fully grasp their meaning. Then Arsan Bey stepped out

* The Constitutional Revolution of 1908 restored the Constitution of 1876, which had been suspended since 1878 when Caliph Abdülhamid II (r. 1876-1909) assumed the full reins of power.

† They were known officially as the Committee of Union and Progress (CUP).

before the crowd. He was himself a Young Turk, native to Constantinople, but had spent many years in exile in Urfa. Shaking with emotion, he began to speak, finding the appropriate, captivating words. He laid out the land's many misfortunes in the now bygone night, all the oppression, injustice and inhumanity that had been inflicted. Everyone had felt it but had never dared to speak out, and it was as if only now, as the proper words were spoken, that they truly saw their past predicament and felt repulsed by it. Now Arsan Bey greeted the dawning day and described how in all its glory they, the people, should live in dignity, not as slaves in fear of spies and gendarmes, but as free men who could defend their rights. He too spoke to them of people's rights, of which they should now partake, and of brotherhood and what it should mean to put loyalty to the fatherland above loyalty to the various nationalities and religions.

Arsan Bey's words broke the spell. The crowd now understood; his words captivated them, unifying them as one in their collective joy about their new life. And as the Young Turk punctuated his speech by first embracing and kissing the *mutassarif* and then Anania Vartabed, everyone broke into celebration and hugs both on the balcony and down below. Marching music played, people laughed and cried, and in the midst of it all the cell doors in the prison, which was located in the government building, flew open. The freed men filed out onto the square and were almost smothered by embraces from the overjoyed crowd.

Misak stood captivated, dreaming a wonderful dream, in the midst of the tumultuous and emotional sea of people. He saw all the possibilities that now presented themselves for his people and himself, and envisioned the way of life to come: beautiful, cozy homes, bountiful fields and gardens, and a pulsating activity in the bazaar. It was the life of Europe, as he imagined it based on his mother's words, that he now foresaw as their future, weaved into and joined with all the wonders of the Orient. And through this new vision ran a central, golden truth, that his life and own accomplishments were up to him alone now that his hands were freed and his people were no longer enslaved.

A youthful Turk soon shook Misak from his daydream, laying his arm around his neck and speaking to him in kind words and with a smile on his lips. Yes, it was indeed true, the Turks too were part of the new vision and all were now to be friends. Misak immediately returned the embrace.

He recognized the young man, as he came quite often to Kullahoghlian's store, and he'd frequently since passed him on the street. The Turk had also always been rather friendly to him, so much so that Misak at times tried to avoid him. Young Armenian men knew well what it meant when a Turk was noticeably friendly towards them, and, if they wished to live a moral life, they kept themselves as far away as possible from such a man. And even in this festive atmosphere, it was painfully clear to Misak that people who were willing to work and wanted to get ahead should never have too close an association with such degenerates who through idleness were driven to the most unnatural of excesses.* Ultimately, it was better for the Armenians, if they aspired to achieve anything in life, to have the Turks as enemies rather than to befriend them too closely.

So, as Misak pushed through the crowd to distance himself from the young Turkish man, he suddenly came face to face with a peculiar-looking figure. What halted him in his tracks was not the man's dirty, ragged clothes, a common sight in Urfa and one with which Misak was well familiar as the city had over the last year become like a vast poorhouse. Neither did the stranger's emaciated, gray face and shabby hair and beard stand out, but rather it was the man's facial expression, the questioning and seeking stare that caught the boy's attention along with the sense that he ought to recognize the man, though it seemed impossible for him to recall who he was.

The man was seemingly being tossed by the crowd first from one side to the other, while Misak followed closely behind. He felt he needed to learn more about him. Suddenly he heard one of the Armenians from Garmuch call out, "Movses, Movses," and quickly approached. Upon reaching the stranger, the man, now sobbing, threw his arms around him, and at that moment it dawned on Misak who the man was and tears too welled up in his eyes. He remembered Movses from the days when he was a boy at the orphanage, a time when that same Movses was a spirited, vibrant person who was like a breath of fresh air whenever he came from nearby Garmuch to visit a relative who lived at the home. Then one day he disappeared, reportedly thrown in jail. No one asked on what grounds,

* Jeppe is here referring to acts of homosexuality.

as there probably were none, and there never was a trial; he was simply incarcerated.

That was at least five years ago, but here he now stood before them, this peculiar, aged man. Misak did, however, gradually come to recognize his facial features once he'd been alerted to his identity. But what had happened to his spark of life in the eyes and his former posture of strength and vitality? His youthful character seemed broken and unlikely to ever return. That was, in other words, the legacy of the infamous Turkish prisons. If only such injustice could be ended, so that innocents would no longer have to languish in jail without their rights or face trial on flimsy charges, then much would have been won.

The large crowds eventually began to disperse and Misak drifted with the mass of humanity in towards the other parts of the city, soon finding himself in the Armenian Quarter. In the meantime, the Turks had headed in other directions, leaving the Armenians alone on their own streets. In fervent discussions, they now congregated in small groups, all contemplating the day's peculiar events as they all headed towards their communal center, the large Gregorian church. As they reached the main entrance, everyone noticed a curious absence. Ever since the massacres, a Turkish gendarme had always been posted there, his mere presence ever a reminder to them of their fate every time they passed through the church door. Now, however, he was gone. It felt as if they all could now stand up proudly again and take a deep breath as they passed by the vacated spot. Did it symbolize the chain of slavery's demise?

On the church square a few youths stood talking and motioning avidly, and around them were assembled several groups of onlookers. The main speakers were part of Urfa's "intelligentsia," young people who normally were away at college but now were home on holiday. They seemed compelled by the circumstances to inform their unenlightened fellow citizens, and the more they used sophisticated and unfamiliar words, the more excited grew the crowd.

Now Anania Vartabed arrived and together with a couple of priests he filed straight past the crowd and into the church. Everyone followed him inside, and there they gathered closely side by side, as the hymns and litanies of this mass of gratitude filled the room.

Then Anania Vartabed spoke:

"My children! It is significant and unique events that have brought us here together today and for which we thank God. Truly we could not have imagined such news would ever be heard by us. We are promised freedom, us of all people, on whom the burden of servitude weighed so heavily. We are to have the right to speak, write, and sing what we wish; we shall be able to travel unimpeded from one town to another, and even journey out of the country without any hindrance. We are to be protected by the law so that no one can ever again take our lives, our property, or our women. We are even to participate in the nation's governance and our young men are to serve as soldiers, carry weapons like the Muslims, and have equal access like them to the highest offices in the land."

"It sounds unbelievable," he continued, "much too good to be true. We must ask ourselves whether this is a dream or if we truly are awake. Our archenemy, Abdülhamid, has fallen, brought low by the Young Turks, those who now promise us all these wonders. Let us believe and hope that they mean it truly and genuinely, but, my children, let us not become wrapped up in illusions. At best, much time will pass before these ideals can be realized."

"Even if the government in Constantinople," the old man cautioned, "issues the grandest orders, who is to implement them? It must fall to those bureaucrats who also carried out Abdülhamid's decrees. They [the new regime] don't have enough new men to occupy even the most important posts. And will those officials who have become accustomed to enriching themselves through bribes be disposed to mend their ways? I don't think anyone believes that."

"Will everyone not always adhere more to their own interests and those of their friends than the laws of the land? And will those peoples who through so many generations have been the rulers, those who were permitted to take from others and act as they pleased, will they now willingly surrender those privileges and deal with us on an equal footing? They will never do that, and if the Young Turks attempt to compel such change, the whole country will turn against them."

"So, my children! Keep from expecting too much, as you will only be disappointed. And disappointment only breeds bitterness and unconsidered, harsh words, which in turn sparks ill will in those on the other side. Know well that we must be as cautious as before.

"Rejoice instead in the easing of our people's fate. Benefits will not fail to appear if just we proceed wisely and with restraint. A new day is dawning and much that has been trampled will be able to grow again. Go with God," the cleric concluded emphatically, "and live joyfully and without worry!"

Along with these closing words, he had lifted his hands to bless the congregation kneeling collectively before him. The choir joined in and with the singing of the final hymn, the people filed out of the church. The senior members of the congregation accompanied the *vartabed* up to the community hall; many others lingered in groups on the church square, while most everyone else headed for home. Misak was among that latter crowd. But as he passed one of the groups on the square, whose core consisted of some of those young intellectuals, he stopped for a moment to listen to their conversation.

"Well," said one of them loudly, "what else can you expect from these old servile minds? They of course believe that we must always bow and crawl before the Turks, but we, the youth, will show them different. We, after all, are people too and we don't cower either before the Turks or the black-robed hypocrites."

Misak then quickly walked on, as he frankly felt those words left him quite unsettled. Just as he passed through the Samsat Gate a carriage rumbled by, headed in the direction of Aleppo.* In it sat a solitary figure, and attached to the rear of the carriage was but a small suitcase. It was Arsan Bey, en route from his place of exile. Earlier, as he stood on the balcony embracing the other leaders, he was also taking his leave of them. Immediately afterwards, he made his way through the crowd and rushed to his house. The residence was built by him and beautifully furnished, but he disliked it so much that he'd promised to give it and all its contents to the first of his friends who informed him of Abdülhamid's fall from power. This pledge he honored, so it did not take him long to put his

---

* A city in northern Syria, located well over one hundred miles southwest of Urfa. It was in this city that Karen Jeppe would establish and operate her rescue center in the years after World War One. Jeppe is also buried in the city's Armenian cemetery.

local affairs in order. A carriage was immediately hired, he climbed in carrying just the bare essentials for the journey, and now he didn't even give Urfa a second thought. Instead only visions of Istanbul's minarets and the beautiful coastline of the Bosphorus danced before his eyes, the places he had longed for during his years of exile. And now, as he felt them so close within his grasp again, the longing seemingly intensified, and it was as if his sheer eagerness gave the horses wings. In fact, Misak had hardly time to see and recognize the man before the carriage was gone in a cloud of dust.

The subsequent weeks constituted an emotional time for all, but most significantly for the Armenians. The sudden and so alien sense of freedom virtually intoxicated them; they expressed their joy in the most peculiar ways, especially the young, who acted like foals when first freed from their stalls in the spring. But everything passed without incident, as the Turks were at this time quite subdued and uncertain about the future. There was change underway throughout the empire, a real springtime atmosphere, so therefore everyone understood the position of each community.

One of the concessions granted to the Armenians, and one of lasting significance, was the establishment of a public lecture association. It was housed in one of the classrooms overlooking the church square, and every Sunday after mass it hosted gatherings at full capacity. Speeches were given on any and all subjects, public discussions and debates were held, and there were public readings from newspapers, the latter having greatly proliferated in number. Singing too went on in the new forum.

The lectures were frequently amateurish, and the speakers often relied on flowery language to compensate for the absence of deeper thought. But the quality of song shared no such shortcoming, and it attracted many people to the gatherings. For it was Armenian songs that here could be heard. From every corner, where these songs had been secretly hidden away, they now sprang forth, sung by a boys' choir instructed by one of the school's teachers. It was the words of their great poets that the Armenians now were permitted to hear, sung to the music of their own composers. These jointly spoke to their hearts and strengthened their sense of national identity. That feeling the Turks had never been able to stamp out; it had burned on intensely beneath the ashes that the Armenians had very carefully strewn about to hide it from view. But now the ashes had been swept aside, allowing the flames to again burn brightly. And nothing better reflected these passions than precisely the songs, those which belonged to all the people and shone a light into even the darkest corner.

A few of the Young Turk officials, ordered by the senior committee in Constantinople to travel across the empire to secure party rule in the provinces, made their way also to Urfa. And, on their very first Sunday in town, one of them came to speak at the main church. He highlighted the key events of the revolution and stressed in particular how the Armenian Dashnakists* had on this occasion loyally supported the Young Turks. That, he stressed, was promising for the future and he hoped for good ongoing cooperation with the Armenian community so that the Ottoman Empire could be strengthened internally and present a united front. Abdülhamid's misrule had brought the realm to the brink of ruin, having choked off its natural strengths to the point that not only was the empire dependent on Europe politically but also economically. It would necessitate great efforts to right the ship, and it was particularly in this regard that the Young Turks looked to the talents of the Armenians. The people had to strive jointly to displace the foreigners under the rallying cry of "The Ottoman Empire for the Ottoman people."

The speech was very well received by the audience. And afterwards the crowd made their way from the church to the Dashnak club, where with much fanfare and words of encouragement its new quarters were inaugurated. In earlier days, the Dashnakists had been outsiders and even the slightest suspicion about people's ties to the group was enough to get them thrown in jail or even exiled. However now, under the constitution, everything was different and it was even fashionable to be a Dashnakist.

* They were members of the Dashnak Party (Armenian Revolutionary Federation), a nationalist and revolutionary movement founded in 1890. Intent on resisting the oppression imposed on them by the regime of Abdülhamid II, the armed members of the party staged spectacular attacks against the government, most notably the 1896 takeover of the Ottoman Bank in Istanbul (Constantinople), and eagerly joined forces with the Committee of Union and Progress in a bid to end the autocratic rule of the caliph.

Many, especially young men, joined the club, even though only few of them actually knew what the organization was all about. They felt it was just a party in opposition and that their watchword was freedom, but what they specifically wanted to be free from was unclear. Under the Dashnakist banner, the youths fiercely criticized all forms of authority, the church included. Luckily, however, they only used words, but if people could die from simply being chastised, then there would have been many fatalities during those times.

Yet anyone who studied the Dashnakist program could plainly see that it was in effect part of the socialist movement. It had, however, due to the state of affairs and desperate conditions been focused on just improving the lives of the Armenians. With that singular objective, they had joined forces with the Young Turks and given them their utmost support. And they would remain loyal even as the Young Turks failed to deliver on their promises, continuing to hope for and acting to create the "The Ottoman Empire" that was envisioned and described to them during the early days of revolutionary fervor.

Gradually national calm was restored under Young Turk rule. Only the troops of the Hamidiye had offered armed resistance, but they were soon defeated. Rumor had it that Ibrahim Pasha was taken prisoner, though later accounts alleged that he had fled and subsequently drowned while attempting to swim across the Euphrates.* This formerly powerful man's days were at an end, his name was forgotten, and his sons came to live a wretched existence, while his bitter rivals, the Karagetchili, became the dominant figures among the more independent tribes. Moreover, the provincial government in Mesopotamia largely came to reassert its authority over the Kurds and Arabs in the countryside; the people remained relatively calm, the pillaged villages were rebuilt, and crime along the rural roads in the better areas was limited to only scattered, rare occurrences.

Soon elections for parliament were called and scheduled to proceed in accordance with the most proper European standards. But, however the process now unfolded, the fact was that two Young Turks won the seats representing Urfa, and rumor quickly spread that this pattern was

* The exact manner of his death in 1909 is still disputed.

repeated in most places. There were some who grumbled over these results, but the wider population cared little about it all. To most it was clear that the country needed to be governed, so what did it really matter to them whom Allah chose in his wisdom to perform that task? Self-rule as a concept, it seemed, was still beyond their intellectual horizons.

Of greater significance to many were the allegations that the Young Turks were weak of faith, as they in the early, heady days of the revolution had made plain that they gave all religions little credence. The leadership, however, quickly realized that they needed to address these concerns by emphasizing overt acts of devotion, such as public prayer and fasting. But the suspicions lingered, and it seemed obvious to many that if the Young Turks were true Muslims, it would never have occurred to them to give infidels and believers the same rights under the law. This was an issue that unsettled Muslims widely as they considered the reforms taking hold. On the one hand, people acknowledged that Abdülhamid had erred in dealing with the Christians, as they were not pagans deserving of eradication, but rather "People of the Book," who should enjoy the protection of the true believers provided they lived as subjects and in accordance with the law.* But to now make them equal with the believers was indisputably in conflict with the Sharia.†

Particular controversy surrounded the decision to obligate non-Muslims to serve as soldiers. The Muslim army was after all intended to be used only against the infidels, so what would now happen when it also included infidel troops within its ranks? They would surely all defect and eventually work to assist their co-religionists. After all, in the past only Muslims had served; the Christians had been considered unworthy to bear arms. In contrast, they did have to share the costs of maintaining the

* Jeppe is referring to the so-called *Ahl al-Kitab* (people of the book or monotheists who embrace God-given, recognized scripture). In traditional Muslim practice protected status was extended to those subjects, mostly Jews and Christians, who agreed to accept Muslim rule but also retain their religion in exchange for paying a special poll tax, known as the *jizya*. Those who secured this status/protection were known as the *Ahl al-Dhimmah* or simply *Dhimmis* (people of the covenant or obligation).

† Islamic law, which at its core is based upon the Holy Quran and the Sunna, the collective traditions about the life of the Prophet Muhammad (570-632 C.E.) and the advice/insight he provided to Muslims.

armed forces through an annual head tax assessed to each of them from the moment they were born. This head tax had been difficult to pay for the poor, but it was only a nuisance compared to the burden imposed on the Muslims, as their young men had to serve in the military for seven years, much of it under terrible conditions. The soldiers were poorly dressed and suffered in every regard, but worst of all was that many of them were sent to Yemen in southern Arabia where Turkey was fighting an unending war with the Arab tribes.* There in the deserts, thousands of young Turkish men found their graves, and even those who returned after many years were often so broken down that they never amounted to much of anything.

It was, therefore, little wonder that everyone sought to avoid military service. Those who could, scrounged up the funds necessary to buy themselves free from the obligation, while others tried to bribe their way out of it, or, when all else failed, simply fled. On occasion, and in response to such resistance, state "conscription" raids were instead conducted in the regions of pressing need, targeting the nearest town and those villages closest at hand. The result was repeated scenes of young and even older men being marched off in columns and chained together, escorted by soldiers brandishing bayonet-fitted rifles, and followed by wailing women as they all headed towards the nearest army base. They were to be the future defenders of the homeland.

But now this shameful and inefficient practice was to be abandoned. The time of service was reduced to three years, the soldiers should be treated well, and all should serve, infidel or believer, rich or poor, as no man should be able to buy himself free from service and shift the burden over on the underclass. Only one exception endured: if the conscripted man was a head of household but lacked adult relatives to assume his responsibilities, as the law mandated, then he could avoid service.

Among the Armenians the changes were embraced with enthusiasm. It was now plain as day that their freedom was real, as their young men were to carry arms in service to the sultan. The first in line were the twenty-

* Ottoman control over the Yemen was much contested early in the twentieth century. Serious revolts in 1905 and again in 1911 led to the loss of tens of thousands of Ottoman soldiers. Moreover, Ottoman claims to the region were further challenged by Britain's control of the strategic southern port of Aden.

one-year-olds; the older men were not to serve directly, as they were exempted by the head tax already paid before the constitution's reinstatement. However, while all Armenians indeed seemed thrilled, precisely those individuals conscripted were less so; for many of them such developments were terribly disruptive. In fact, those who were registered as twenty-year-olds in the official records were often at least thirty or even forty, with both personal businesses to run and families, as no one had foreseen ever having to serve in the military.

Fortunately, the stipulation about heads of household was in effect. There were many of them and those who didn't qualify moved quickly to rectify their circumstance. However, not all wives could exempt their husbands from military service; if her father or brothers were alive, she could simply be sent back home while her husband was away. So, the situation called for finding young women who had no male relatives. The mothers of the young men scoured the town's streets and every nook and cranny, and even the poorest girls, who had always been rejected before and pushed aside, were now valued and coveted. They became downright besieged with offers and were married off every single one, however homely and unattractive they may have been.

But it was quite a calamity for the town with the establishment of all these new families. The Armenian Quarter was already overcrowded and there were limited monies for setting up additional households. Poverty and misery spread during those years and ultimately the Young Turks worsened the situation by abrogating the law exempting family providers from military service. Hence, the husbands were forced away, leaving these young wives, many with a child to care for, entirely on their own and without any family to turn to.

So, those Armenians eligible for conscription did everything to avoid having to serve, but failing that and recognizing its inevitability, they did not resort to flight. Instead, on the appointed day, they turned up on their own to their assigned bases. Such behavior impressed the Muslims, so customarily on the day when the local Armenian contingent, as the first of them all, made ready to set off, the whole town, including the Muslims, turned out to watch. The Armenian women had said their goodbyes without making a scene, and now the men marched off in step, singing an Armenian song; out from the barracks, down through the

Samsat Gate, and headed off to Aleppo, the destination for all the region's new conscripts.

It was no wonder that the Young Turk officers praised the Armenians and held up their discipline as a good example for the Muslims. And for a time this had a positive effect, as one no longer witnessed the lines of chained conscripts on the rural roads.

Misak was not part of the first contingent of conscripts called up. When his name was originally registered with the authorities, he was recorded as being a bit younger than he was in actual fact, so matters were not as pressing yet for him. But the day was approaching, and in the meantime the country was in many ways sliding back to its old conditions. Even the army officers, who in the beginning had made every effort to improve the conditions of the soldiers, were failing in their responsibilities. Life in the barracks was again deplorable where brutality reigned supreme. In short, Misak was in complete agreement with his mother that he should not spend three years of his youth in the military.

To that end, they one day managed to convince Chalil Effendi, who had retained under the new regime his position as manager of the passport office, to visit them at the orphanage and present to him their situation. He was happy to extend "Chanum Effendi" that small favor, and he found a way.

Hagob's son, "Misak," as he appeared in the official registry, was dead! After all, such a fate struck even the best in society. Certainly, a couple of male witnesses were also needed to verify the death, but those Chalil Effendi felt confident he could easily produce.

"All right, but under what name," asked the bureaucrat, "does Chanum Effendi now want 'Misak' to be reborn?"

The answer to that question was already clear in her mind. He should be registered as Misael, son of Melkon, from Avran near Musch; that was, after all, his true name and birthplace.*

However, Chalil Effendi was naturally curious about why the young man had used another name, something that now warranted an explanation. Hence, the story followed, about how Misak in his earliest childhood had come to Urfa with some relatives and how he'd been

---

* Misak, born around 1891, would eventually immigrate to the United States after the Second World War and settle with his wife in California.

adopted by Hagob but then was orphaned again by the massacres. All traces of his other relatives had since disappeared.

But just within the past year, an Armenian woman had come from Musch in search of him in Urfa and had, of course, at last found him. She claimed to know his relatives and to have been sent by them to try and find him; she said his mother and sisters were alive and longed greatly to be reunited with him. Misak had his doubts, as he suspected the woman was just seeking some charity from him. After all, he thought, if he had relatives and they indeed cared for him, would they not have sought him out long ago? Yet, he still gave the woman a letter and a little money for the return journey to Musch. And with that, he didn't dwell on the matter again.

However, six months later the *vartabed* summoned Misak and handed him a letter sent from Musch and addressed to him. It was the letter of reply from his family.

It related how Misak's father had been killed in a Kurdish ambush. Afterwards, his paternal uncle, who had survived, married off Misak's young mother but took away her children. They, along with his father's property, belonged to his uncle who had become head of the family. Misak's older brother ran away and rejoined their mother who had remarried and lived in another village; the stepfather subsequently took him in lovingly. Misak, however, was quite little, so him they could not recover; instead, his older sister stayed with him and endured all their aunt's demands in order to look after him. But eventually, as the family opted to move to a different region, Misak's sister too seized the opportunity to flee, abandoning him to his fate.

A few years later, the uncle and aunt returned, this time without the child and claiming that he had died. And only recently, on her deathbed, had the aunt told the full story. All the family's efforts had since been devoted to finding and recovering the missing child.

The letter closed with expressions of gratitude to the foreign woman who had cared for Misak and calls on her to allow them to recover him.

Chalil Effendi was quite visibly moved by the account. It was indeed deplorable that such tragedies had unfolded under Abdülhamid's regime. Thankfully those days were in the past and every one could now tend to his affairs in peace and without fear of being attacked or some such.

Their collective attention now returned to the matter at hand; they had yet to resolve the most important question, namely what age to record for Misak.

"Let's put twenty-nine years old," suggested Chalil Effendi, "because then we'll be sure that he won't be conscripted."

That brought the clerical matter to a close. Chanum Effendi rose and retired to the other room while Misak paid the agreed upon five gold pieces for the services rendered. Coffee was then served after which they parted company according to tradition and exchanged assurances of mutual friendship. Just a few days later, Misak received his new papers, recording him officially as Misael Melkonian from Avran near Musch, aged twenty-nine. In addition, his name was registered in the logbook for visitors; the people listed on those pages were assured of being overlooked on all occasions, unless they inadvertently called attention to themselves.

Chapter Ten

The Final Feast

The winter of 1909-1910 brought about a time of terrible suffering in Urfa, a time of virtual famine. The weather became unpredictable, locusts ravished the region, and grain speculators ultimately aggravated the conditions. Worst affected was the Armenian Quarter, for the people there had essentially only their labor to sell, but prices quickly outpaced their ability to buy even meager provisions.

Gradually, Armenian eyes turned to the potentially fertile wheat fields surrounding the town that either lay fallow or were woefully underproductive due to the inefficient farming methods employed by the Kurds and Arabs. How different things would be if they, the Armenians, were able to farm and live out on the open land rather than in the narrow confines of the Armenian Quarter, where they almost couldn't avoid trampling on each other and where starvation touched them all.

The Armenians brought this proposal to the government, and it was received favorably. Land was plentiful and quite affordable, so it was just a matter of seizing the moment and setting about developing the countryside. After all, the people already resident on the land were still using farming techniques dating to the time when Arabs ruled the region, so the present government could benefit more than anyone if a modern system of agriculture existed in the rural areas.*

A small core of Armenians willing to pursue this venture soon emerged and they managed to raise the funds needed to buy the land. The initial sum was not large, but some of the town's more affluent citizens extended the group credit to help cover their expenses. The pioneers settled along the Euphrates, constructed the simplest of houses, and began laying out gardens and planting the soil.

* The exact period which Jeppe is referring to is unclear. However, the region had been under Ottoman rule for about four centuries by the early 1900s, suggesting, at least in Jeppe's mind, that there had been no significant agricultural improvements in the area for at least that long.

But the Armenian settlers had failed to anticipate the impact of the Arab nomadic tribes. As soon as the first crops appeared in the gardens, the Arabs came calling and behaved not unlike locusts, as they descended on the fields and stripped them bare. And if this was not enough, they allowed their animals to graze in the wheat fields, stole the few possessions owned by the settlers, and generally harmed the farmers in every conceivable way.

The Armenians could not drive off the Arabs, either through enticements or by force. They next turned to the authorities, but they simply ignored the situation, leaving the settlers no other option but to return to Urfa even poorer than when they set out; the debts accrued were to burden them all for the rest of their lives.

Better luck fell to those who sought lands closer to Urfa. Misak was to play a leading role in this effort, having set his sights on a region in the nearby mountains, not too far from Garmuch; this area was a former river bed called Medjeide. There were, in fact, still people around who remembered the river, which during the rainy springtime seasons had filled the ravines and valleys with thundering and foaming masses of water as it rushed out across the plain and emptied ultimately into the Djulab, a tributary of the Euphrates. Left behind, at the foot of the ravines, were scattered boulders and gravel, while across the heights spread lush greenery interspersed with fragrant flowers.

The area, however, did not lend itself to growing wheat, but rather was ideal for the establishment of vineyards and the planting of orchards. Years ago, the place had even been known as a virtual garden, the loveliness and bounty of which was legend. And numerous vineyards were still scattered across the region, many owned by the Armenians from Garmuch, others by the local Kurds or the Turks of Urfa. But presently all were of limited value, largely neglected and overgrown, as the whole area had been notoriously dangerous during the era of the Hamidiye regiments; entire caravans of men and beasts had disappeared, so everyone had avoided traveling through those parts. The scourge of those sinister Hamidiye forces was now at an end, but people still viewed the Medjeide region with apprehension. Only the occasional shepherd ever ventured into the area and then it was simply because he and his flock couldn't resist the lure of the verdant pastures.

Misak had since set his sights on this area and he spoke frequently with his mother about how wonderful it would be to spend the summer months there in the countryside. After all, she didn't cope well with the heat in Urfa, and the sojourns to the Lebanon or the Taurus mountains were ever so costly and inconvenient. So, she was already becoming quite convinced of the soundness of Misak's plan, but she needed just to be prodded ever so gently by external factors. This came in the form of the suffering witnessed during that winter. During those months, they were visited by farmers from the "Black Ruin," a Kurdish village lying just on the outskirts of Medjeide and very aptly represented by that the name. The villagers offered to sell Misak a large tract of land for the measly sum of six Ottoman pounds or one hundred Danish crowns.* It was a matter of pure desperation that drove them to this decision, as they needed money to buy seed grain. In short, it was not every day that such an offer would present itself.

Subsequently, one sunny and clear winter's day, Misak took his mother on horseback out to visit and explore Medjeide. They jointly inspected the site and considered all the local conditions, and upon their return that evening it was decided that the area should be developed as their "colony." They purchased the land and then set about planting grapevines in the river valley during the spring. The vineyard eventually came to number four thousand plants, but that was just on the smaller part of the property.

In the meantime, rumors swirled that "the Girl," Misak's mother, planned to live in the countryside during the summer months. This news caught the attention of everyone who owned vineyards around Medjeide, as now perhaps the soil could again be cultivated in peace. The plows returned to the valleys and Medjeide awoke to a new day; however, the workers still ventured out there fully armed and in groups, as no one yet dared to be alone in the area.

"The Girl" first arrived in early June.† On a hill right by the main road that passed through Medjeide, a large tent, visible from all across the area, was put up; there she moved in and established her household. A lone

* This amounted to approximately twenty U.S. dollars.

† We should assume this refers to 1910.

Armenian shepherd with his goats occupied an area just to the west of the hill by a well, but otherwise not another person stirred in Medjeide.

"She naturally has troops with her," said the Kurds as they looked suspiciously up at the tent above.

Eventually one of them, who happened to have his military documents in order and didn't otherwise have any outstanding issues with the government, climbed the hill to bid her welcome to the area. He soon returned with the surprising news that rather than soldiers there was just a large dog, even though it was indeed a most fearsome animal.

"There're no soldiers!?" they burst out in surprise.

"Just think," they speculated, "her king* must be mighty that he can protect her even so far afield, for she would surely not be here otherwise. We must certainly do our utmost to ensure no harm comes to her, because we will surely be the first to suffer the consequences as we live nearby."

The Kurds speculated intensely about this remarkable "girl," who seemed so utterly fearless. Often there appeared not to be a single man in the camp, only a few women, and the more the tribesmen discussed the matter the more the rumors grew about the means she had at her disposal. Certainly, when her son was with her no one posed any questions, as he was very well armed and had permission to shoot whomever without being held to account. The encampment also didn't lack for weapons, as they seemed to hang from every tent pole, including even a curious contraption that she just turned to fire bullets all around.†

Whoever was anyone in the area made sure to pass their way by Medjeide and visit "the Girl." She, in turn, welcomed them warmly, offered them coffee and cigarettes, and felt greatly delighted by their

---

* "Her king" in those very years was King Frederick VIII (r. 1906-1912). He was the eldest son of the famed King Christian IX (r. 1863-1906), who was known across the continent as "Europe's Father-in-law" by way of the prominent royal marriages and status of his children. Most notable among them were his daughters Alexandra (married to King Edward VII of Great Britain) and Dagmar (married to Czar Alexander III of Russia and was the mother of the last Romanov czar, Nicolai II) and his son Vilhelm, who reigned for fifty years (1863-1913) as King Georgios I of Greece.

† The description suggests that Jeppe perhaps had some type of machine gun at her disposal!

company. They, in turn, felt honored by such treatment and did not neglect, whenever they returned home, to instruct those under their authority to leave "the Girl" and her property in peace. But what exactly constituted "hers"? It seemed that came to include all the territory around Medjeide, and it was hardly worthwhile for anyone to dispute that claim. Further, it soon became evident to all that it was now safe to pass by that way. Gradually, more and more caravans chose to do so, and the Kurds from the surrounding villages too travelled that way whenever they headed to and from Urfa. It was also always so nice that one could stop by there and get something to drink and quench one's severe thirst in the summer heat; after all, there was no other place for far and wide where water was available.

Over time, the demand for water grew as the number of travelers increased. But it was hard work to carry it up the hill by mule from the well far below. Misak realized something needed to be done, so he resolved to buy a large water container, which he set up by the road and everyday had it filled with fresh water. It was still a bit of distance to transport the water, as one now had to go around the hill, but it had been made easier for both the travelers and his mother.

The new amenity caused a stir across the region. Just think, people observed, "the Girl" had acted like a *Sheirat,*[*] overseeing the creation of a well of mercy, an action highly regarded among Muslims. So those who drank from it did not neglect to pray for heaven's blessings to be bestowed upon her and especially her father. Medjeide was now regarded by everyone as a sanctuary, not just during the summer but all year round; attacks or thievery became unthinkable there. It too followed that within just a few years there remained only two or three Muslim-owned properties in the area; all the others had been bought by Armenians and were now managed diligently by them.

Misak was the soul, the spiritual core of all these developments. Bolstered by his mother's regional respect, he wielded great authority and worked tirelessly to help everyone get settled and to seek out new and

* Essentially a woman of respected piety and virtuous action, sometimes also referred to as a female shaykh or shaykha. Water is in Islam symbolic of knowledge but also mercy, suggesting that the construction of a well is a dutiful action to bring good to others and to generally benefit the community.

innovative ways to improve conditions in Medjeide. For instance, the road running from Urfa to Medjeide was no more than a trail, even a poor one at certain points as it was strewn with large rocks. Each summer Misak traveled the road on a daily basis, and he never neglected to get down from his horse in order to roll the odd obstructing rock out of the way. It did initially seem to him rather fruitless to try to remove them all, but soon he discovered that others were doing the same and the road began to gradually improve year by year.

Over time, all those who at first had only taken notice of the “Girl” and her efforts, eventually also came to appreciate Misak. He soon gained a wide circle of friends across the countryside, as he had a great ability to converse with people from all walks of life. And the ideals alive in him and inspired by his mother he understood well to instill in the locals and make relevant to their lives. Thus many a tiny seed, though some were blown wayward, took root in peace time and grew, bestowing on life in the countryside greater comfort and tranquility.

But handling affairs in Medjeide wasn’t Misak’s prime responsibility, as he spent far more time focused on another role. This did not, however, involve politics, as he was never even a member of any political club. In fact, for him these affairs were entirely too strife-riven and dominated by disagreements and limited clarity. He instead turned his attentions towards the town’s commercial life and found much there to inspire his efforts. And while Misak had never learned the silk weaving trade well, as events had repeatedly interfered in his plans, he did successfully complete training in cotton weaving. That expertise had given him much to focus on and accomplish in the town since the local cotton trade, like most, was struggling.

The generation that dominated Urfa’s commercial life at this time was aged only about thirty. Beyond them was the gaping generational hole caused by the loss of older men during the massacres. The younger people had therefore missed out on receiving a shaping influence, since their fathers, the skilled craftsmen and the town’s leading men, had died before their sons could mature and stand on their own. They had consequently grown up either cut off behind the walls of the orphanages from their promised futures or had been condemned to struggle under deplorable conditions, oppressed and humiliated by their enemies, until their passion for life and sense of dignity had been undermined to the point that they cared only to sustain themselves by whatever means possible.

Further, the fairly few master craftsmen who remained labored against the odds to succeed under the domination of the Turks. Their apprentices, of course, fared worse, focusing wholly on just freeing themselves from their masters and becoming independent. As quickly as possible they sought, with a modest, even measly, loan to just set up a small workshop. So, even as the veteran masters struggled, the fate of the novice craftsmen was even more precarious. They were constantly backsliding and ever worsening the quality of work in order to sell on the cheap. And as a consequence, people no longer had any respect for Urfan craftsmanship as it descended deeper and deeper into mediocrity.

Misak recognized these conditions more acutely than others of his generation, for he knew that people could live and conduct their affairs in a better way. He also saw how his mother worked tirelessly to foster better prospects and brighter horizons for the people in certain specific areas. Naturally, he sought to emulate her efforts and strove to achieve them by way of similar means.

After all, for years people had habitually frequented the orphanage's weaving mill to purchase quality textiles. And even though the prices were high, reflecting the workmanship, the buyers were not put off by the expense. Likewise, poor Armenian women, the seamstresses, many with tears in their eyes, were quick to thank the Mission for its work. Only through them, the women asserted, had they been able to keep the clothes on their backs.

But the circle of satisfied customers, those who benefited from access to the mill store, was small since the orphanage was off the beaten path. So Misak was determined to shift the focus to the bazaar, the very heart of the Turkish world in the city; he meant to make his mark in reviving the commercial life of his native town. He started small, in a modest corner stall, but the textiles he offered for sale displayed beautiful patterns and were expertly woven with the best threads available in the region. Quickly his business became well-known and there was no shortage of people stopping by to browse and consider the items on display.

One of the first to stop by was a young Turkish man idling in the market, who found it a nice diversion to chat for a time with Misak. By and by, one particularly fine textile caught his eye and he decided to buy it. He inquisitively asked the price.

"Twenty-five piasters," answered Misak.

Well, sure, the Turk thought, and instead counter-offered just fifteen, because he just figured that they were simply negotiating to reach an "agreed" price of twenty. But Misak didn't budge and rather reiterated that he had already quoted the set, non-negotiable price. This insulted the Turk. He found it a particular case of disregard towards him that Misak was so stubborn, namely towards one not from the street but rather of a good family and someone with whom he should negotiate. While voicing his considerable displeasure for all to hear, the Turk abruptly walked off. A few hours later, however, he came back.

"Seventeen and a half," he barked tersely just as he passed the open stall.

"Twenty-five" Misak shot back determinedly.

Twice more he returned during the day, each time marginally increasing his bid, until finally by evening, just as Misak was closing up, he stopped by a final time, threw twenty-five piasters on the counter, grabbed the cloth in question, and stormed off in a huff, complaining and condemning.

But a couple of weeks later the young man dropped by again, and this time he had a friend with him. The item he had purchased – a washable cloth for a summer outfit – had since been washed and sown to fit, turning out wonderfully, so everyone said. He now praised Misak to the sky, said the material had been well worth the money, and pledged to recommend his business far and wide.

"But why," he asked searchingly, "were you so stubborn? You should have asked for thirty, then I would have offered twenty, and we could have settled on twenty-five."

Misak now answered that such an outcome was exactly what he had sought to avoid. He wanted to conduct business as they did in Europe, where merchants sold goods for a set price and not at twenty piasters to one customer and then at thirty to the next based simply on negotiation or tradition.

"That's not right," remarked the Turk. "One must take all conditions into consideration because how else will one win friends and generally deal with people? In fact, it's never been tradition in the East to treat everyone the same, to do so is simply bad form."

A crowd of passersby now began to build as the discussion continued and people stopped to listen in and take sides. Among them eventually were also two leading Turks, and with their presence the others soon fell silent out of deference. They, of course, wanted to hear what all the commotion was about, so Misak quickly offered them two of the few seats available and set about explaining the situation. They in turn considered the merchandise before them and his words. They also probed him about the cost of producing his fabrics and the specifics about the weaves (these Turks had business sense; under such primitive conditions it was, of course, simpler to understand the market).[*]

"Sure, this is a very solid business you have started, but it's impossible for you to sustain it. After all," they pointed out, "people have little sense. When they find that they can buy almost as much, even comparable, clothes somewhere else for only seventeen-eighteen piasters, do you think they will pay twenty-five for yours even if it might benefit them to do so? And if you don't bargain with them, if you just stand firm, then they'll naturally and understandably be insulted as that's no way to treat people."

"Just act like everyone else," the Turks beseeched him. "After all, why insist on ramming your head against the wall?"

Misak now responded in nationalist overtones, playing on its great contemporary popularity.

"Just look around town!" he urged. "What has this attitude led to? Is there today even one single reputable workshop left here? Hasn't it resulted in us buying everything we need from Europe because whatever we produce no one wants? If we want to get anywhere, we must improve our skills and set up workshops of consequence. That's exactly what I'm working to accomplish."

"You speak the truth," remarked one of the Turks in agreement. "It is utter scandal that we are so at

the mercy of the Europeans. They simply export everything they don't want, thinking that must be good enough for us. We should, in short, support such an initiative as yours."

* This parenthetical is original to the Danish edition.

And in a gesture to emphasize his words and agreement, the Turk took with him a sample of fabric to show his associates over at the café; then they'd have something to discuss.

Soon Misak's place of business became a favored meeting place for the Turks. Many stopped by to examine his textiles and consider his points of view. He subsequently engaged with them in ever more lengthy conversations on topics from business to politics, particularly and naturally focusing on the Ottoman Empire and how best to foster a renewed prosperity and revival. Meanwhile, Misak's commercial fortunes flourished and he could soon rent a larger space, combining workshop and store at the same location. This was a marked improvement because now the customers could also see for themselves how and with which types of materials the fabrics were made.

The nationalist fervor not only buoyed Misak's progress but also that of many others within the Armenian community. In fact, the more secure the Young Turks felt in the seat of power, the more they strove to diminish European dominance over the realm. They felt confident enough in their political and administrative abilities to consolidate control over the empire but were also very conscious that their national economic future depended upon the Christian peoples, particularly on the Armenians as regarded affairs in the interior of the country. So these communities received just enough room to operate and prosper as permitted by the leadership's short-sightedness and inherited, historical tendencies to oppress.

And even as the Armenians had to endure injustice and discrimination, since equality before the law was absent, their lot in life was still much improved from the days before the constitution. The community now grasped those opportunities and seized the moment. If the Turks were of the opinion that they could do without the Europeans, then the Armenians were conversely most anxious to learn from them. Progress was evident in the schools, in commerce, and people's general living conditions.

When Misak set about expanding his workshop, he convinced his apprentices to invest their savings too, and soon his business prospered further as all the employees now had a greater stake in its success. This innovation caught the attention of many, and it did not take long before groups of young men joined forces to found similar cooperative businesses. Misak was also part of the efforts to introduce other new approaches to improve the state of artisanship in the area. Namely, he looked to the proper treatment of his apprentices and was ever attuned to developments in the West, a perspective through which many learned something new.

Misak's attraction to Western ideals did not, however, negate his deep-rooted attachment to Urfa and the people within its walls. But, at times, he felt frustrated by their pettiness and lack of vision even as he still loved them and excused their faults. In fact, he attributed those failings to the conditions, to, as he put it, the shallow waters having allowed nothing but small fish to evolve; under better conditions, fish of greater size and quality would have been the norm.

Ultimately, in 1913, Misak and his mother agreed that now was the time for him to marry, leading them to make preparations to realize this goal. The easiest part was finding a bride because Misak had been secretly engaged for a few years. And even though such private arrangements had no precedent and legitimacy in the region's traditions, as an engagement was by nature as public an event as a wedding, the fact that Misak's mother was European meant that they could take upon themselves certain liberties. It was, in short, an action *à la franca* just like so much else that was cutting edge and gradually, little by little, becoming acceptable.

But regardless, the selection had been made long ago. Lucia, Misak's bride-to-be, was a young girl from the orphanage who had always been close to his mother. Ever since the day when the foreign lady took up residence in the home, Lucia had been assigned to look after her room all the while also being supervised in her training to teach at the orphanage school. Over time, their relationship was reinforced by Lucia's prolonged service as leader of the school alongside also running the household with only one assistant. They all lived together as a family in harmony and joy and naturally sought only to continue that state of bliss.

So when Misak and his mother sat down to discuss the matter of his marriage, the choice was really not a difficult one. They recognized quickly that their lives were good and stable, and that introducing a woman outside their circle might be disruptive to the family. And when she then posed the question to Lucia, she answered, "You know well that my greatest wish is to always remain by your side."

For the next few years, they continued their lives as if nothing had changed, until in 1913 when it was decided that the wedding should go ahead; they selected the 2nd of November as the date, the ten-year anniversary of Misak's mother's arrival to Urfa. The couple was to marry in the abbey church outside the city, and the *vartabed* and Misak's mother had already discussed the preparations thoroughly, aiming to ensure that it be the most wonderful and respectable event possible. The *vartabed* was in particular very attentive to such matters and was intent on demonstrating for the whole town what the Gregorian Church could muster.

The last week before the ceremony was filled with festivities as was customary in the preparations for a large Eastern wedding. One party of guests followed another, eventually reaching a number of around three hundred. The hosts butchered and roasted, cooked and baked, and Misak kneaded the bread dough just as tradition demanded. And everyone in the household got dressed up as finely as their means allowed and busied themselves in helping with the many activities, all the while laughing, singing, and chatting. A great deal of commotion was everywhere afoot; all the while, a steady stream of presents poured in. An Eastern home hosting a wedding simply couldn't be any more vivid and alive.

Amidst all this celebratory commotion, the preparations for the actual wedding day were also unfolding apace. Most vexing was the challenge of securing an appropriate bridal carriage as what was available fell short of the expectations. Urfa's wagons were fine and adequate for long-distance travel, but they lacked charm. There was but one attractive carriage in all the town, but it belonged to a wealthy Turk and therefore wasn't available for their use. So everyone was greatly surprised when the selfsame fine carriage, polished and shining brightly, suddenly passed through the gate and being pulled by a team of magnificent black horses finely decorated with red streamers. The final piece was now in place.

When the day arrived and the wedding train's twelve coaches, all led by the fine carriage, headed off for the abbey church around noon, the entire town's residents were on the streets. The Armenians were out to see the wedding procession while the Muslims were gathered to greet a

Kurdish chief who was arriving that very afternoon. However, the latter community was displeased not to find a single wagon available to receive their guest, and the *mutassarif* felt much aggrieved that he couldn't hire the carriage, but it was, of course, already spoken for and the owner wasn't inclined to renege on that arrangement.

Outside the abbey's walls a gray mass of humanity stood assembled while inside the women's multi-colored dresses brightened the scene. The fortunate ones were the invited guests, the ones who'd been lucky enough to receive the much coveted little card decorated with the *Dannebrog* flag in the corner.* For everyone else, the doors were closed, as there wouldn't otherwise have been room inside for all the guests. However, some gained access by other means. Namely, the abbey housed a number of rooms that were only available to the congregants under specific conditions. So already a week prior to the festivities all the accommodations were reserved for people who wouldn't want under any circumstance to miss the wedding.

Upstairs in the *vartabed's* offices everything was ready to receive visitors. He had made all the proper preparations and was much satisfied to host the occasion. The bride and groom entered and sat down just across from the *vartabed's* official seat, while everyone in attendance greeted each other. And both the *vartabed* and Misak's mother strove to ensure that all were shown full respect and enjoyed all measures of proper hospitality.

The couple, after Eastern custom, did not at all participate in the celebrations. They should instead remain quietly seated and contemplative of the blessed transition they were embarking upon. It was in this somber atmosphere that the memories came rushing back for Misak.

He'd been in that room before, had stood on that very spot where he now sat, in front of the *vartabed's* chair. On that day it hadn't been the young Ardavast Vartabed in the chair, but instead Bishop Choren with his long, snow white beard. Misak was then just a small boy, anxiously clasping Hovagim's hand, just observing while his protector negotiated

* *Dannebrog* is the nickname for Denmark's flag, comparable to the terms "Old Glory" in the United States and "Union Jack" in the United Kingdom.

his fate with his uncle and aunt. That was the day when his future became forever tied to Urfa.

Hovagim and all the events surrounding those days were still so vivid in Misak's mind that they almost overshadowed the present. His mother now gently touched his arm and brought him back, saying softly:

"We should head for the church now."

She then took Lucia, who was clearly moved, by the arm and led her down the stairs. Almost mechanically, Misak followed with Mr. Eckart at his side.

When the wedding party arrived, people had already gathered and been seated in the quaint little abbey church. And despite being filled to capacity, a profound quiet dominated the assembled crowd. Walking in front of the bride and groom were the children of the missionaries, dressed in white and wearing crowns of flowers in their hair and carrying lit candles in their hands. As they reached the main doors of the church, the organist began to play, spiriting the procession down the aisle to the sound of "Your House Shall You All Build."*

That melody and song was, of course, not part of traditional Gregorian Church ritual, but the *vartabed* had translated it from Danish and subsequently allowed for a girls' choir to now sing it as part of the marriage ceremony. He was also himself present, standing in full regalia up front by the altar beside the presiding priest. This too was unusual as only rarely did the *vartabed* take part in such events, but his wonderful singing voice only heightened the beauty of the wedding.

The entire ceremony was, in fact, a great honor for the church, as something so refined and proper was a rarity in Urfa, and the event made a profound impression on all in attendance. But the two who perhaps least sensed or appreciated the full spectacle of the occasion were ironically the couple themselves.

In Urfa, people say that whatever a bride wishes for during the ceremony, when she lays her hand in the groom's, will surely be granted. So as Lucia stood there, she concentrated and prayed intently. What she asked for no one knew, not even her husband, but so focused was she, feeling as if their entire future life together was in her hands, that she

* A famed Danish hymn (*Jert hus skal I bygge*) composed in 1878 by Jacob Paulli.

afterwards couldn't really remember anything of whatever else had happened in the church. In a way it was as if she'd been entirely alone in the building. But she was now convinced that as Misak led her away from the altar, the foundations to their future had been properly and firmly laid.

The day's event too had a profound effect on Misak, giving him an opportunity to come to terms with his past. His memories of Hovagim had been intense, with him reliving everything right from the time when as a small boy he was near death and sat begging before the church gate right up through all that had occurred until this very day, when everyone who was anyone in town now gathered for his wedding. Fate and good fortune had ultimately carried him far over those years and he felt quite humbled by it all. His heart was full of gratitude towards providence and towards the people.

And many of them were with him, in a sense, on this occasion, including all those who had played a role in his life. Hovagim was, of course, dead, but Chanum and Kevork were both there in the church. It was precisely in light of his wedding that he had reestablished his ties with them and had asked his mother to grant Chanum that very place of honor to which she was entitled. Misak was also very much in the company of the orphanage, which he in a sense had never really left. And right behind him stood his mother, she who had been like a fairy tale in his life and had elevated his existence to a level well beyond the commonplace.

How clearly he remembered that day, ten years ago, when he first saw her. It was indeed in the late afternoon, much as it was now on this very day. He could still see her clearly before him, smiling and sitting on her white donkey, and he relived again his utter disappointment when he saw someone else be presented as her son. But what had now become of that other boy? What might that other child have experienced with her? Regardless, Misak thought, she was today his, his above and before anyone else; he had truly secured the prize. That happenstance was after all his life's greatest fortune.

But now on this day she had bestowed on him another woman, and upon sensing her hand in his, a powerful feeling came over him. He was to love and protect this woman, and through her he should become a father. He was essentially having a woman bestowed upon him. A deepening understanding of the moment's intangible significance took hold of him and his hand closed more firmly around hers.

The day's formal festivities were now at an end. Misak led his bride out of the church and, after a brief goodbye with the *vartabed* in his quarters, onwards to the bridal carriage and the procession en route to the evening's celebration. Soon the orphanage's rooms and halls were filled with the many joyous guests.

That day was to be Urfa's last true celebration, the last of my happy memories from there. The promising Young Turk era became like one of those foreboding spring days that sometimes occur in the East, those that begin so wonderfully, but end with utter destruction.

On such a day, the radiant sun rises into a cloudless sky, shining across the beautiful landscape of verdant gardens and vineyards, abundant fields of wheat, and flowering, fragrant meadows. Here the deer graze peacefully and the people go about their day smiling and carefree, taking in the sweet breath of spring.

By mid-morning a few clouds begin to appear, be it only small and innocent-looking white ones, like little lambs, moving across the light blue vault of sky. More clouds follow, and by noon it is overcast. Gradually the cloud cover becomes heavier and heavier and rolling thunder sounds in the distance. People and animals look up for only a moment but then go about their business as such weather is commonplace in springtime.

But the sky becomes ever more ominous and day almost becomes like night. And then suddenly the deluge is unleashed. In a frenzied scramble everything living runs for cover. Uninterrupted the thunder rumbles, lightning and hail hurl forth, and chunks of ice as big as pigeon eggs are hurled by the raging storm towards the ground, which is soon covered by an inch-thick layer.

Through the great din of noise every anxious creature hears a roaring and rumbling that almost drowns out the thunder. It's the seasonal streams that with a rushing and foaming fervor are filling up, overflow their banks, roar forth ripping away bridges and dams like playthings, and transform whole fields into lakes.

Suddenly, as quickly as it began, the storm is over. But in the world that it leaves behind nothing is as the morning promised. Stripped bare of leaves, the trees stand as in winter and branches lie strewn all around on the ground. Where earlier was a vineyard there now is a raging river. Where the unharvested grain stood tall, it now lies trampled and flat along the ground never to rise again. The meadows are robbed of their beds of flowers, replaced now by the carcasses of animals that failed to find timely refuge.

For that year, the summer is as if at an end.

Such a storm was what beset the Armenian people under the Young Turk regime and inflicted upon them great injury. And even the most barbarous acts of Abdülhamid were minor compared with the coming actions of his opponents and successors.

I was there when the great calamity descended on Armenia. Together with the unfortunate people, I experienced tragedy, conditions that almost robbed me of my life, and witnessed bloody events that were forever seared in my mind; events about which I have had a great deal to tell.

– THE END –

Gomidas Institute
42 Blythe Rd.
London W14 0HA
England
www.gomidas.org

www.ingramcontent.com/pod-product-compliance
Ingram Content Group UK Ltd.
Pitfield, Milton Keynes, MK11 3LW, UK
UKHW041856190726
13854UKWH00002B/940